"*A Lighter Side to Cancer* is a treasure of information. Sandra Miniere's thorough research shows in her clear explanations of conventional procedures and even more alternative treatment options, and in the numerous enlightening quotes she includes from well-selected experts. She reveals how she combined a variety of useful strategies to ensure her own long-term healing from stage I breast cancer, and candidly shares the mental and emotional journey she went through as well. Being a psychotherapist, Miniere already understood the mind/body/spirit connection and the way she put what she knew into action to manifest a complete recovery and become even stronger and happier is important wisdom for everyone. This book will help many, many people!"

— Tanya Harter Pierce, MA, Author of *Outsmart Your Cancer: Alternative Non-Toxic Treatments That Work*

"I was quite taken by Sandra Miniere's book, *A Lighter Side to Cancer*; a stunning alchemy of wisdom, humor and insights that makes for a most compelling read... for everyone. Sandra fully understands the mind-body-spirit dynamics and she serves as an excellent guide for your journey into optimal health."

— Brian Luke Seaward, PhD, Author of *Achieving the Mind-Body-Spirit Connection: A Stress Management Workbook*

"I am happy to say that a book like this one is necessary to help us get through the cancer journey. It does have a beginning, and the end comes much later AFTER you live your life. *A Lighter Side to Cancer* helps make that easier for all of us.

— Ms. Ann Fonfa, Founder and President of The Annie Appleseed Project

"Sandra Miniere's open and loving heart is right here for you to benefit as well as her clients. Lucky you!"

— Joel Chudnow, Wholistic Health Educator, Tampa, FL

A Lighter Side to Cancer

From Wake-up Call to Radiant Wellness

By Sandra Miniere, M.Ed.

Printed in the United States of America

A Lighter Side to Cancer: From Wake-up Call to Radiant Wellness

ISBN-10: 0615642713

Published by:
Integrative Choices, LLC
Wesley Chapel, FL
www.integrativewellnessexpert.com

First Printing 2012

Dedication

To my beloved father and mother who died
while I was writing this book.
Lung cancer took my father, and
my mother died one year later because
her heart just stopped beating.
They will never hold my book in their hands,
but I know they have it in their hearts.
I miss them every day.

Acknowledgements

Many wonderful people have been a part of my cancer journey and/or this book project. I value and appreciate all of them. Here are a few I want to mention.

Thank you to the authors, doctors, and other health care experts who allowed me to share their wisdom in this book. They contributed to my taking the mystery out of cancer. A special thank you to their assistants too.

Thank you to the book publishers for allowing me to use book excerpts and quotes by their authors that highlight valuable information relevant to my story.

Thank you to the cancer patients who shared their personal cancer stories and healing approaches in this book. They exemplify what is possible when a person takes responsibility for his or her own health and wellbeing.

Thank you to the authors and experts who gave me a statement about my book because they saw something of value in the message. A special thank you goes to Tanya Harter Pierce who gave me feedback that clarified cancer in my mind and in my writing.

I could not have produced this book without the guidance and support I received from the coaches and consultants in Steve and Bill Harrison's Quantum Leap program. Geoffrey Berwind, my QL coach, was a guiding light throughout the process.

Thank you to my book editor, Deb Bush. She allowed me to be meticulous and obsessive with the layout and copy until we got it right—an incredible undertaking. We took the journey together, and she encouraged me every step of the way.

Thank you to Dotti Albertine who designed the book cover and jacket. She was patient with me throughout the process, and we came up with an image that says radiant wellness. Awesome!

Thank you to my book agents, David and Joel Dunham. They believed in this project and got me started on the path to becoming an author.

To my husband, family members, friends and colleagues who reviewed my book and gave me constructive feedback, you are the greatest! Your belief in me and your encouraging words inspired me to stay focused on telling my story and completing the book.

Thank you to the doctors and health care experts who took the cancer journey with me. My heart is filled with gratitude for the late Dr. Douglas Brodie, Dr. Glenna Wilde, and Auntie Margaret Machado. Their wisdom enabled me to heal.

To all of the courageous children, women and men who have taken on cancer, they are all heroes in my eyes.

Table of Contents

Introduction
Wake Up and Pay Attention!

Arms raised to the sky and feet touching the top of Mission Peak, I had a panoramic view of the area near my home. In spite of the dark clouds, the southern tip of San Francisco Bay was visible. Surprise, excitement, wonder and high energy filled me. I almost said aloud, *"I can't believe I am standing here. Oh my God, I made it! There is no way that I should be standing here."* The years of stress before my move to California two months earlier had compromised my health and fitness and made me doubt my ability to climb this 2,500-foot hill in Fremont California. The buoyancy of accomplishing "mission impossible" lifted me beyond myself. I felt invincible in that moment.

The excitement lasted only moments. My next thought was *"Wait a minute; something does not feel right. The sun should be shining because I've reached my six-week goal of climbing to the top of Mission Peak."* But as I looked to the sky, all I saw were dark clouds. I became somewhat alarmed that I couldn't see the sun. I strained and tried to pierce the clouds with my eyes in search of that sun. After several minutes, a little break in the clouds appeared. The sun smiled on me and let me know it was there. I felt relieved because this experience would not have been the same without the blessing of the sun, even if only for a brief moment.

There I stood at the summit with a young man who had a deformed foot. The only two people on the mountain that day, we made our mark on a pillar with the pen he brought and said a few words to each other. Perhaps, that was my first clue that we should not have been there. In fact, the closer we got to the peak while climbing, bursts of cold rain and wind tried to discourage me, but I just kept walking. Once I stood three-quarters of the way to the summit, nothing could stop me. Some inner strength, that I didn't know I had, took over. Suffering from debilitating asthma and in weak physical shape, I had to use asthma spray about a quarter of the way into the climb. But, once I broke into the high energy of the "zone," I felt lifted beyond limitation. I am not a hiker, and I knew this was a once in a lifetime opportunity.

The young man and I began to climb down the mountain, walking at our separate paces. Suddenly, I became aware that the clouds seemed to be coming closer. Before I knew it, I had zero visibility and began to panic. I had no idea where I was putting my feet on the narrow path. For a brief moment, I feared I might become lost on the mountain. Somehow, I let that fear go and concentrated on slowly placing one foot in front of the other while trusting the process and the path. After about fifteen minutes, I could see again. At that point, I definitely knew the universe was trying to speak to me. However, I didn't know what it was trying to tell me, and I certainly did not have the time to figure it out right then. Once I could see, I needed to pay careful attention and get myself off the mountain without getting hurt.

Somehow, I let that fear go and concentrated on slowly placing one foot in front of the other while trusting the process and the path.

One-half hour into the descent, the rain poured down on me. I was getting drenched to the skin since all I had on were lightweight long pants, a short sleeve polo shirt under a sweatshirt and my favorite hiking hat, which did keep the rain from my eyes. Knowing I had at least another hour of walking ahead of me was too overwhelming to think about. I had to stay in the moment and get off the mountain as quickly as possible. When my feet started sticking to the muddy earth and I could hardly walk, anxiety overwhelmed me again. Steep muddy sections had to be navigated, and I had to be careful not to slip or fall. After one such steep decline, I looked back and saw the young man with the deformed foot struggling to get down. Afraid he would fall and be left on the mountain until the next day, I stood at the bottom of that area and waited for him. The rain continued to pound me. At that point all I could do was laugh. I was so wet it just didn't matter. His safety had become more important. I slowed my pace, and we walked together for another 20 minutes back to our cars.

When I reached my car, I struggled to untie soaked, muddy sneakers with fingers too cold to function. I threw the sneakers in the trunk of my car, drove the five minutes to my home and jumped into a hot shower. I was so excited that I could hardly contain myself. I felt energized and omnipotent. *"I did it!"* kept repeating itself in my mind. *"I did it!"* I reached the peak and made it off that mountain without any injuries. In my current state of health and physical strength, this seemed like a miracle. I called Paul, my significant other, at work to share my good news and realized that I felt so high there was no way I was going to get a cold or pneumonia. I never even sneezed.

From Clouds to Clarity

Two weeks later while watching television, I casually pressed my fingers around my chest and discovered two small lumps high on my left breast. At first I denied that they could be cancerous, especially since I had had a mammogram back home in New Jersey two months before this discovery. At that time, everything had looked normal. *"Besides,"* I told myself, *"with my disciplined lifestyle and spiritual practices, I cannot possibly have cancer."* I hadn't taken my gynecologist seriously several years earlier when she warned me that the way I was taking the hormone replacement therapy (HRT) put me at a 50 percent risk factor for getting breast cancer. Convinced that I wouldn't develop cancer, I actually stayed on HRT for a total of ten years. Three and a-half months after I moved to California and six weeks after climbing Mission Peak, I was diagnosed with stage I invasive tubular breast cancer.

My body revealed its secret only two weeks after the adventure. I must have heard the subtle message at some level of my being. My intuition and fingers did the rest. This early detection gave me a great prognosis. Something was looking out for me.

I received that diagnosis while living in my landlord Lala's house. I am still amused when I see how the universe works through its subtle messages. What an appropriate name to get my attention! Finally the time had arrived to stop living in "lala land" and deal with the real world; I had to face a life-threatening disease and make important decisions in order to save my life. I immediately made the commitment to find the right treatment and also explore my part in getting breast cancer.

Not for one minute did I feel that my body had betrayed me. I really do believe that my body reflects how I live my life, including what I put into it. Right after the diagnosis, I remember asking my body to forgive me for not listening and taking better care of it. I was willing to acknowledge anything I may have done to contribute to the cancer. I could look back at all of the subtle and not so subtle warning signs I had not seen, or had chosen to ignore.

3

Fortunately, the cancer diagnosis released me from a naiveté that almost cost me my life. I could not be angry or blame anyone. I just felt sad that this was happening to me and that I could possibly have prevented such a health crisis. Following the diagnosis, my first words to God were, *"I cannot believe You are asking me to walk this path; I know there is a reason. I will do my best to discover what this is all about."* In the grace of that moment, I felt connected to a Higher Power, and so began the next phase of my life: my journey through cancer. The journey proved to be filled with lots of laughter, tears, and miracles.

From Awareness to Action

Through synchronistic events, I was led to an amazing team of doctors and healers who saved my life. I also did my own soul-searching work to free myself from past emotional baggage that weighed me down and prevented me from living abundantly. During that first critical year of cancer treatments, I found the courage to do what I had to do. From mastectomy to vitamin infusions to internal cleansing to life changes, I followed my inner guidance. And when I discovered the specific doctor mentioned in a psychic reading, who used natural approaches to healing cancer, I knew I had found the proverbial needle in the haystack. The surprise ending at the Hawaiian Cleanse may have saved my life. Inner exploration and lifestyle changes gave me a new career and contributed to my deeper connection to a Higher Power. I became filled with unshakable faith after observing how the universe guided and supported me on my quest for healing.

When there is no path, what do we do? We create our own. That is exactly what I was forced to do. From my perspective, cancer treatments performed by the conventional medical community, like radiation and chemotherapy, often do a lot of harm to the body without impressive results. Consequently, I could not completely turn my body over to mainstream medicine. Compelled to take control of my own healing, I explored options, made choices and created a healing path that worked for me. The choices and decisions that would save my life had to be made by me alone, and I stepped up to the task.

Perhaps I am more courageous than I think, but I could not have done this alone. Grace supported me the whole way.

Blazing my own trail proved a major challenge, but I was committed to using my wake-up call as an opportunity to achieve optimal health and wellbeing. Eleven years later it is time to share my grace-filled story about this unique cancer adventure.

Chapter 1
This Can't Be Happening to Me!
(Breast Cancer Diagnosis)

October 2000

"There is good news and bad news: You have breast cancer; but… it is a 'friendly' cancer." This devastating message, given to me by a charismatic, golden-haired pixie in a sun-filled examining room, pierced the illusion that I was in charge of my body. At that moment I felt stunned. How could this be happening to me? Evidently, all I was doing to take care of my body and soul had not protected me from cancer.

As I walked down the long dark hallway after receiving the diagnosis from my surgeon, I thought, *"What a major hassle!"* I would have to take a detour from building a new life in California to saving my life instead. I could already imagine all of the research I needed to do. My surgeon's message left me with the opinion that I had a "mild" form of cancer, which the conventional medical community could easily treat with surgery, radiation or chemotherapy. However, their treatment approaches were not in alignment with my plan to get healthier. On the other hand, taking charge of healing my cancer through natural approaches meant more work for me.

Comforted that Paul was with me at the time I received my diagnosis, I still felt alone in this cancer adventure. (Paul is now my husband, but during the time around diagnosis and treatments, he was my significant other of fourteen years.)

Driving home alone in the car after receiving the diagnosis, the realization hit me: *"You are on your own with your cancer."* I had to take charge of treating this illness because no one had as much at stake as me—my life. Decisions had to be made by me alone. The feeling of being on my own and taking care of myself is a very old life pattern. I learned early to live by my wits and figure things out. I can remember at the age of three or four opening the back door and entering an empty house; I was hungry. No one was around, but I spotted a loaf of bread on a counter in the kitchen. I dragged a heavy chair over to the counter, climbed up, opened the paper wrapper around the bread and ate a slice or two. I climbed down and went back outside to play with the other kids. Being on my own and taking care of myself are what I do best. Cancer provided another opportunity to relive that script and also gave me an opportunity to change the distorted belief that I had to do everything myself.

Stage I cancer would not kill me if it was treated properly, but what lay ahead seemed overwhelming. In addition to having cancer and being a new resident of California, I had no business or career. Mental health counseling in California was not an option for me because I did not have the proper credentials. I had no local support system in place and was dependent on Paul financially and emotionally. *"Unbelievable!"*

The Truth Shall Set Me Free

After the surgeon biopsied two small cancerous tumors from my left breast, she told me I was very fortunate because my cancer had been detected early. The damage to my body was minimal. However, once she recommended a mastectomy with reconstruction, I did not feel lucky. A lumpectomy was never suggested. I remember her saying, *"Something is going on in that breast."* I had two tumors in one breast, and my breasts were small. Getting clear margins and breast appearance were probably considered too. It felt like my health-conscious, disciplined lifestyle for the past twenty years had just been defeated. Adequate nutrition, yoga, and meditation had not prevented this health crisis. The alien world of cancer had found its way to my front door, and I couldn't slam the door in its face. Those pamphlets on breast surgery, neatly stacked in a small wooden shelf on the wall in my surgeon's office, were about to become a part of my realty.

The surgeon instructed me to take several weeks to educate myself about treatment options. My life depended upon making an informed choice. Surgery, radiation, chemotherapy, or non-invasive alternative treatments were possibilities. I got my first assignment from my surgeon: Read *Dr. Susan Love's Breast Book*—all 700 pages. I asked Paul to buy this breast cancer bible on his way home from work because I did not want to deal with it. He held the book first and began reading it before me. The book lay on my kitchen counter. Each time I walked by it, I reminded myself, *"I should be reading but I am just not ready."* I needed more time to recover from the shock. Two days later, I picked up the book. It was my turn to make choices like all the women who have gone before me. I felt some embarrassment that I had become one of them. In my work as a holistic, body-centered mental health counselor, I had helped cancer patients. I was not supposed to become one. Clients and students looked to me as someone who had it together. The illusion of invincibility was crumbling fast, and I had to face it.

When I finally emerged from the false security of denial, I sprang into action. First, I faxed the biopsy report to two experts for second opinions. Then I read the treatment section of Dr. Love's book, contacted support centers, bought books, scanned the web (before the Google phenomenon), called friends knowledgeable about cancer, and consulted a holistic doctor. Each contact gave me a list of more contacts. Within two days of taking charge, I was inundated with resources for traditional and non-traditional treatment options. My dining room table became a smorgasbord of cancer information. Cancer had invaded my home.

While adapting to this uninvited guest, I had difficulty releasing the tension from my body. My insides were quietly trembling as if I were in the aftershocks of an earthquake. I seemed to be able to keep the feelings under control while I stayed busy, learning all I could about the causes of cancer and treatment options. But, the shock and trauma were rumbling around in my body anyway. Yoga stretches, meridian tapping and meditation provided minor relief. However, after one visit to Dr. Xie, my new Chinese acupuncturist in California, I felt optimistic and in charge. With thin needles in my feet, abdomen, and head, he reconnected me to my peaceful center. When I left his office, my body and soul were calm for the first time since the earth-shattering news. Grace enveloped me, and I felt more connected to a Higher Power.

As I walked to my car after that treatment, I told myself, *"You can do this."* I just didn't know what "this" would entail.

Overwhelmed, but motivated, I continued to gather information and speak to other women who had survived breast cancer. One of the women's cancer support centers gave me a buddy. She listened to my cancer story and shared hers. We discussed doctors, surgery, recovery, alternative medicine and prevention. She spoke in a matter-of-fact way about sleeping in a chaise lounge for three months after her breast reconstruction. The assurance and confidence in her voice gave me hope. It placed a solid foundation under my feet. Real people had successfully survived the havoc of treatment. The world of cancer was becoming familiar, and a women's support network was nurturing me.

Some Cancer Statistics

◆ The American Cancer Society 2010 Cancer Statistics reveal that one out of three women in the US is at risk for developing some form of cancer in their lifetime. That number increases for men to one out of two.

◆ The National Cancer Institute reports that more than 11 million Americans have a history of invasive cancer, while the American Cancer Society estimates that in the year 2009, over 1.4 million Americans will receive a diagnosis of invasive cancer with over a half million cases resulting in death.

◆ In 2012, the American Cancer Society estimates that about 226,870 new cases of invasive breast cancer will be diagnosed in the United States—and about 53,300 new cases of carcinoma in situ (noninvasive). About 39,510 women will die from breast cancer, and 2.6 million survivors currently live in the United States.

◆ A study by scientists at Imperial College in London confirms the link between lifestyle and breast cancer. A woman can significantly reduce her risk of getting breast cancer if she limits the amount of alcohol she drinks, maintains a healthy weight and is physically active.

Just when I thought I was coping effectively, I received a telephone call from a friend who worked in cancer research. *"This is Vicki. You have to have your breast off!"* I was sitting on my bed listening to her with my free arm wrapped around my stomach while she told me, *"All the women I know who had lumpectomies are dead, and those with mastectomies are alive."* As soon as we hung up, my body began shaking. Paul found me lying on the bed trembling in a fetal position. My body seemed to be resisting this truth. I could not accept that the body I had tried to protect with hormones and healthy lifestyle would be mutilated by a surgeon's knife. This thunderbolt of reality shattered the fragile armor I had erected to keep going.

I calmed down enough to fall asleep that evening only to awaken abruptly at 3:00 a.m. As I opened my eyes and I sat up, I could still see the dream image even after blinking a few times. The scene in front of me reflected an ethereal substance with natural color. It revealed my surgeon standing next to a hospital gurney with me lying on it. We were getting ready to go into surgery. I couldn't see my face, but I felt safe. She stood confidently by my side. The truth encoded in this vivid image got my attention. In that moment I decided to have a left modified radical mastectomy. It felt right.

The truth—distasteful as it was—set me free. Peace replaced the turmoil in my mind and body. I fell back to sleep with a profound sense of relief. In the morning I would discuss my decision with Paul, begin to grieve the loss of my breast and explore breast reconstruction options. Gratitude filled me because the decision had been taken out of my ego's hands by the truth and guidance of my soul. I began to feel that I was not alone on this cancer journey. A power greater than myself appeared to be helping me take each step. A process that could have consumed my energy for weeks resolved itself within five days after the diagnosis. In my hour of need, my body and soul spoke to me—and, I listened. I never doubted their profound wisdom. The memory still brings tears to my eyes.

Finding Doctors in a Strange Land
(Weeks Before the Diagnosis)

At the time I found the two lumps in my left breast, I had to spring into action and find a local gynecologist sooner rather than later. Before moving to California, I had taken care of all my medical business, including the mammogram, which showed nothing. Without anyone to ask for a recommendation, I had to rely on myself. I wanted someone who did not perform obstetrics and worked primarily with menopausal women, similar to the doctor I left in New Jersey. After checking the yellow pages of the phone book, I called the office of the doctor who fit that description and decided this two-doctor office was the place for me.

When I met my doctor, I felt an immediate connection with her. After all, she had gone to medical school in New York. She tried to put a long needle into one of the lumps to discover whether it was a cyst. The procedure was not successful. I had to find a surgeon to perform a biopsy, and she suggested two doctors in Freemont. I was not happy with those options because they were general surgeons, not breast surgeons. And, they were men.

After all of my reading and discussions with breast cancer survivors who were in the know, from my perspective, I wanted a woman surgeon who only worked on breasts. If I had been in New Jersey, I would have gone to a local female breast surgeon who had an impeccable reputation. I knew they existed, and I would find one. I went against the gynecologist's recommendation, and searched for someone who fit my criteria. I made some phone calls to get the search started. How I found Dr. Lebovic grabbed my attention.

I had been speaking to a good friend in New Jersey, who had lived in San Francisco with her husband for one year when he was on

9

a sabbatical there. He taught clinical psychology at Rutgers University. She made a call to a doctor she had met in San Francisco, and he gave her Dr. Lebovic's name for me. As soon as I met her, I knew she was the doctor I needed. She had a positive outlook, and I learned that she was skilled at making sure women looked good after breast cancer surgery. After all, I was in the Stanford University area of California, and she was the best of the best. I felt so blessed and thankful to have found her. Once I put my body in her hands, my cancer burden began to feel lighter. Once again, grace was smiling on me.

Looking Back: Warning Signs and Subtle Messages
(Years Before the Diagnosis)

Before I moved to California and received the cancer diagnosis, life screamed to get my attention. I just was not listening, or I was not able to listen. The overt and covert signs did not register. I still wonder about how deaf and blind I had been during those years prior to my diagnosis. Could I have prevented breast cancer? Because of my own denial, I have learned to have compassion for people who cannot hear what they do not want to hear. Most people are not aware that the universe is trying to get their attention with subtle messages. I was one of them once and could be again if I stop being alert.

Hormone Balancing

In 1997, about seven years into hormone replacement treatment, I met a woman at a holistic health conference who warned me about pharmaceutical HRT. She suggested I see a practitioner who specialized in natural hormone balancing. I did not understand that natural hormone balancing is still considered HRT, so I did not take her seriously. (Today they call it bioidentical hormone therapy.) I remember taking the piece of paper she offered me knowing I would not follow through. I did not want to hear about going off HRT. When I got home, I threw the information in the trash. Denial and ignorance prevented me from listening to other options. The research today is clear. Long-term use of pharmaceutical HRT increases the risk of breast cancer. But, I was too bull-headed to take her warning seriously and change my ways. Today I understand that any hormone balancing therapy requires close monitoring of a woman's hormonal levels by the experts who know how to prevent breast cancer.

Yellow Mucous in My Lungs

About two years before the diagnosis, I had a lot of yellow mucous in my lungs. I was not coughing, but it constricted my lungs and breathing. I noticed it when I cleared my throat and brought up mucous, and even with the asthma medicine my breathing was compromised. As an asthmatic living in polluted central New Jersey, this mucous situation was not good. I did not want to go on a steroid spray so I kept looking for a natural treatment approach that would clear up my lungs. For example, I went to a holistic practitioner while visiting my daughter in California who did Iridology and some other minor health assessments. He never mentioned cancer as a possibility, nor did any of the other practitioners I had seen for several years before the cancer diagnosis. (I now realize that the mucous was a sign of chronic inflammation, which no one mentioned.) He put me on a treatment plan, which included the herb Pau de Arco. I had to sprinkle the herbal remedy on my salads every day.

The mucous kept getting worse on that herb, but I decided to stay with it and give the remedy a chance. After one month on this powerful herb, a friend and I walked the boardwalk at the Jersey shore. I could not walk very far without having difficulty breathing. I used my spray at least once an hour. In serious trouble, I just needed to get home. Right then I decided to stop the herbal treatment because it was doing me more harm than good. But, I knew something was wrong with my body, and I had to get to the bottom of it.

All the drug-free approaches I had tried to get my body healthy were not eliminating the excessive yellow mucous in my lungs. However, I never had to go on a steroid spray. Acupuncture, chiropractic adjustments, diet, supplements and Nambudripad's Allergy Elimination Techniques (NAET) (an acupuncture protocol) seemed to be having some effect on my lungs. Using the non-steroid asthma spray three times a day kept me breathing. However, my body was still in trouble.

Three weeks after moving to California, I went to a local acupuncturist to help clear my lungs of the yellow mucous and improve the asthma. With no one to ask for a recommendation, I checked names and pictures in the yellow pages of the phone book. I used a pendulum to help me pick the right doctor. I held the crystal pendulum by a thin chain between my thumb and index fingers. If the pendulum rotated in a clockwise direction over the doctor's name or picture, that meant yes. If it rotated counter-clockwise that was a no. The pendulum spun the fastest in a clockwise direction over Dr.

11

Xie's picture, an elderly Chinese gentleman. (He was the acupuncturist who helped me get through the shock of the diagnosis and continued to be a great support throughout my cancer journey.)

When he inserted needles and twisted them, I felt pain, but he would just smile and keep going. He was aggressive, but really good. I began to feel better and my breathing started improving. (The excessive yellow mucous in my lungs eventually stopped being a health challenge after the mastectomy and my immune boosting treatment in Nevada.)

Medical Warning Signs

Two or three years before diagnosis, I had to have my left breast radiated about three times in one mammogram screening. Feeling annoyed that I had been detained, I sat in a confined area waiting for the technician to return with the verdict. Anxiety and agitation set in. She finally returned and told me everything was okay. What a relief. I was home free—or so I thought. When I looked at the x-ray she showed me, I could see the left breast had streaks of light going through it, but I thought that was a good thing. I told myself that perhaps more subtle healing energy was moving through my breast. (Today there is evidence that excessive radiation from mammography screening may lead to breast cancer.) Something was going on in that breast, but did I take it as a warning sign? No. I did not want to stop taking those hormones!

Around that time, my gynecologist told me I had a 50-50 chance of getting breast cancer. My hormone protocol continued my menstrual cycle, which also raised the risk factor. I used an estrogen patch and natural oral progesterone. I told myself the closer I stayed with my natural hormone cycle, the better off I would be. I denied what the research was saying and told my doctor that I would take my chances. There was another important issue to consider. I doubted that I could take small doses of progesterone every day, which was the alternative hormone protocol at the time. I noticed that when I took the progesterone orally for ten or fourteen days each month, my asthma got worse. For me, taking the progesterone orally increased the amount of mucous in my lungs. To avoid any change, I did not address the important progesterone issue with my doctor. (I was ignorant about the estrogen/progesterone issues for safe hormonal balancing and the risks associated with having an estrogen dominant body.) I really thought spirituality and positive attitude would save me. Unfortunately, pride went before my fall into breast cancer, but I still love and accept myself anyway.

Ambulance Crisis

About six months before my move to California, I had bronchitis and needed to take an antibiotic. The doctor prescribed Cipro. I could not remember whether this medication was a problem for me, but I gave it a try. I was too preoccupied with other things to give it much thought. Paul was living in California and I was living in our home in New Jersey, which wasn't selling. One evening around 10:00 p.m., I began having shortness of breath right after taking the medication. It kept getting worse, and I was getting concerned, so I called 911. When I spoke to the gentleman on the phone, I told him that I did not know whether I needed to go to the hospital, but that I was having trouble breathing. He could hear that I could hardly breathe and speak. After assessing the situation, he said they would send an ambulance, and I told him, *"Please do not have the ambulance come to my home with the sirens blaring."* I did not want to wake up my quiet neighborhood, but I was living alone and there was no family member or friend close by to take me to the hospital. I do like to feel in charge—a strength and a weakness.

When the medics arrived, they checked my breathing and without my knowledge called the hospital ambulance (…so much for not wanting to make a scene). There were two ambulances in the street when I walked out of the house and five men stood by to help me. I went into the hospital ambulance, and the local ambulance followed. A short while in the ambulance I was gasping for breath and starting to panic. The medic immediately hooked me up to an IV with Benadryl, and my breathing began to stabilize. By the time I arrived at the hospital, my breathing was normal. Here I was in a life-threatening situation, six months before my cancer diagnosis. I knew even then that my body was trying to tell me something; I only wish I had known what it was, but I did not have a clue at that time. I just remember waking up at night sometimes with a feeling that something wasn't right.

Grace to the Rescue

As I look back over the several years and months before my cancer diagnosis, I see signs that something very serious was wrong with my body. Did I contribute to getting breast cancer? The answer I tell myself is *yes* and *no*. Could I have done more to protect my body from contracting this disease? I believe I could. (My ignorance about what causes breast cancer had severe consequences.) Was it my destiny to have breast cancer so I could achieve optimal health and help other people? (I am now off daily asthma medicine.) I believe that is possible too. I cannot know exactly why something shows up in my life. I just know that my body, soul and life are constantly guiding me toward living my greatest good. Acceptance and grace light the way.

I have learned to be naturally curious in order to understand the messages that life is sending my way. No longer do I anxiously strive to know and control the future. I just allow the clues to come to me easily in a relaxed state of open awareness; and hopefully, I get the message, most of the time.

In addition, I have more love and acceptance toward myself even when I make mistakes. I take responsibility for the life I am creating. True responsibility means I am able to respond to any situation that is placed at my feet without blame and condemnation. I am willing to ask myself the difficult questions to get to truth. I have found that grace enters when I am in a state of acceptance. I did not resist cancer or blame my body, my God or myself. Perhaps that is how grace became my constant companion throughout my breast cancer adventure. I was guided through the jungle of treatment possibilities, made choices and came up with a healing plan that felt right for me.

The Gift of Grace

by Sandra Miniere
Author of *A Lighter Side to Cancer:*
From Wake-Up Call to Radiant Wellness

Paul Tillich in his "You Are Accepted" essay describes grace as a light that breaks through our inner darkness and reminds us that we are accepted by that which is greater than ourselves. At those times we should not ask questions or do anything, just allow this divine acceptance to unite us with ourselves, others, life and God.

Grace brings divine unconditional love into our souls and lives. It operates behind the scenes until we awaken to the oneness and gifts it offers. Grace intercedes when we are open and available. It cannot be earned by striving toward some perfectionist ideal. It happens in moments of inner darkness and outer turmoil.

We may talk about grace casually in a crisis: "By the grace of god I made it." "God was looking out for you." However, when the crisis is over, we often forget that something remarkable intervened. Once we acknowledge grace as a spiritual resource, we may decide to make it our ally. We can work with grace consciously by acknowledging its existence, invoking it by request, giving thanks when it touches us, and having faith in its mystery.

Acknowledgment: Grace is present in our lives and souls whether we recognize it or not. It is a force waiting to be harnessed and cultivated, not controlled. Once we acknowledge and work with it, we will witness miracles consistently.

Invocation: We may ask for a divine intervention to spare us from a negative consequence, guide us when we are lost, comfort us when we feel despair, or strengthen us when we feel overwhelmed.

Gratitude: If we are filled with gratitude when the miraculous shows up in our lives, grace will continue to shine upon us, light our way and unite us with a Higher Power.

Faith: Grace intervenes in its own way and own time; we need to believe in it anyway. As we accept and work with this sacred resource, grace lifts us from the havoc we create or tragedy we encounter.

Grace takes us beyond the limits of human love into the transforming power of unconditional love. When we see ourselves and the world through the eyes of acceptance and gratitude, grace will become our constant companion.

Chapter 1 Lessons Learned...

- When you are making plans, life may take you on an unexpected adventure. Go with the flow!

- Bad news can shatter you. But purposeful actions, support from others and grace will put you back together.

- Your wake-up calls are usually a signal that something isn't right. Pay attention or the soft ring can become a loud blast.

- The easy path is not always the best path for a positive outcome.

- Risk takers often finish ahead of the pack.

- Herbs, supplements and medications may have negative side effects. Be aware and speak up!

- When you do not know the way, ask for support and guidance from your intuition or Higher Power.

- Self-love and acceptance is the key to healing and personal empowerment.

- Ask questions and be willing to hear the answers. The truth will lead you toward more aliveness.

...a time to pay attention, ask questions and be intentional

Chapter 2
Where Do I Go from Here?
(Treatment Options)

October and November 2000

The surgeon scheduled the modified left mastectomy with reconstruction approximately six weeks after the diagnosis. She gave me time to do my cancer research and take my parents to Hawaii the middle of November. They were celebrating their 60th wedding anniversary. While I had the dread of a mastectomy hanging over me, I did not want to cancel the trip. My father had not been back to Honolulu since World Word II, and my mother had never been there. It seemed like a great way for them to celebrate their marriage of sixty years. Plus, it provided a good distraction for me. While researching cancer treatment options, I was planning a vacation to Hawaii. It took some of the heaviness out of my body and soul.

Getting the Whole Story

After the biopsy and breast cancer diagnosis, the surgeon requested that I get an oncologist. She would not operate unless I had one. Because she was a breast surgeon, I assumed that she needed a cancer doctor to confirm her treatment plan. I could understand that, so I did some research in the book, *Third Opinion (Third Edition)* by John Fink, an international directory of alternative therapy centers and doctors. I found an oncologist about 30 miles from my home. From the description about him and his work in *Third Opinion*, I was willing to make an appointment. When I walked into his office, I received another dose of reality. It felt strange to be in the office of *my* oncologist. This was the last place I expected to find myself. I like to feel in control of my life; clearly, my body had other ideas. Rather than dwell on feeling like a failure, I looked around the waiting room and felt grateful that my cancer was stage I.

The oncologist also agreed that a mastectomy would be his choice. On my post-surgery visit with him, we would explore treatment options based on the pathology of the breast tissue. He was also optimistic about my prognosis. The mastectomy should be all that was required. (Later, we would find out that was not true.) The most important news I received from him that day was his suggestion that I use a cortisone (steroid) oral spray to control the asthma. It was getting toward the time for me to use the asthma spray, and he could hear the slight congestion in my lungs and throat. I took his advice. My lungs had to be healthy enough to get me through a four-hour operation, plus hours in recovery. (I was taking the non-cortisone spray three times a day.) The cortisone improved my breathing, which got me through the surgery without any breathing complications. Even though I had an oncologist, I still had a lot of reading and exploring to do. No matter what the surgeon found, I would be treating my whole body in order to heal the physical terrain that produced two cancerous tumors in my left breast.

The six weeks between diagnosis and mastectomy were filled with learning about alternative treatment options. Conventional approaches were relatively straight forward—surgery, chemotherapy or radiation. I could put that aside while I read several books on alternative treatments. I discovered that the alternative experts have a very different philosophy about cancer than the conventional medical community.

The alternative medical community views cancer as a systemic disease, not just a cancer site. Cancer cells develop and interfere with normal cell reproduction, especially during the aging process. A compromised immune system cannot detect and destroy these developing cancer cells fast enough, and eventually they clump together to form a localized cancer.

Most medical practitioners and researchers agree that, in fact, we all probably have cancer cells developing in each of us all the time, but our bodies are able to dispose of them before they rage out of control. In other words, a healthy body can normally defend itself quite well against the development of cancer because it knows how to deal with these natural occurrences.

—Tanya Harter Pierce, MA, MFCC, *Outsmart Your Cancer: Alternative Non-Toxic Treatments That Work* (2009, p. 21)

Alternative doctors and other health care practitioners believe a breakdown in the systems of the body, particularly the immune system, allows the body to produce a cancer. Therefore, their treatments often focus on strengthening the immune system. A healthy immune system not only destroys developing cancer cells, but also kills cancer cells that have formed a tumor and/or have spread to other parts of the body. I began to understand that natural killer cells protect the body from getting cancer and also eliminate the cancer once it has taken up residence.

Conventional medicine is focused on naming diseases based on geography, body location, and specialty, instead of by the cause, mechanism, or pathway involved. Doctors say you have a liver, kidney, brain, or heart disease. But this approach to naming disease tells you nothing about the cause, and it is quickly becoming obsolete as we understand more about the mysteries of human biology...Functional medicine gives us a method for identifying the conditions in which disease arises and shows us how to begin changing those conditions.

— Blog Post by Dr. Mark Hyman November 6, 2010:
*Cancer; New Science on how to Prevent and Treat It—
A Report from TEDMED by Dr. Mark Hyman*

Options: The Alternative Cancer Therapy Book by Richard Walters explains the underlying rationale, proposed actions, supportive evidence and the course of treatment for the many alternative approaches. It was a guiding light for me in 2000. However, Walters encouraged his readers to approach all traditional and alternative therapies, as well as remission and cure rates, with caution. His message was not what I wanted to hear. It left me longing for certainty in an uncertain world. I wanted to be guided to the right option for me.

After reading the book and being bombarded with so many options, I could not connect with one approach that *felt right*. Some of the approaches seemed to call for a commitment which I was not prepared to make, like totally changing my already restricted eating habits along with numerous coffee enemas every day. If I had stage IV cancer, I might have been more inclined to try some of the approaches that required drastic lifestyle changes. Or, perhaps, I was just being lazy or timid about my treatment. This whole process was pushing me against myself. I had to keep asking, *"What are you willing to do to heal the cancer naturally?"* And, *"How much are you willing to spend?"*

I learned that conventional treatments focus on destroying the tumor, and surgery has the highest survival rate. Their standard of care does not address or treat the underlying causes of the cancer. For example, what causes the systems of the body to break down in order for cells to produce cancer remains a mystery in mainstream medicine. In contrast, alternative treatment approaches address the tumor as a symptom. Their treatment aims at correcting the root causes of the disease, which include how the mind, emotions, body, spirit and environment affect the cells and genes. Lifestyle—which includes nutrition, stress, thoughts, emotions, toxic exposure and more, appears to influence whether the body produces cells that promote or prevent cancer. This empowers the patient to participate in the healing process and make lifestyle choices that contribute to cancer recovery.

Alternative and integrative health care providers address the whole picture. They focus on strengthening the body's ability to destroy cancer cells, as well as eliminate the tumor through a variety of modalities.

Regardless of the new wisdom I gained while exploring the natural approaches to curing cancer, I stuck with my decision to have the left breast removed. I totally accepted and honored the message in my divinely inspired dream image. My body and soul spoke; I listened.

Throughout my research, I learned that many cancer patients who were pronounced "terminal"—dying within weeks or months, went on alternative treatment approaches and fully recovered. To my way of thinking, if it can happen to just one person, it becomes possible for others to outlive their prognosis. Even though the research was somewhat lacking at that time regarding alternative and integrative therapies, I was curious. The anecdotal stories of cancer remission got my attention and gave me hope. Today many books and studies are available for those who are willing to do the research

The Problem with Most Cancer Treatments

**by Raymond Francis, MSc, Founder of Beyond Health International,
Author of *Never Fear Cancer Again, Never Be Sick Again,*
and *Never Be Fat Again*
(www.beyondhealth.com)**

Conventional cancer treatments are aimed at the wrong target. Surgery, radiation and chemotherapy may remove tumors, but they do nothing to address the true causes of the tumors. A tumor is merely a symptom—a product of the cancer process. Yet all the attention goes to the symptom. You can poison, slash and burn the symptom all you want, but unless you turn the cancer process off, you still have cancer and it will come back.

What we call cancer is actually a process that can only occur when certain conditions are present in the body. In this process, cells malfunction in a way that interferes with their normal communication and growth-control mechanisms, so the cells grow uncontrollably. To rid the body of cancer, we must shut down this process by removing the conditions that support it.

Cellular malfunction is what disease is all about; it's what causes all symptoms, whatever disease you may have. There are only two causes of cellular malfunction: deficiency and toxicity. Either cells are getting too little of what they need or too much of something they don't need.

The human body is a truly magnificent self-regulating, self-repairing, and self-healing machine. It knows how to get well and stay well—if only we would provide the support it needs. Rather than attacking symptoms, we have only to assist the body by supplying cells with all the nutrients they need and keeping them free of toxins that can interfere with their proper functions.

We have much more control over our health than is widely believed, and we don't need to fear cancer or any other disease. It is possible to prevent and reverse most disease simply by supporting "the doctor within" and allowing the body to do what it already knows how to do.

To learn more about how to prevent and reverse cancer, read *Never Fear Cancer Again.*

to find them. Alternative treatment approaches offer non-toxic, non–invasive modalities that support the body's ability to heal itself. I wanted to give them some credibility, even if the medical establishment did not. I began to understand the politics of cancer medicine and the conflict between conventional versus alternative. It was and still is filled with ignorance, fear and hostility from the medical power structure, including the drug companies, Food and Drug Administration and cancer foundations. The red flag question: What will happen to the billion-dollar cancer industry if cancer is eliminated?

In 2000, I found detailed descriptions for many alternative treatments in the book titled *Options: The Alternative Cancer Therapy Book*. The author, Richard Walters, compiled a comprehensive list of treatments by doctors, scientists and other health care professionals. He included the theorists and their theories as well as protocols, research and outcomes. A few of the treatment options that I reviewed and considered 11 years ago are summarized at the end of this chapter on page 27. These brief descriptions are inadequate to describe the protocols and theories by the experts who developed them.

The newer book, *Outsmart Your Cancer*, by Tanya Harter Pierce also describes many of these treatment approaches and some new ones. Suzanne Somers's book, *KNOCKOUT*, includes interviews with prominent doctors who use innovative approaches to treating cancer. Research continues to support the effectiveness of alternative and integrative cancer treatment approaches (used independently or in conjunction with conventional treatment).

Time to Take a Stand

The world of alternative cancer treatments had to be explored and evaluated in a short period of time. A woman on a mission, I had to find the best way to treat my cancer. I kept my feelings in check while I immersed myself in the research. I really could not accomplish this task in a few months, but I gave it my best shot. If ever I needed a divine intervention, it was then. I put forth my plea for help as I faced this mountain of life-enhancing therapeutic approaches. Each treatment approach appeared to have something of value to offer. A picture was forming in my mind about how emotions, thoughts, nutrition, spiritual practice, physical environment and lifestyle influence the body's biochemistry. I learned that the medical establishment labeled many alternative approaches as quackery. They threatened and closed down doctors who were getting too powerful outside of the established procedures and theories. They forced some doctors to go underground or leave the country. A few fought back and won.

Because of all this controversy, I had to be on this journey without much guidance and support in 2000. I felt like I was dealing in the "cancer black market." Some of the time I felt sad about this situation, and other times I felt really angry. Too many people were dying of cancer, and no one seemed to have the answers. I would have hoped that for the greater good of healing cancer, the two worlds could merge and learn from one another. But it was not happening then and still is not happening now. I approached my own healing with the desire to understand how my body broke down to produce cancer and how my soul and lifestyle may have contributed to this dilemma. I chose to take myself out of the box imposed on me by the medical power structure and find treatment options that made sense for me and my finances.

Alternative Treatment Statistics

◆ According to the National Cancer Institute's 2007 *Complementary and Alternative Medicine in Cancer Treatment PDQ®*, a large survey of cancer survivors reported 38.3% of adults (about 4 in 10) used complementary and alternative medicine.

◆ This 2007 PDQ® reported 61% used prayer and spiritual practice, 44% relaxation, 42% faith and spiritual healing, and 40% nutritional supplements and vitamins.

◆ According to a 2005 study conducted at Ohio State University, about 70% of adults fifty or older used some kind of alternative medicine, such as acupuncture and herbal medicine. This is higher than the general adult population.

◆ According to The World Health Organization, an estimated 65% to 80% of the world's population (about 3 billion people) relies on holistic medicine as their primary form of health care. (Reported by Dorothy M. Neddermeyer, PhD, *Holistic Health Care Facts and Statistics,* www.disabled-world.com, January 16, 2009).

◆ *Newsweek* (December 2002) reported that Americans make more visits to holistic health care providers (some 600 million a year) than to MDs and spend more money out-of-pocket to do so, about $30 billion a year.

With a commitment to find my own answers and chart my own course, I intended to discover how I could improve my health. The messages of fear and control within the medical establishment would not stop me. I spent six weeks before my surgery learning all I could from people, books and magazines. Whenever I could speak with someone who had success with an alternative treatment, I listened and learned. One of my former clients with breast cancer chose not to have any traditional treatment. She went to a doctor who treated her cancer naturally. Her tumor and cancer disappeared. When I met her ten years after her diagnosis, she told me she was still cancer free. The truth that cancer is a systemic problem took root in my awareness. Her story inspired me to take some risks and follow my gut instincts.

Along with my research, I contacted Nicole, an intuitive, who was excellent at picking up clues about the future and giving me wise guidance. In the past she had been right about many important life decisions. If I ever needed her to be a guiding light for me, it was now. I was inundated with information and had to decide how I wanted to deal with my cancer. Nicole came through for me again, but when I hung up from our one-hour consultation, I was laughing out loud and walking around the house repeating, *"Oh my God!"* She described a short, male, bald-headed doctor about 200 hundred miles from my home. OK, I was living in the southeastern San Francisco Bay area. I could not drive that far west, but north, south and east covered a lot of possibilities. She saw me driving three to four hours to his office. He would help me, and that was all the information she could provide.

Wow! How on earth was I going to find this man? I could not even comprehend how to begin. This felt like a treasure hunt to me. A few days later, I decided I could not do it because it would require finding "a needle in a haystack" of possibilities. So, I told the Universe: *"You need to bring me the information that will lead me to this doctor who will play a major role in my healing."*

Nicole also saw a female Hawaiian healer that would be helpful. Well, that one was a little more tangible. I knew who she was, but I had no idea how I was going to track her down. It was Auntie Margaret on the big island of Hawaii. I had read a magazine article about her 12 years prior to my cancer diagnosis. The article described her internal cleansing program for cancer patients.

After speaking with Nicole, I began to get more clarity. All my investigating was paying off. My three-step healing program began

24

to emerge in my mind. I began to develop "Sandy's treatment plan," which had three distinct phases: have a mastectomy, boost the immune system with an integrative cancer specialist, and participate in a deep cleansing program to detoxify my body. Of course, I would do the deep emotional, mental and spiritual cleansing as well, which is what I do for a living. With my plan in place, I felt energized and confident instead of weary. The world of cancer, its causes and treatments, started coming into greater focus. With my antenna of awareness up, I would do my best to ask people about these two healers. I wanted to find them even though it seemed like "mission impossible." While I had some apprehension, mostly, I was also curious about how this "trust walk" would play out. The search took a back seat as I prepared myself for a vacation in Hawaii and a mastectomy.

I realize that I chose this three-phase treatment approach because my beliefs and lifestyle were more in line with holistic and integrative medicine than conventional medicine. I worked as a mental health counselor in a medical center with doctors who practiced integrative medicine and acupuncture. I served on the board of directors of an organization in Princeton, New Jersey, that also focused on promoting holistic wellness. I also worked with the clients of a local chiropractor. My very being was immersed in holistic medicine, so that is the path I chose and trusted. I went into surgery with this three-fold treatment plan formulated in my mind. It gave me a sense of control and hope.

Chapter 2 Lessons Learned...

◆ Explore, explore, explore. Do your research because informed choices lead to the best cancer outcomes.

◆ Put your attention, time, energy and money into getting the whole story.

◆ Think outside of the box. Creative solutions may come from unexpected places.

◆ With trust, a positive attitude and persistence, you will reach a destination that is right for you.

◆ Divine interventions happen. Invite Spirit into your healing adventure.

◆ A health challenge can become an opportunity for personal growth.

◆ Be willing to change.

◆ The biggest get-well question is: "What am I willing to do to participate in my healing?" Getting well and staying healthy is a life-long inquiry.

*...a time
to explore,
be open
to change,
and
participate
in your
healing*

Alternative and Integrative Approaches to Treating Cancer

*These brief descriptions of the approaches available to me in 2000 are based on information I currently obtained from the books **Options: The Alternative Cancer Therapy Book** by Richard Walters (1992) and **Outsmart Your Cancer: Alternative Non-Toxic Treatments That Work** by Tanya Harter Pierce, MA, MFCC (2009); and also official websites. Only the book **Options** was available to me in 2000.*

— Sandra Miniere

Pharmacology

◆ **Dr. Stanislaw Burzynski, MD, PhD — Antineoplaston Therapy —** In 1967 Dr. Burzynski discovered a group of peptides (short chains of amino acids) and amino acid derivatives occurring naturally throughout the human body that inhibit the growth of cancer cells. Peptides offer a biochemical defense that is separate from the immune system. Antineoplastons reprogram and destroy cancer cells and do not interfere with normal cell growth. Treatment involves oral supplements and intravenous infusions, as well as customized nutritional programs to complement the treatment. After an initial stay at the outpatient center, people continue their protocol at home. His treatment could cost as much as $5,000.00 per month for intravenous therapy. He has survived many government attempts to shut down his Houston clinic.

◆ **Gaston Naessens (Biologist) —** 714X is a camphor-nitrogen compound that is injected into the body's lymphatic system. It is designed to strengthen the immune system and unclog lymphatic fluid. 714X enables the leukocytes (white blood cells) to resume their activity and destroy foreign cells. 714X is self-administered through injections in the groin area about once a day in 21-day cycles. It may also be inhaled through a nebulizer as additional treatment for certain types of cancer. Through the microscope he developed, the Somatoscope, Gaston Naessens observed live blood samples and discovered somatids, microscopic subcellular living and reproducing organisms. Somatids circulate within the blood and have life cycle patterns that influence the reproduction and growth of cells. A breakdown of the healthy somatid cycle can lead to cancer and other diseases. He is still harassed for his theories and treatment approach.

Immunotherapy

◆ **Dr. Lawrence Burton, PhD — Immuno-Augmentative Therapy (IAT) —** Dr. Burton's therapy consisted of four blood proteins—substances occurring naturally in the body—that caused tumors to grow and shrink. IAT was

(Continued on the next page...)

developed in the 1960s. It aims to restore normal immune functioning so that the patient's own immune system will destroy the cancer cells. His therapy involves replenishing the deficient blood fractions by injecting patients with them in amounts based on a blood analysis taken once or twice a day. Patients are injected with a non-toxic serum to keep the immune system in balance with these proteins, much like a diabetic with insulin. As a result of continued harassment for his work, Dr. Burton left the country and relocated to the Bahamas. The Immune Augmentation Therapy Clinic continues to help patients control their cancer.

◆ **Josef Issels, MD — Whole Body Therapy** — Dr. Issels's immunotherapy program is designed to stimulate the body's immune mechanisms to recognize and eliminate cancer cells. He treats all of the organs and systems of the body that affect the immune system. His complex healing approach is designed to remove causal factors, repair damages to organs and organ systems, as well as prevent disease progression and recurrence. Individualized treatment plans include cancer vaccines; organic foods; intravenous nutrition and nutraceuticals; Co-Enzyme Co-Q10; digestive enzymes; ozone therapy to improve cellular respiration; glandulars to help regenerate the liver, thyroid and thymus; Laetrile; chelation therapy; colon hydrotherapy; and more. His treatment facilities are located in the US and Europe.

Herbal Therapy

◆ **Harry Hoxsey (1901-1974)** — Harry was the son of a veterinarian. He had little formal education and originally used the family herbal remedy to treat animals. When he began treating and healing human cancer patients, he was hounded by the authorities for practicing medicine without a license and eventually left the country. The Bio-Medical Center in Tijuana, Mexico, uses his approach today. Their treatment includes the original internal tonic and external salve, as well as diet, vitamin and mineral supplements and attitudinal counseling. Hoxsey's remedy for external cancer consists of a red paste made with bloodroot, mixed with zinc chloride and antimony sulfide. The basic ingredients of the internal tonic are Red Clover blossom, Licorice root, Buckhorn bark, Burdock root, Stillingia root, Poke root, Barberry root, Oregon Grape root, Cascara Sagrada bark, Prickly Ash bark, Wild Indigo root and potassium iodide. In 1953, Hoxsey's clinic in Dallas, Texas, treated 12,000 patients. These herbs were also used to treat cancer by Native American healers.

◆ **Rene Caisse (1888–1978)** — During the 1920s, a Canadian nurse developed an herbal tea formula—Essiac. This remedy contributed to many cancer cures and gave cancer patients symptom relief. On the way to developing her final formula, she experimented, tested and refined the mixture of burdock root, sheep sorrel, slippery elm bark and Turkish rhubarb root. When the herbs were blended and brewed in a certain way, they reduced tumor growth, purified the blood and strengthened the immune system. She initially gave the tea to her aunt who outlived her cancer death sentence by 21 years. For many years she treated thousands of patients. She was allowed to give her remedy to patients because she did not charge for it. She never received the recognition and approval she wanted for Essiac. A year before her death she gave the secret recipe to a Toronto-based company. Today many Essiac products are on the market.

◆ Not included here but worth mentioning: Chinese medicine uses herbs to treat cancer successfully.

Nutrition

◆ **Macrobiotics** — Michio Kushi is the author of *Cancer, Diet and Macrobiotics* and a leader of the macrobiotics movement. According to Michio, cancer results largely from improper diet and is classified to be predominantly yin or yang, contraction or expansion of the organs. Once the yin/yang diagnosis is made, specific dietary recommendations can be targeted to the individual. A general macrobiotic food plan would include replacing a high-fat, low-fiber diet with 50 to 60% whole cereal grains, 25% to 30% vegetables, smaller amounts of soup, beans and sea vegetables, plus occasional fish, seasonal fruits, nuts, seeds and condiments. Foods to be avoided are highly processed foods, meat, poultry, eggs and dairy, as well as fruit juices, canned and frozen foods, coffee and commercial tea, and refined sweeteners. Many foods in the basic macrobiotic diet have reduced or inhibited cancer growth. It is a philosophy and a way of life, as well as a nutritional system. In the book *Cancer Free*, Vivien Newbold, MD, presents six case histories of patients who overcame incurable cancer through macrobiotics. She wrote the book because the American Cancer Society and The National Cancer Institute, as well as medical journals, were not interested in her findings.

◆ **Moerman's Anti-Cancer Diet** — According to Cornelis Moerman, MD, cancer develops as the result of a disturbed metabolism arising from a long period of malnutrition. His healing approach creates an oxygen-rich bodily environment that is hostile to cancer cells. The basic diet includes fresh organic vegetables and fruits, fruit and vegetable juices consumed in place of water and other beverages, whole cereals of all kinds, whole-grain breads, buttermilk, other dairy products in small amounts and natural seasonings. Dried green peas eaten in a vegetable soup, red beet juice and egg yolks are included. The diet forbids eating foods believed to damage the body and prevent nutritious foods from being properly absorbed. His patients avoided meat, fish, shellfish, animal fats, cheese with high fat and salt, egg whites, alcoholic beverages, coffee, tea with caffeine, cocoa, hydrogenated vegetable oils and shortenings, most beans and peas, all added salt, refined white sugar, sugar substitutes and all food containing them. Dr. Moerman was rejected by the Dutch medical community despite the remission of hundreds of incurable cancer patients.

Metabolic Therapy

◆ **Max Gerson, MD (1881-1959)** — Dr. Gerson theorized that cancer results from faulty metabolism due to poor nutrition and long-term exposure to pesticides, chemical fertilizers, air and water pollution and other irritants in the environment. If the systems of the body are healthy, especially the liver, pancreas and immune systems, cancer cannot invade the body. Dr. Gerson's therapy focuses on restoring the body to health and supporting each metabolic requirement by drinking almost 20 pounds of organically grown fruits and vegetables daily. The daily protocol consists of drinking 13 glasses of juice and taking five coffee enemas to detoxify the liver. His protocol also involves injections of liver extract, high doses of thyroid extract, Vitamin C, digestive enzymes and niacin. All salt added to foods is eliminated, and fat protein is restricted. Thousands of cancer patients have reported being cured by the Gerson Therapy over the past 60 years.

◆ **William D. Kelley, DDS (1925-2005)** — Kelley's Nutritional-Metabolic Therapy is based on the premise that a deficiency of pancreatic enzymes contributes to a faulty metabolism. These enzymes are required to attack and destroy the protective coating around trophoblast-like cells—cells naturally produced for healing purposes within the body. However, when these cells multiple out of control, they eventually turn into cancer cells. Pancreatic enzymes keep this destructive process in check. Kelly's therapy combined large doses of pancreatic enzymes and other supplements intended to allow the body to naturally destroy cancer cells. He also prescribed vigorous detoxification of the liver, gallbladder, intestines, kidneys and lungs. He suggested at least one coffee enema a day. He individualized dietary requirements for each patient based on the ten metabolic types he developed and categorized. The psychological-spiritual aspects of healing were also addressed. Despite his outstanding success in treating cancer for 25 years, he was harassed and forced to shut down his business in 1986. Dr. Nicholas Gonzales in New York City currently uses a modified Kelly approach in the treatment of cancer.

Energy Healing

◆ **Royal Ramond Rife (1888–1971)** — The Rife Generator was a device that destroyed cancer-causing microbes using specific electromagnetic frequencies. Rife successfully treated many cancer patients in the 1930s, but the American Medical Association worked to destroy his therapy and technology. Doctors who used Rife's instrument were harassed. Rife's device used a plasma tube modulated with a frequency that was precisely tuned to the resonant frequency of the targeted pathogens. It destroyed the pathogens, but not the other cells because of the differences in their respective frequencies of resonance. The original Rife treatment consisted of using a specific frequency three times a day for three minutes. Today many types of Rife boxes are on the market; however, there is little data to support their effectiveness. In addition, there is controversy regarding their duplication of the original device.

◆ **Homeopathy** — Samuel Hahnemann, MD (1755-1843) was the founder of Homeopathy in Germany. To stimulate a person's natural healing response, a homeopath dissolves in water minute dilutions of natural substances from the plant, mineral and animal kingdoms. The more the solution is diluted, the greater its potency. Homeopathy considers cancer to be a symptom of an underlying imbalance associated with poor diet, chronic exposure to toxins, genetic disposition, and repressed feelings and thoughts, to name a few. A homeopath treats the person and their disease by using a client's unique symptoms (considered "strange, rare and peculiar" to the disease) to select a remedy. Homeopathic treatment is intended to strengthen the cancer patient's immune system, reduce or eliminate tumors, and control metastatic processes. Homeopathic remedies bring a person's "lifeforce" back into a balance that promotes wellness. If the resonance of one specific remedy is incorrect, the person will require a new remedy to get well. Individual remedies have demonstrated prolonged survival and symptom relief. In the early 1900s the pharmaceutical industry in this country got stronger, and Homeopathy as a legitimate medical treatment was shut down.

◆ Not included here but worth mentioning: Chinese medicine uses acupuncture to treat cancer successfully.

Mind-Body Healing

Mental patterns stored deep within the subconscious mind have a powerful influence over the body. This unconscious programming is formed from the situations, traumas, emotions and interpretations an individual experiences from birth into adulthood. The experiences from birth to approximately seven years of age form rigid scripts and beliefs that can interfere with a person's health and wellbeing. An important part of healing involves uncovering and clearing this subconscious programming because it influences a person's thoughts, feelings, behaviors and spirituality on a daily basis. Cutting edge research is revealing the role cellular memory plays in the disease process.

Negative emotions, like hate, anger, resentment, frustration, fear, depression, helplessness, sorrow, guilt, and shame, to name a few, can produce harmful changes to the body's biochemistry. In contrast, positive emotions produce life-enhancing biochemical changes. These chemical changes are documented in scientific research. Neuropeptides demonstrate that the body is fluid enough to match the mind. Neuropeptides move with thoughts and affect the body's chemistry to promote health or destroy it. Chronic stress is another documented source of biochemical changes that interfere with the body's ability to heal itself. The latest research on stress reports that 80% to 95% of the time stress is the underlying cause of illness. Long held negative thoughts and emotions and chronic stress, whether conscious or unconscious, weaken the immune system and disrupt normal processes within the body. When people change habitual negative thoughts and beliefs to positive thinking, they are changing their emotions and chemistry. They are promoting a healthy body.

According to mind-body therapies, people are able to contribute to their recovery by improving their emotional, mental and spiritual practices. The techniques of visualization, affirmation, meditation and energy psychology can change the course of a disease. A small number of people have healed themselves of cancer through mind-body techniques alone. They remind the health care community and people who are struggling with a disease that anything is possible when mind-body-spirit techniques are brought into the healing equation.

◆ **Ayurveda Medicine** — Ayurveda medicine treats disease holistically by including physical, mental and spiritual factors. From the Ayurveda perspective cancer has many causes—toxic environment, devitalized foods, negative emotions, sedentary lifestyle and lack of spiritual purpose or fulfillment. Emotional, mental and spiritual stagnation contribute to a weakened immune system.

A person develops cancer as the result of biological, emotional and spiritual imbalances. Treatment involves diagnosing the patient's constitutional type (humor) and state of bioenergetic balance. Three stages of treatment include removal of the accumulated toxins in the body, balancing the excess biologic humor (constitutions—air, fire, water) and rebuilding and rejuvenating the body. Treatment includes herbal medicine, diet, massage, detoxification, breathing exercises, yoga, meditation and mantras. Ayurveda offers a holistic lifestyle of wellness.

◆ **Carl Simonton, MD** — Dr. Simonton, the Father of Psychosocial Oncology, died in 2009. He generated a new level of awareness and understanding concerning the mind's role in healing. In *Getting Well Again* (1992), he highlights the role of emotional stress in the development of cancer. Through relaxation and visualization, people worked to overcome their cancer. Cancer Recovery Foundation continues his legacy today.

◆ **Louise Hay** — Ms. Hay guides many toward wellness. Her book, *You Can Heal Your Life* (1984), her affirmation tapes and DVDs associated with this book, as well as other books, offer insights and techniques to heal the body, mind and soul. Louise Hay healed herself of terminal cancer with mind-body techniques alone, a great inspiration for other cancer patients. Self-love and ownership, not blame and condemnation, enable people to look within themselves to uncover the psycho-spiritual causes of their illness and work through them.

◆ **Deepak Chopra, MD** — Dr. Chopra describes in *Quantum Healing* (1990) how the individual is central in the process of creating the universe that exists within the individual's perception and without in the physical world. Awareness, attention and intention are an important part of the physical healing process. He describes the individual going to the deepest core of the mind-body system to the point where consciousness starts to affect healing. Bringing the body back into balance and harmony reawakens its own healing ability.

◆ **Lawrence LeShan, PhD** — Dr. LeShan encourages cancer patients to cope with the losses and disappointments of their past and do what makes them feel more alive. In *Cancer as a Turning Point* (1994), Dr. LeShan describes how people can make psychological shifts and create lives with personal meaning and passion. This mind-body approach influences the body's ability to heal itself. Many of his clients with late stage cancer go into remission.

34

Chapter 3
Don't Think or Feel; Just Do It!
(Surviving a Mastectomy)

November and December 2000

The morning I entered the hospital to have a left modified radical mastectomy with reconstruction, I was plummeted into a stunning reality. Nothing and no one could rescue me from this assault to my body and wellbeing. Once again, I had to endure a traumatic experience that left me feeling vulnerable. There was no escape. Surviving two divorces and repressed memories of sexual abuse prepared me to face life's challenges courageously. Over time, I learned to trust that everything would work out OK.

Paul drove me to the hospital on November 29, 2000. My other support people were thousands of miles away, which did not seem to matter because I felt alone in what was about to happen. People offered to be there, but I thought I would need them when I got out of the hospital. Wrong!

As I entered the large bathroom off the surgery waiting room with its eight curtained stalls, I was stunned that I could be so calm. Observing myself, I thought, *"Would I be this calm if my life were in serious danger?"* I only had stage I breast cancer and had to cope with having a mastectomy with reconstruction, about a four-hour procedure. The surgeon would remove the breast tissue from the left breast, including the nipple and place an implant under the chest wall muscles. On the right side she would insert an implant so the two breasts looked symmetrical. She would remove the nipple and take a piece of skin from my abdomen to place over that opening. I would come back six months later so she could take another piece of skin on the other side of my abdomen to build a nipple.

Once inside the bathroom, I had to strip naked and put on the white elasticized stockings and a gown that opened at the back. I placed my underwear, jeans, sweater, socks, and shoes in a paper bag with my name on it. I walked to my gurney with the bag in my hands and gave it to Paul for safekeeping. Reality set in. At that point, I told myself, *"You just have to do this. You'll cry about it later. Now, you must stay positive and visualize a positive outcome."* I had to do this to save my life. And, it felt like I was doing it rather well. Grace carried me.

Oncoplastic Surgery: A Creative Surgical Approach for Breast Cancer Patients

by Gail S. Lebovic, MA, MD, FACS
For Additional Information visit: www.ASBD.org

The term *Oncoplastic Surgery* describes an evolution within the field of breast surgery that was started in the late 1980s by a few pioneering surgeons. Concerned with the disfiguring surgeries commonly associated with breast cancer removal, these individuals sought a more creative surgical solution. Basically, the idea behind Oncoplastic Surgery is to combine the principles of surgical oncology (cancer removal) with techniques from plastic and reconstructive surgery. In this way, the surgeon plans the cancer-removing portion of the operation while keeping in mind the aesthetic outcome, and utilizing techniques to improve the appearance of the breast(s) afterwards. Oncoplastic Surgery does not describe a particular surgical procedure; it represents a comprehensive approach to surgical planning intended to achieve:

1. Wide surgical margins free of tumor

2. Reduced risk for local recurrence

3. Optimized cosmetic outcome by preserving more skin

4. Breast volume reduction for patients with large breasts and breast cancer

5. In general, fewer surgical procedures overall

6. Prophylactic removal of the breast tissue with reconstruction for patients at high/serious risk of breast cancer (i.e., genetic)

Studies have demonstrated that the Oncoplastic approach adds to the oncologic safety of breast-conserving treatment, and ultimately better cosmetic outcomes following breast cancer surgery. This occurs because a larger volume of breast tissue can be excised and wider surgical margins free of tumor can be obtained. Oncoplastic techniques can be utilized routinely, and they are especially useful in specific cases such as removal of large tumors, when standard breast-conserving approaches have a high probability of leaving positive margins behind. By obtaining a "cleaner" margin, the associated risk of local recurrence can be diminished without creating an unacceptable deformity of the breast.

A preoperative assessment includes a discussion regarding the cancer, but will also include the details of methods of breast reconstruction and whether surgery is needed on the opposite breast such as reduction, lift, or augmentation in order to achieve breast symmetry.

Over the past several decades, techniques for breast reconstruction have undergone dramatic improvements. With the advent and integration of breast implants, tissue expanders and new methods for natural tissue flap reconstructions, there have been dramatic improvements in the appearance of reconstructed breasts. However, even though plastic and reconstructive surgery has seen and achieved great success, recent studies reveal that most women undergoing mastectomy (as many as 80%) are not having breast reconstruction. Unfortunately, fewer and fewer surgeons are committed to this highly specialized area leaving far too many women with little or no option for reconstruction.

This phenomenon has stimulated a tremendous interest in the field of Oncoplastic Surgery, with many breast surgeons seeking additional training in order to offer full and comprehensive management to their patients. Since there are many various clinical practice settings within the United States, sometimes surgeons will work as a team, and in other situations, a single surgeon may have the skills to perform both the cancer surgery and the reconstruction as well.

As mentioned, in some cases the primary surgeon may not take on the additional responsibility of performing the breast reconstruction; however, if the surgeon has an intimate knowledge of the various techniques, the risks, benefits, and timing of each type of reconstruction, this can help the patient take a more active role in planning the overall surgical approach. This allows for integration of all aspects of the surgery. In many cases, immediate breast reconstruction can at least be started at the time of mastectomy with placement of an implant, expander, or flap. This ultimately helps the patient emotionally through the loss of the breast, and in most cases, decreases the number of surgical procedures the patient ultimately needs to undergo.

In this manner, the field of Oncoplastic Surgery will help surgeons learn and apply creative surgical solutions that simultaneously improve oncologic outcome and surgical cosmesis. These techniques are broadly applicable to all patients undergoing breast surgery, and it is most likely that university training programs will soon offer specialty training for surgeons in Oncoplastic Surgery. The American Society of Breast Disease has dedicated significant resources to teach surgeons these unique skills in a unique annual program called the "School of Oncoplastic Surgery."

Dr. Lebovic is Past President of the ASBD, and founder of the School of Oncoplastic Surgery.

Men to the Rescue

Before the surgery, I asked my female surgeon to request a female operating team. I wanted the sacrifice of my left breast to be a women's ritual. It felt like a private female thing. When I received a telephone call the evening before surgery from a male anesthesiologist, I was upset. While I was not rude to him, the conversation lasted two minutes. I told him not to over medicate me, and I would see him in the morning. The disappointment hit. I felt weighed down because my ritual was not being honored by the "powers that be."

I reminded myself: *"You believe in the divine right order of things, so you really need to let this negative attitude go."* I had to get past my sense of dread. The inner turmoil lasted a few hours, and I finally fell asleep surrendering to the inevitable. When I met the anesthesiologist the next morning in his funny green shower cap, he seemed quite harmless. He was tall, blonde and had bulging muscles on his thin frame. I liked him in spite of myself. He appeared centered and calm like someone who meditated as well as lifted weights. He exuded confidence. I gave him a slight smile, as a truce offering between us. He passed the test of a *painless* IV insertion.

My female team took another hit when a short, dark-haired, body-builder type man walked over to introduce himself and offer his assistance as my surgical nurse. I was too preoccupied with staying positive to have an emotional reaction to him. I did not have the time or luxury to get tense and upset. I wanted the energy to stay high and positive so the surgery would be flawless. (I believe that our attitude affects outcomes.) My job was to remain centered and calm while I waited to go under my surgeon's knife. The nurse appeared gentle in spite of his strong masculine appearance, and he spoke to me with genuine concern. Instead of females, I attracted two muscular men who were gentle and caring. I began to get the picture. I was in the best of hands regardless of the demise of my ritual. I got what I needed, instead of what I wanted.

I did manage to become slightly agitated when Paul could not find the healing mantra tape I wanted to hear before being wheeled into surgery. I quickly settled on my second choice—*Triple Mantra*, designed to eliminate negativity and prevent accidents. As I began listening to the trance inducing sounds, my body relaxed. I was able to transcend the voices, smells, and activity in the room. Within five minutes of focusing inward my surgeon showed up. She was all smiles and positive about the surgery. She looked like a little happy pixie, so I am thinking, *"How bad could this be?"* I reminded her not to take too many lymph nodes because I was going to do something systemic to heal my body. My plan was to treat my body as though the lymph nodes were positive no matter what they actually found. Plus, I had heard horror stories of women suffering without their lymph nodes, and I did not want to become one of them. It was time to go. It all seemed so rushed. I forgot to tell her to keep my breasts small with the two implants she would be inserting. I just wanted to look normal, not buxom.

Soon after she left, the anesthesiologist came over to me and injected medicine for nausea into the IV bag. I didn't have much time to dwell on what was about to happen to me. When I got a farewell kiss from Paul, I thought, *"The next time he kisses me I would have a different body."* With my headphones on, the Walkman lying next to my body and listening to the chant, I was wheeled away from the curtained stall. Before we reached the end of the room, I was unconscious.

The Worst Is Yet to Come

As I was preparing for the surgery psychologically, I realized waking up in pain was the thing I dreaded most. I regained consciousness in the recovery room moaning incoherently that the pain medicine was not working. I felt an excruciating burning pain in my chest. I lost consciousness again. I regained some awareness when Paul was next to me holding my hand. The contact helped me slip into reality for a few moments. The next thing I remember he was sitting next to me in a hospital room. Voices were coming from a TV clamped to the wall in front of my bed. I was complaining, *"This isn't working; I am still in pain."* He called the nurse. She tried to teach me to push a hand-held button for pain medicine, but my fingers wouldn't work. I still felt an oppressive, painful weight on my chest, and I could not move my arms and hands. I thought, *"I just have to get through the next 24 hours."*

Before breast cancer, I was very healthy even though I had asthma. I stayed a long distance away from hospitals and traditional doctors most of the time. But here I was in a prestigious hospital, and the quality of care was a surprise to say the least. Late in the evening of the surgery, my surgeon came to visit me. She had me press the button to call the nurse for something. When no one came to me after about ten minutes, she got angry. She had me moved into another wing, which was not much better in terms of my care.

When I woke up the next morning, I was still in mild pain and could not move my body in the bed. Two implants were placed under my chest wall muscles. The left one became a prosthesis after she removed the tissue of the left breast and the right one a "boob job." I had no idea how much pain and restriction the surgery would entail. I went into the surgery and reconstruction very naive. I trusted my surgeon's reconstruction recommendation. She was just going to "pop" two implants under the muscles of my chest wall. It sounded so simple and still makes me smile. If I had known more, I might have thought twice about the procedure. But, I might have caused myself even more stress living with the alternative. All the options were awful. In this case, ignorance got me to do what was best for me. I just had to suck it up and make the best of my decision.

Initially, my efforts to get help in order to control my pain and adjust my body in the bed did not produce results. I lost my composure. I finally got a hospital staff member to call Paul at 6:30 a.m. and tell him to come to the hospital as soon as possible. He was planning to go to work that day, but he came to be with me instead. While I waited for him, I kept trying to get help from the staff for the pain, but my voice was not being heard. Finally, I said I wanted to see the head nurse. When she arrived in my room, I told her I wanted a private duty nurse because I needed help and no one was available to help me. The sponge bath that morning consisted of a warm, wet facecloth put on my tray. I could not use it because I could not use my arms. I could not feed myself either. Fortunately, food did not appeal to me because I still felt slightly nauseous from the anesthesia. The IV method of pain relief had limited effect on my pain level.

We ultimately discovered that with my arm bent, the flow of the IV liquid was constricted going into my veins. Consequently, the pain medicine was not doing the job adequately. The level of care contributed to my feeling helpless and agitated. Once Paul arrived that first morning, I felt a sense of relief because the reinforcements had landed. I had someone to help me move my body on the bed and make sure the pain level was under control. Once the pain medication finally started working, I calmed down. Paul went to work around noon and returned that evening. He could see that I was coping at that point. When my surgeon showed up around 10:00 p.m., I was able to sit up with my legs over the side of the bed. We had a nice half hour visit. I asked her why she was still working in the hospital at this hour. (Less than two days post surgery, I watched myself trying to take care of my surgeon. *Helper* is in my DNA.) I never did get the private duty nurse because the crisis appeared to be over and I would be leaving the hospital the following day. None too soon!

The two days I spent recovering in that hospital were more stressful than going into surgery, but I survived both. The serenity of my home embraced me when I walked into the house. My cousin would arrive that afternoon. She would nurse me back to health for a few days, and my daughter would take over when she left. I remained in physical distress even with the loving care of the two women closest to me. I slept sitting up with five pillows under me in order to feel somewhat comfortable. Once I got settled into a position, I could not move, but I was sleeping. Within a few days of being home, the high of the pain medication kicked in. I was laughing and joking about my "boob job"—a sign I was getting better.

My Aching Breasts

My breasts were huge. In my robe all you noticed were my breasts. I thought, *"How could she do this to me."* I deliberately told my surgeon in her office to keep my breasts small. (What I did not realize at the time was that my chest was swollen from the surgery.) The implants were also causing the muscles to spasm, and even with mild pain medication, I wasn't pain free. Dr. Lebovic informed me that the muscles would spasm and be painful until they relaxed and acclimated to the new position. If that were the case, I suggested that I take some Valium to relax the muscles. A half of a Valium did the trick. The pain lessened. Being my own advocate paid off.

About one week post hospital stay I was on my own. The loneliness and feeling sorry for myself set in. My high school girlfriends sent me a plant. It made me cry. I called one of them and tried to thank her for thinking of me, and I could not stop crying. It was comical. My friend could not understand a word I was saying, but she listened and loved me. The outpouring of love from my family and friends surprised me. A few days after my daughter left, I realized that I was feeling homesick and needed some nurturing food. I found an Italian restaurant in the phone book, called them and asked if they had ravioli on the menu. They had a special three-cheese homemade ravioli. Bingo! Ravioli would become my teaspoon of sugar. Paul picked up an order on his way home from work. Eating that ravioli, I felt like a kid again. I could picture myself surrounded by my wonderful Italian clan and feeling their love. I was home, and I felt safe!

For almost one month the pain had my attention. For the first two weeks I could not focus enough to read. Watching movies on television took my mind off of the pain and stress of recovery. I watched the six-hour video of Pride and Prejudice with Colin Firth. It got me through two lonely, uncomfortable days. I observed myself sitting in front of the TV smiling through the physical discomfort while I watched movies that kept me amused. Talking to people on the phone helped too. I felt connected to others even though we were thousands of miles apart.

Almost three weeks after surgery, I was still on pain medication and could not move my left arm easily. The implant placed under the muscle of the left breast affected all of the muscles in my left shoulder and upper back. Moving my left arm gave me pain, and I had little range of motion. Paul was still washing my hair in the kitchen sink. When I went to see Dr. Xie, my acupuncturist in California, he told me not to worry, he would fix it, and he did. In one session he put needles in that shoulder and upper back, and I left his office almost pain free with a great improvement in my range of motion. The needles that day really hurt. I almost jumped off the table with a few of them, but they did their magic, and I left with a different feeling in my body. I was totally surprised that he could do this. I finally put aside the pain pills and replaced them with over-the-counter pain relief medication. Amazing! Thank you Dr. Xie. I do not know what I would have done without you during my cancer recovery.

Time for Me

When I moved to California, I still worked with some of my clients over the telephone and saw people in person on visits to New Jersey. For the two weeks during the surgery and recovery, I did not have any client telephone consultations. And, I did not return to New Jersey to celebrate Christmas with my family that year or work with clients. I could not tell my clients about the breast cancer because I did not want them to worry about me. I lied and said I would not be back for my December visit because I was attending a workshop around the Christmas holidays.

Looking back, I can see the benefits of my being diagnosed and treated in California. I would not have wanted an active psycho-

The Benefits of Acupuncture in Cancer Care

by Dr. Nalini Chilkov, LAc, OMD, Traditional Oriental Medicine, Biomedicine and Cell Biology
Integrative Cancer Care and Optimal Health Collaborative
(www.doctornalini.com)

Acupuncture is an ancient system of healing with modern applications. Many leading edge cancer centers today include acupuncture therapy for cancer patients. For the cancer patient or cancer survivor/thriver, research supports the use of acupuncture for the following concerns:

Pain Management: Acupuncture is very effective for managing pain related to tumors, surgery, chemotherapy, radiation and inflammation. Patients who receive acupuncture may be able to use lower doses of pain medications.

Immune System Modulation: Acupuncture increases blood cell production and enhances Natural Killer Cells and Lymphocytes which lead to increased immune response and decreased risk of infection.

Inflammation: Many of the treatments for cancer such as chemotherapy, radiation therapy and surgery also cause painful inflammation. Acupuncture reduces the pain and swelling related to inflammation.

Nausea and Vomiting: Acupuncture has been shown to reduce the intensity and frequency of nausea and vomiting in cancer patients receiving chemotherapy.

Dry, Painful Mouth and Throat: Cancer patients receiving radiation to the head and neck experience dry mouth due to the reduction in saliva production. Acupuncture has been shown to decrease these side effects.

Sleep: Cancer patients suffer sleep disruption and insomnia. By relieving these symptoms the cancer patient is able to get the deep sleep and rest required for recovery and healing.

Hot Flashes in Breast Cancer Patients: Many women undergo hormonal treatment for breast cancer. Acupuncture has been shown to decrease the frequency and intensity of hot flashes for breast cancer patients.

Neuropathy: Nerve damage and numbness are common side effects of chemotherapy. Acupuncture supports the healing and repair of nerves and the restoration of normal nerve function.

Quality of Life: Eugene Mak, MD, oncologist, states that acupuncture *"can also add to the patients' sense of wellbeing and decrease the malaise associated with any chronic disease, especially cancer... and imparts a sense of wellbeing and accelerates patients' recovery."*

Acupuncture Therapy uses very thin needles inserted into acupuncture points throughout the body. During a treatment, the patient will slowly drop down into a pleasant state of restful relaxation. In order to create deep lasting change, acupuncture is done as a series of treatments.

therapy practice while going through this. I had all the time I needed to heal with few responsibilities. I guess there was a divine order to things. I felt lonely, but I was free of responsibilities and did not have to explain anything to anyone. I *did* tell my clients about the breast cancer when I saw them during my April visit to New Jersey in 2001, and they were all shocked. One client said, *"If it can happen to you, it can happen to anybody."* I do not know how true that is, but I do believe being on HRT the way I was taking it for ten years contributed to my getting breast cancer.

Back into Life

Attending Paul's company Christmas party three weeks after surgery distracted me from my physical discomfort and loneliness. An enchanting dinner cruise around San Francisco Bay was exactly what my body and soul needed. The over-the-counter pain medication helped me stay focused on pleasure. I sat there quietly taking in everything—the people, the ship, the food and the magnificence of San Francisco Bay. I said no to the dancing, but I had one glass of champagne to celebrate life. Being on the cruise felt like a gift for all that I had been through. I remember walking down a long gangplank next to the young CEO and congratulating him on his success in creating a business that was about to be sold. I suggested that he would do it again. I began to act as a success coach even before I knew what that meant. Attending this event was a wise decision on my part. It got me back into life and gave me the emotional lift I needed to keep going and get through the Christmas holidays without my family.

On Christmas Day, 2000, I dressed in a navy blue silk pants suit, and Paul and I had Christmas dinner at a hotel in San Francisco. The food was delicious and the place was elegant and festive. I missed being with my family (my first Christmas without them), but I felt good to be pain free and at peace. My body and life felt quiet for the first time in a few months. I could feel the surgery ordeal receding as the joyful mood of Christmas wrapped itself around me. Two instead of ten people were sitting at the table. I took my focus off the loss and felt deep gratitude to be in a beautiful place with my very special partner. He did not become my husband until the following December. As we held up our glasses filled with golden sparkling bubbles and wished each other Merry Christmas, life felt sacred and so did our love.

After several months, the swelling went down, and I looked like the new normal. I still feel as though I am wearing a breastplate, and I wonder what people feel when they hug me. But, the two breasts look similar with and without clothes. What is done is done, and I am grateful that my skilled surgeon remained a beacon of optimism throughout the process. She was a blessing in my ordeal. My decision to have implants in both breasts at the same time served me well. If I only had the left breast done during the mastectomy, I do not know whether I would have had the courage to get back on the operating table and have an implant inserted in the right breast.

Three months post surgery I returned to Mission Peak. I needed to reconnect with the victory energy of reaching its peak and return to climbing as a form of exercise. I hoped to climb a fifth of the way to the top that day. On my way up I stopped to visit with a black calf with a cute white face. He stood as still as a statue staring at me. His fur looked so soft and cuddly; I wanted to walk over and pet him. Instead, I asked him, *"Do you think I can make it to my marker today?"* My new friend just continued to stare at me. I did make it to my goal. When I turned around and looked at the view of the south point of San Francisco Bay in the distance, the view was spectacular. The sun reflecting off the water gave the scene a mystical quality. In that moment the mastectomy became a part of my history. My life was returning to normal. Implementing the important second phase of my recovery plan loomed before me—to eliminate any traces of cancer in my body and restore it to radiant health.

Chapter 3 Lessons Learned...

- Your naiveté can get you into trouble; sometimes the trouble leads to a positive outcome.

- When "what you need" instead of "what you want" arrives, find a way to accept and work with it.

- "Pity parties" and "temper tantrums" are normal; just move through them quickly.

- When things are bad in the present moment, focus on the positive possibility that is on its way to you now.

- Staying calm and hopeful, no matter how dark it gets, will attract grace into your life.

- Appreciate what is working and what you do have, especially the people who support you.

- Smiling and laughing are good for the body and soul.

...a time to focus on the positive, work with what is, and appreciate all that you have

Chapter 4
Choice and Trust Pay Off
(Alternative Treatment)

February and March 2001

Life feels magical when I observe a mysterious force working behind the scenes to guide me. How it works eludes me most of the time, but I acknowledge its presence when I feel directed to the people and places that benefit me in some way. My intuition and instinct usually help me make wise choices. However, finding the alternative cancer doctor after my mastectomy felt like a miracle. Without my trying to control things, I was led through the maze of possibilities right to his door.

As stated earlier, my research for natural approaches to treating cancer led me to explore nutrition, vitamins, herbs, vaccines, detoxification, mind-body approaches and immune boosting procedures, just to name a few. I read several books highlighting nontoxic treatment options. *Third Opinion*, by John Fink, listed hundreds of doctors and centers throughout the world. Resources on the Internet (before the Google explosion), as well as personal referrals, made the task monumental. At one point, I just stared into space while sitting on the step of our deck and thought, *"This is more than I can do; I don't know which way to turn."*

Nicole's intuitive reading about a short, bald, male doctor gave me more stress, not less. Was the doctor she saw in her mind's eye located several hundred miles north, south, or east of my home? And, how could I possibly find him? Praying for guidance while exploring all of my options seemed the reasonable thing to do.

Five weeks after the mastectomy, I decided to find a new hair stylist. Two previous attempts at getting my hair cut since moving to California had been disappointing. A neighbor gave me the name and telephone number of her stylist, but the person she recommended did not return my call. I decided to make an appointment with the owner of the hair salon instead. When I saw the owner, a middle-aged woman with an attractive hairstyle, I had a good feeling. Her welcoming smile and genuine interest in me made it easy to tell her that I was recovering from a mastectomy. Sharing such a story with a stranger was out of character for me, but I could not stop myself.

She did a good job with my haircut. Better still, she recommended a book by a doctor in Reno, Nevada. One of her clients had gone to him and had been treated successfully by his cancer protocol. She offered to get the information for me, and the next day I picked up Dr. Douglas Brodie's book. His picture on the back page of the book indicated he was bald. I wondered if he was short, too. After reading his book in one day—and liking what he had to say—I thought, *"Could he be the one?"* It would be nothing short of a miracle if my first encounter with Dr. X took place only five minutes from my home. Unbelievable actually!

Meanwhile, the pressure to do something was getting more intense. Based on the pathology report of the left breast tissue, the oncologist informed me that the margins were not clear. Microscopic cancer cells had traveled beyond the removed breast tissue into the muscles of the chest wall and perhaps the lymph nodes in the center of the chest. However, all of the lymph nodes under my arm and in the removed breast tissue were normal. My oncologist recommended radiation, which might affect my lungs and heart. I did not want to think about what it would mean for the implant under the skin of the left breast. This was not good news. My life was still in jeopardy, and I had to do something. From my perspective, radiation was out of the question. I did not want to encounter the harmful effects it might inflict on my body. In addition, my surgeon did not think I needed radiation, but I agreed with the oncologist that something more should be done to protect my body from a cancer recurrence. My strong belief that I could heal my body of cancer naturally and systemically was about to be tested.

From what I learned about cancer, I had to improve my immune system and clean up my body of any remaining cancer activity. Six weeks after surgery, I went to a physician in San Francisco who specializes in complementary medicine. He was tall (not my short bald doctor) and spoke in a pleasant, calm manner. He listened with compassion as I explained my health history. He recommended a thyroid test and supplements to get the asthma and digestion under control. He also suggested I pick up the current issue of *Alternative Medicine Digest* because it had an article on cancer vaccines.

Scanning through the magazine, I spotted a full-page advertisement with a picture of Dr. Brodie, whose face reflected wisdom and confidence. This man had managed to get my attention a second time. I went to his website to learn more. I was close to picking up the phone to make an appointment, but instead, called Dr. Schachter, an alternative cancer specialist in New York. A colleague of mine had received treatment from him for breast cancer, and she became cancer free. Since it was inconvenient to see Dr. Schachter in person, I set up a telephone consultation in order to get his assessment of my cancer situation, as well as his treatment recommendations.

The radiation option created a sense of urgency and major distress. While on a weekend family vacation in Las Vegas, I had a telephone consultation with Dr. Schachter from my hotel room. After our conversation I felt relieved. He helped me understand that I could eliminate any cancer residue and restore my body to optimum health. He gave me hope that there were alternatives to radiation treatment that would clean up my margins. When I told him I was thinking of going to Dr. Brodie, he said enthusiastically, *"He is me in the West. We have been doing this work for the same length of time. I know him well."*

Three indicators pointed to Dr. Brodie. That was good enough for me.

When I hung up the telephone, I decided to call his office on Monday morning to make an appointment. I felt ready to make the financial commitment that would cost me thousands of dollars. His immune enhancing and detoxification approaches promised to be the right approach to prevent a recurrence. The cancer situation did not seem so life threatening when I left that hotel room. As I entered the large elevator vestibule on the floor of my hotel, I noticed one open elevator door with the indicator light going in my direction, down. No one was waiting for an elevator, and the seven other doors were closed. The foyer was filled with bright golden/white light from a huge crystal beaded chandelier. *"Could this be a sign that I was making the right choice?"* I gave a silent *"thank you"* as I stepped into the welcoming elevator. In that moment, all seemed to be in divine order.

Reno Bound

Paul and I made reservations to stay at one of the large casino hotels in Reno, Nevada, on a Sunday evening in February 2001. After my Monday morning appointment with Dr. Brodie, we would drive back to California with his treatment recommendations. It certainly felt strange to be checking into a casino hotel to see a doctor about saving my life. Fortunately, the festive mood of the city with its glitzy lights took the heaviness out of my heart. We looked like other visitors in search of fun. On the inside, however, I had some apprehension about what the next day would hold for me.

After signing in at the reception desk of the clinic, we got a tour and saw one large treatment room with about twelve overstuffed reclining chairs, a waiting area, large business area and small examining rooms. Patients were hooked up to IV drips in the large treatment room where nurses monitored them. They were reading or speaking quietly. The room had no TV only a large tropical fish tank. The setting, as well as the patients and nurses, all seemed pleasant enough. When I met Dr. Brodie in one of the small examining rooms, I knew he was the doctor who fit Nicole's description. How I found my way to him was beyond my rational comprehension!

We listened to each other, and I learned how he would treat my current cancer status. He recommended ten days of treatment on his protocol, which primarily consisted of vitamin and mineral intravenous drips and shots of peptides. The approximate cost was ten thousand dollars for ten days of treatment. His objective was to get my immune system functioning; mine was to clean up my margins. I would need to go to Reno and stay in a hotel for two consecutive five-day periods. The clinic was only open Monday through Friday.

Dr. Brodie gave me hope that my body could heal itself, and I could beat the cancer that was still a threat to me. Motivated and optimistic, Paul and I came up with a plan that worked. I took a plane from Oakland to Reno for the five-day treatment program. Driving alone near Donner Pass in the Sierra Mountains in February and March would have been too risky because of possible snowstorms. In addition, we could not predict whether I would be alert enough after the treatment to drive home. I flew out on a Monday morning and returned on a Friday afternoon. I rented a car to get around locally. I also decided to skip one week between the two five-day treatments.

When my dear friend in New Jersey heard that I would be going to Reno alone, she wanted to join me for a few days. This particular friend had also held a vigil with another friend, sending me love and healing energy for several hours during my surgery. When she called the hospital the day of surgery, the operator had put her call right through to the recovery room, and she spoke with the nurse. She had really taken this journey with me. I was deeply touched that she would put her business and life on hold in order to accompany me to Reno. I did not know how to accept her offer. This was an inconvenience and expense for her, but she insisted, and I accepted.

50

The Body's Immune System and "Terrain" Promote Wellness

by Robert A. Eslinger, DO, HMD
Reno Integrative Medical Center
(www.renointegrativemedicalcenter.com)

Our therapies support and enhance the body's natural defenses against cancer, while, at the same time, target the cancer. We offer treatments that strengthen and balance the immune system and improve the "terrain" or internal environment of the physical body. This approach plays a significant role in a patient's ability to heal from any health challenge, especially cancer.

Immune System: The immune system is designed to detect "foreign" invaders whether they are external or internal (normal cells becoming abnormal). It can also become part of the problem (i.e., "autoimmune disease") so it must be kept in balance.

When the immune system is not functioning properly, there are ways to stimulate it. Smart pathogens have a way of hiding or disguising themselves within the body to prevent obvious detection and common treatments are usually ineffective. It is a constant quest for researchers to find new ways of exposing these pathogens and eliminating them from your body.

Our Biological Response Modifiers are remedies and substances that are given orally and intravenously to increase the sensitivity and strength of the immune system as well as other systems of the body. This could be thought of as a "wake-up call to the body."

Terrain: The "terrain," the internal environment, is everything inside your body but outside the cells. It is where all the nutrients and waste products are transported to and from the cells. It can get "clogged up" with waste even in a healthy person. It is composed of many different substances and helpful micro-organisms. If it is kept in balance, it helps everything to function normally. If it gets out of balance, it can become a contributing factor to the development of disease.

Before Dr. Brodie died in 2005, I had the honor of working with him for two years. Dr. Brodie believed that cancer is not a death sentence. With the latest scientific information and belief in the natural healing impulses in the human body and mind, nothing is impossible. I believe that the future of medicine lies in working with the healing capabilities of the body, not working against them.

It looked as though I would not have time to feel sorry for myself and cry if I needed to do that. She would be there to keep me distracted and smiling—a better plan than having a pity party of one.

Lifeline to Health

The first day at the clinic was a bit traumatic. I do not like having needles inserted in me, and everyone in the large room was being injected or having the needles removed. I had to get used to this protocol and stop being a baby about it. I reminded myself, *"It could be chemotherapy."* So I just looked the other way, took some deep breaths while the nurse inserted the IV needle and hoped she knew what she was doing. Most of the time, the nurse inserted the needle without a problem. When the IV drip burned, she would put something in it to relieve the pain or slow the drip. The IV was expected to take about three hours. Some of mine took close to four hours. I often monitored the drip to be sure it wasn't going too fast or too slow. I got pretty good at assessing the right rhythm for me. And, of course, I adjusted my own drip sometimes. After the IV came a shot of peptides in the buttocks. Every day I walked into one of the small examining rooms, dropped my pants and got the shot.

Twice a week I received a darkfield microscope live blood cell analysis and a consultation with Dr. Brodie. On a computer screen I could see the shape, mobility and number of my red blood cells and the sparkling white blood cells (leukocytes) that were protecting my body against disease. I could also see what was floating around in the plasma. The number of leukocytes, as well as their activity, indicated the strength of my immune system. Dr. Brodie would analyze the written report on how my red and white blood cells were functioning, as well as my liver, metabolism, digestion and oxygenation. The report gave him a picture of whether any bacteria, fungus, parasites and more were compromising my health. Based on what the report indicated, I would be placed on specific supplements and a food plan. He reported that I had no signs of cancer in my blood, but my immune system was weak and my liver had some challenges.

Sitting in the bright, serene atmosphere of the IV room that first week, I looked around to see who my companions were. They had come from many different parts of the country. Each one had their unique cancer story. Some of them tugged at my heart. One young man looked like he was near death; he was so thin and pale. Fighting for her son's life, his mother would hover around him

Darkfield Live Blood Analysis

by Robert A. Eslinger, DO, HMD
Reno Integrative Medical Center
(www.renointegrativemedicalcenter.com)

A darkfield live blood analysis, by a trained practitioner, can provide clues as to what is currently happening in the persons "terrain" or internal environment. For example, it can reveal whether the person's immune and digestive systems are operating at an optimal rate to maintain that persons' health. Below are several important findings gained from a darkfield microscope:

Immune strength can be inferred by the size, shape, brightness and activity of the polymorphoneucleocyte (or "polys") white blood cells. They are the cells responsible for protecting you from invasion by any "foreign" organism or substance.

Inflammation in the body appears in the blood as a "stickiness" of the platelets. The platelets normally have much to do with clotting; but with inflammation, they get sticky and form what are called "platelet aggregations."

One drop of blood can reveal if parasites or allergies are interfering with healing by showing a predominance of certain kinds of white blood cells.

The first thing that happens to the red blood cells when the pH (acid/alkaline) shifts into acidic is they get very sticky and start forming into clumps. This can be deceiving because everyone's blood will eventually become sticky, but the issue is "how fast" it occurs. Cancer patients are already more acidic due to the waste products of their abnormal anaerobic metabolism, a process in which parts of their bodies burn sugar without oxygen.

Impending infection usually causes an increased number and activity of the polys and a much higher concentration of the "endobionts" (or healthy microbes) that inhabit our blood. This appears as what is called a "snowstorm."

Sequential live blood analysis provides clues as to whether the person is improving or not. Patients can observe the changes because of the use of a video camera and TV monitor connected to the microscope. This is a great motivator to help them stay on the rigorous program of supplements and therapies that are necessary to treat aggressive cancer.

The benefits gained from the blood analysis are very dependent on the training and experience of the practitioner. At Reno Integrative Medical Center, I have performed over 5000 darkfield live blood analyses since 2003.

getting him whatever he needed. Another woman had a five-year-old son at home, and she was doing what needed to be done to ensure that she would be around to raise him. One man had been poisoned by his work environment and was building up his immune system before he went for chemotherapy. Another beautiful young woman had tongue cancer, and conventional doctors wanted to remove her tongue. Her mother stayed right there by her side trying to protect her from this fate.

Everyone in that room looked for hope from Dr. Brodie's treatment. We had different agendas based on our specific illnesses. Hopefully, some of us would get the healing we wanted. Talking among ourselves, we got to know each other's story. Within a few days I learned that people's tumors were shrinking. A thought occurred to me, *"If Dr. Brodie could shrink tumors, he could clean up my margins."* When I told him this, he just smiled. He never promised that would happen, but he left me with the impression that I was in competent hands.

Throughout this time, my friend and I were staying at a casino hotel near the cancer clinic. In order to save money, I made a $40.00-per-night room reservation at a casino hotel. Great rates are available through the Internet. While registering on our first day, my attention was drawn to the smell of smoke in the lobby. After we checked in, we had to walk through the smoke-filled casino to get to the elevators that would take us to our room. Here I was hanging out with the smokers, while paying thousands of dollars to clean up my body and save my life. Something seemed wrong with this picture! I had no time to take on the task of changing hotels while under the stress of my first week of treatment, but I resolved to make a wiser choice for the next five days of my adventure in Reno.

After the treatments, I felt tired and needed to rest in the late afternoons. I wasn't much fun to be with some of the time, but my friend was not concerned or disappointed. We had breakfast and dinner together and kept each other amused. She stayed with me at the clinic and sat in the waiting room most of the time. She brought me lunch from a nearby restaurant and came into the consultation with Dr. Brodie. When there was room, she sat next to me while I was getting my IV drip. I like to think we added some positive energy to that treatment room. My cancer situation was so much less threatening than others around me. Gratitude, optimism and compassion filled me because I was only preventing a recurrence instead of treating an active cancer.

Relationships Are Important

A 2006 research study in the *Journal of Clinical Oncology* by Candyce H. Kroenke, *et al.*—"Social Networks, Social Support and Survival after Breast Cancer," reported that women with breast cancer who could name ten friends had a four times greater chance of surviving their disease than women who could not. Physical proximity was not a significant factor in these women feeling connected to their friends.

Medical setting by day and casino environment at night felt a bit strange. Neither one of us cared much about gambling, but we did play a few slot machines while exploring Reno. We drove around and checked out some of the other hotels. The Silver Legacy became my first choice of places to stay when I returned to Reno. It had a mostly smoke-free lobby and restaurant area. As long as I could get a decent hotel rate, I would be staying there for the last five days of treatment. It even had an indoor promenade that connected two hotels. We walked and we talked as friends do, and before I knew it, she was heading home, and I was approaching my last day of the first week's treatment.

Hitting the Jackpot

For my second week of treatment, I stayed at the Silver Legacy and had dinners sitting in the courtyard restaurant within the indoor promenade. Again, the contrast between being in a life and death environment during the day and sitting next to the ding, ding, ding of the slot machines and the colorful sparkling lights in the evening proved disconcerting. What a dichotomy! But the child in me loved it. I would walk the promenade every night and take in the sights and sounds of Reno. I felt peaceful for some strange reason. I was alone, but I did not feel alone. Grace must have been carrying me.

One evening, while having dinner, I became aware of a sensation of tiny needles pricking me around the area of the tumor incision. At first I did not know what was happening. I did not feel sick; I just had this sensation in my chest. The thought crossed my mind that I might need medical attention, but nothing else felt wrong with me. I quickly finished my dinner, left the restaurant and went to my room. I called Paul to let him know what was happening and then quietly lay on the bed in my room with the phone next to my hand in case I needed to dial 911. Something significant was occurring, but it was beyond my realm of possibilities. The best scenario would be that my margins were being cleared of cancer. The pricking sensation lasted on and off for about one hour. When it stopped, all seemed normal. I could not wait to tell Dr. Brodie what had happened. When I spoke to him the following day, he just smiled and said that was very interesting in his noncommittal way. But, I thought, *"This is what I came to Reno for. Yeeeaaah!"*

During the second week of the ten-day program, Dr. Brodie gave me a special blood test, an Anti-Milignin Antibody in Serum (AMAS). This test determines the presence of antibodies to malignin, a substance present in patients with cancer. It is a test that can detect cancer in its early stages, possibly before clinical manifestations appear. When he received the results of my blood test, my numbers were elevated. I had too much of these antibodies still in my blood. He placed me on peptides, which cost $430 for one tiny bottle, which lasted several months. I did not know how expensive supplements could be until I began treatment with Dr. Brodie. He put me on Laetrile, high doses of vitamin C, a Thymus extract, digestive enzymes, Co-Q10, soy protein, Oncoplex (broccoli), DIMension 3 (curcumin), Calcium D-Glucarate, Indoplex, progesterone cream and more. I began paying approximately $500 per month for my supplements. Of course, part of his treatment included the cancer prevention diet, a regimen of foods to eat and foods to avoid. Following his dietary recommendations felt easy for me because I had already been doing most of them. I do not remember him stressing the importance of exercise, which I now understand to be a critical element in healing and wellness.

Leaving the ten-day treatment program in Reno, I believed that my margins were clean and I had beaten the need for radiation. Dr. Brodie appeared to incorporate the basic philosophies of the alternative approaches I had researched. Based on what I had learned, I felt confident that he was an expert in integrative cancer medicine. I never went back to the oncologist, and I announced to Dr. Brodie that he was now my cancer doctor. He allowed me to do that because he understood my frustration over trying to explain to conventional doctors the approach I was taking. Besides, the focus of treatment had become prevention. For the first year after the ten-day program, I went to see him quarterly for a live blood cell analysis, IV drip with peptide injection and consultation. The following two years, I saw him twice a year until I moved to Florida in 2004.

In saying our goodbyes, we just gave each other a big hug, and I thanked him for saving my life. It had been quite a journey. A few years later, I learned that he died—a great loss to the cancer community.

Through the Looking Glass

Dr. Brodie's treatment approach also emphasized the mind-body-spirit connection. He suggested that his patients consider making lifestyle changes and finding better ways to manage the stress in their lives. He was not content to have his patients focus only on the physical aspects of healing cancer. Regarding this integrated approach to healing, we spoke the same language. We connected because we could speak about the mental and spiritual aspects of healing.

Most people have not yet learned the healing secret of the ages—that health is basically an inside job, mentally as well as physically. No matter how successful a treatment is in time of illness, a person often becomes sick again and again, because he has not gotten at the cause of his illness—ill thoughts and feelings about himself, others, his Creator, and the world in which he lives. These ill thoughts constrict the life force within him, causing disease, or lack of ease.

— *The Dynamic Laws of Healing* by Catherine Ponder |
9780875161563 DeVorss Publications www.devorss.com
(1966, p. 8)

I assured him that I was going to take a good look at the unresolved mental, emotional and spiritual issues plaguing my body and soul. Before I could make the necessary changes in my lifestyle and myself, I needed to understand the psychological issues and life stressors that had undermined my immune system and may have contributed to my getting cancer.

Chapter 4 Lessons Learned...

- When you stop trying to control people and outcomes, a higher order takes over.

- Miracles are visible when you take the time to notice them.

- Road signs and messengers appear once you place your feet on your "yellow brick road." Trust your next step will be revealed.

- Friends and family are an important part of the healing process. Receive what they offer.

- Even during a dark hour, allow the "lighter side" of life to uplift you.

- Building a strong immune system is a full time job that requires discipline and persistence.

- Gratitude, optimism and love are important elements of the healing formula.

- When you follow your inner guidance, you are destined to hit a jackpot.

- Special people come into your life for a purpose; treasure them.

...a time to trust a higher order, witness miracles, receive help, and embrace the lighter side of life

Chapter 5
What Is My Cancer Trying to Tell Me?
(Psychology of My Cancer)

March through September 2001

While the conventional medical community is slow to realize that cancer is a multifaceted disease, I fully embrace this truth. In some way, my body, mind, spirit and environment contributed to my getting cancer; therefore, I chose to do everything within my power to address all of these factors. Before I got cancer, I had done a lot of self-examination. I now realize that self-discovery and personal growth are a life-long commitment, and I am in for the long haul. My body also wants that kind of commitment in order to stay healthy and active.

Dr. Brodie's psychological and spiritual approach to healing was in alignment with my beliefs and values. I felt blessed to have him as my doctor. He encouraged me to examine more closely the personal patterns and life situations that were compromising my health. After the ten-day treatment program in Reno, I turned my attention to the psychological issues that needed my attention. The life disappointments and challenges I endured and overcame throughout my life prepared me for the task. I also had a lot of experience helping former clients discover how they were sabotaging their emotional and physical wellbeing.

My cancer was a signal that I had to look at myself and life through a more powerful microscope. I needed to put myself under the darkfield microscope, not just my blood. I wanted to understand the whole message my body conveyed when it whispered cancer. Stage I breast cancer felt like a whisper that compromised my body. Early detection prevented the cancer from becoming a serious life threat. However, I took the stage I message very seriously. I needed to understand how my thoughts, emotions, personality and past experiences might have contributed to the cancer. I was willing to clean up any unfinished business and change my lifestyle in order to stay cancer free for the rest of my life.

> *The symptom is only an outer effect. We must go within to dissolve the mental cause...The mental thought patterns that cause the most disease in the body are criticism, anger, resentment and guilt.*
>
> —Louise Hay, *Heal Your Body: The Mental Causes for Physical Illness and the Metaphysical Way to Overcome Them* (1982, p.7)

Life Is Just Too Hard!

In my early forties, I dealt with repressed memories of childhood sexual abuse. This discovery shook my world. I had no idea this had happened to me. I moved through negative feelings of fear, sadness, powerlessness and anger as these memories and images emerged from my body into my conscious awareness. The hidden traumas were revealed while I received therapeutic touch sessions from an energy worker. At that time, I was becoming an energy worker myself.

I spent about four months clearing these cellular memories. (I am grateful that the perpetrators were not emotionally close to me or still a part of my life.) As a result of clearing this, I emerged with more unconditional acceptance. I actually could love more deeply and feel more connected to myself, others, life and God. The protective shell around my heart was disintegrating. (The immune system cannot detect and destroy cancer cells because of their protective protein coating. Hmmm!) I knew I was free of this trauma because I could counsel victims of sexual abuse without having my own emotions triggered.

Cancer became another earthquake in my life. Once again, life challenged me to dive deep into myself and ask some thought provoking questions that would change me even more. Perhaps, my heart—my ability to love and accept, needed more healing.

Four months after surgery, I had the time and desire to deal with the personal wounds of the past, repressed feelings and lifestyle issues that may have contributed to my breast cancer. Cancer gave me an opportunity to explore the messages being spoken by my body, and I heard the wake up call. Taking the cancer journey with some of my clients better prepared me for the task at hand. I helped them explore the underlying messages their bodies were trying to tell them. My time had arrived.

Workshops I had attended with leaders in the energy medicine field shed some light on the disease. One leader in particular got my attention. She stated that *"cancer is associated with change."* I remember her saying that if the person could not make a necessary change, death could become the change. This interpretation felt right to me. I believe the change can be an internal shift in perception, emotion or behavior—less resentment, guilt or helplessness. But, it could also mean an external change—a new job, relationship, location or personal habit. The bottom line is that feeling trapped and powerless in a negative situation for a prolonged period of time can make a person sick. Chronic stress and negative emotions compromise the immune system. It was now my turn to become more aware, shake up the status quo and make some positive changes in my life.

In response to stress, your body releases a flood of hormones into your blood. Hormones are part of your body's communications system. They deliver messages to genes and cells and act as genetic switches, turning genes on or off. They directly influence important cellular processes, including those that regulate cell growth and help to protect against tumors.

—Raymond Francis, MSc, *Never Fear Cancer Again: How to Prevent and Reverse Cancer* (2011, p. 224)

Cancer Cells Have Adrenaline Receptors

In his book, *The Genie in Your Genes: Epigenetic Medicine and the New Biology of Intention*, Dawson Church, PhD, cites research showing that cancer cells have adrenaline receptors! In other words, stress literally feeds cancer according to Dr. Church.

Epigenetics is the science of how environmental signals select, modify, and regulate gene activity. This new awareness reveals that the activity of our genes is constantly being modified in response to life experiences. Which again emphasizes that our perceptions of life shape our biology.

— Bruce H. Lipton, PhD, *The Biology of Belief: Unleashing the Power of Consciousness, Matter & Miracles* (2005, p. XV)

I thought I was doing pretty well coping with my life's ups and downs. But, I was living in Lala's house on the outside and "lala land" on the inside. The time had come to get a grip and take a hard look at what my body was asking me to see. The inner light needed to be turned on, and all I had to do was turn on the switch. Dr. Lawrence LeShan's book, *Cancer as a Turning Point*, and other literature said to go back about two to three years prior to cancer invading the body and look for a major stressor, disappointment or loss. When I did that, two jumped out for me.

Paul and I were living in a very special house on a lake in central New Jersey with a big mortgage. Paul lost his job, and we were having serious financial challenges for years. We lived in a peaceful, beautiful setting, but the financial stress was almost unbearable. The second disappointment involved my career. I came up with what I thought at the time was a great model to help people integrate the world of spirit and the world of form. The six strategies within this co-creating model would enable people to turn their visions into physical realities with more ease. I felt as though these insights came from a place of deep inspiration, but either it was not as good as I thought it was or I just did not know how to market it. I really did not understand the concept of marketing at that time. I was a mental health counselor, and we did not learn to market ourselves.

Feelings of powerlessness, guilt and despair were lurking in my body as a result of these two stressors. The career disappointment added to the dimension of feeling like a failure. (This should have been a clue that my ego was in charge but I did not see it at the time.) Instead of promoting my creative ideas, I put them in a filing cabinet. With the move to California, I intended to retrieve the model from its hiding place and turn it into a book. But, I guess this quiet desperation was eating away at my body and soul without my conscious knowledge. Instead of pursuing my vision three years earlier, I gave up. I settled for the way things were. I did not know that withdrawing would have such a devastating consequence. As I look back at that time, putting my model on hold was the right thing to do. Without the cancer challenge, I may not have gone deeper into myself in order to achieve the spiritual growth and awareness I have today. And, I certainly would not be writing this book. Unfortunately, it is usually through the hard times that people reach for their inner gold. In addition, my co-creating model has taken on new meanings over the years. But at the time, I felt trapped in my inability to touch a larger audience, advance my career and improve my income.

Two Stress Statistics

◆ The Stress Knowledge Company (www.stressdirections.com) reports that 75% to 90% of all doctor's office visits are stress related according to a poll of family physicians.

◆ According to *Healthy People 2000*, a report generated by the U.S. Department of Health and Human Services, 70% to 80% of all visits to the doctor are for stress related and stress induced illnesses.

The financial hardships Paul and I experienced during the years prior to cancer took a great toll on my body and soul. The good in my life—a loving, generous man and beautiful business office in my home—could not make up for this heavy weight I was carrying. This situation drained my energy for years. One of my strengths is that I can cope with just about anything. I reframe things into something positive and move forward with enthusiasm. I have learned to smile through the despair and appear confident. But, I guess some things will not be buried and denied for too long. The body does not lie. It soon rebels; the repressed wound festers and erupts as a disease or accident.

After the cancer diagnosis, I made a commitment to live in close communication with my body. I did not want any more surprises. I would be listening to my emotions, thoughts and physical symptoms on a regular basis.

I had to integrate spiritual optimism and unlimited potential with limited resources and real world challenges. The dreamer had to wake up, take off the blinders and take appropriate actions to accomplish her visions and goals. The cancer forced me to deal with what was in my face. And, it was not pretty. My body spoke, *"Life is just too hard; I would rather be dead."* In that moment, I got it. During the two years before the cancer diagnosis, I was not acknowledging and working through the feelings of dread and powerlessness hiding beneath my coping strategies around money and career. Post diagnosis, I would learn to live fully by the rules of the real world. I would take more purposeful action to achieve business success. I think moving to California and starting over became the first step in my journey of healing and empowerment. Interestingly, the move took place three months before the cancer diagnosis. I was already healing and did not know it.

How Am I Getting in My Way?

As a result of the internal work I had done on myself for twenty years, I could only mildly identify with most of the personality traits that put a person at high risk for developing cancer. Going through Dr. Brodie's indicators of the cancer-susceptible person, I had some insights.

Highly Conscientious, Responsible and Hardworking — I admit to being a dutiful, responsible, hard working person; however, I am not addicted to working. I know how to let go and have fun. And, I usually make sure I have balance between play, rest and work in my life. Did I feel burdened with responsibilities before the cancer diagnosis? Perhaps I did. But, I do not think I would have left my family in New Jersey, if I did not have within me a free spirit in search of the next adventure.

Carry Other People's Burdens and Worry about Them — I was willing to consider that holding the healing space for my clients and carrying financial stress for several years had taken its toll on me. I did love my clients and the work of personal transformation we did together. But, I realized that being a psychotherapist and taking care of and being responsible for other people's problems kept me in the role of the responsible child in my dysfunctional family. I thought I was coping with the financial stress prior to cancer, but my body must have carried this heavy burden more than I realized.

Repressed, Denied and Ignored

Excerpts from *Your Body Speaks Your Mind: Decoding the Emotional, Psychological and Spiritual Messages that Underlie Health* by Deb Shapiro

Deb Shapiro is also the co-author of *Be the Change: How Meditation Can Transform You and the World* (www.EdandDebShapiro.com)

Emotional pain is just as real as physical pain and can be far more invasive. Long-held resentments, anger, bitterness, hurt, fear, guilt, shame, they all play their role in debilitating our energy. Those emotions that are repressed, denied, or ignored, that never found expression or were never fully acknowledged, are the ones that go deepest and need our greatest attention.

Many different emotions get repressed such as hurt, anger and betrayal, to name but a few. Rage is the most obvious of the emotions to be repressed because it is rarely appropriate to release it at the time and after a while we are hardly even aware it is there. Repressed rage gives rise to irrational fear, hate and bitterness, all of which detrimentally influence our health, undermining our strength and resistance.

Grief is also repressed: grief at what has been lost or at what might have been but never will be. When repressed, grief can lead to heart or immune issues or a change in eating patterns. Shame, hurt, shock and abuse get repressed, buried inside where we can delude ourselves into thinking they are gone.

Denial enables us to believe that everything is fine, but beneath the surface is a hidden mass of feelings and traumas. Denied emotions can erupt and spill out through our behavior; they can cause sexual problems, relationship problems, addiction, even violence. The event itself may have gone but the emotional impact can stay with us, affecting the body on the cellular level.

Ignored emotions are equally as detrimental. Ask yourself how you feel when someone is ignoring you, and you will get an idea of how your feelings feel when they are ignored. They have to find some form of expression, which is invariably through your body or behavior.

Our body is constantly changing, forming and reforming the cells. So why do we maintain the repression, denial and ignorance if that pattern is an unhealthy one? It is because the inner programming has not changed. To work with that inner programming means entering into a dialogue of communication so we can come to understand ourselves more deeply.

Need for Approval and "People Pleasing" — In my adult life I was not aware of a pervasive need to make other people feel happy or get their approval. I do believe that was true about me in my childhood. As I approached my late twenties, I did things my way in spite of what others had to say. When I realized that my first marriage was not working, I chose to end it sooner rather than later because it was the right thing for me. As the executive director of a nonprofit organization, I made decisions for the greater good without too much concern for what people thought of me personally. I think my epitaph should be *"She did it her way."*

Harboring Long-Suppressed Toxic Emotions — From childhood into early adulthood, I was filled with toxic shame, anger and resentments. I covered up my anxiety by becoming a take charge controlling person. (At times it was not pretty.) Throughout my twenty-year healing journey up to the cancer diagnosis, I learned to let go of my anger and resentments. Instead of seeing myself as a victim, I made choices and took charge of my life. I found a way to live my truth without shame or guilt. By the time I reached my middle forties, I had more love and self-acceptance than most people I knew. If there were any toxic emotions buried in my body that may have contributed to the cancer, they were self-doubt, despair and powerlessness about building a successful career and improving my finances. On the surface, I looked successful to people. I was not aware that this was a major problem until the cancer forced me to face it.

Fear, doubt, anxiety, anger, resentment pull down the cells of the body, shock the nervous system and are the causes of disease and disaster. Happiness and health must be earned by absolute control of the emotional nature. As man becomes spiritually awakened he recognizes that any external inharmony is the correspondence of mental inharmony. If he stumbles and falls, he may know he is stumbling or falling in consciousness.

— *The Writings of Florence Scovel Shinn* | 9780875166100
DeVorss Publications www.devorss.com (1988, p. 68)

Reacting Adversely to Stress — Dr. Brodie also believed that a stressful event two years before the onset of cancer plays an important role in the disease. He talked about the "last straw" effect. The series of stressful negative events and disappointments in my life must have piled up on me. All the meditation and spiritual practice I did was not enough to protect my immune system. I also realize that I have been most fortunate. Up to that point in time, my stressors were related to two divorces, business disappointments and financial issues. To me that is minor when compared to the illness, death and loss that others experience. But, they played havoc on my serenity and happiness anyway.

Unresolved Deep-Seated Emotional Problems from Childhood — My inability to believe in my gifts, back them with action and turn them into abundant financial rewards definitely stems from my childhood. In spite of my moderate adult successes, I found myself feeling tentative rather than empowered. What happened to the five year old who was able to stand on a big stage all alone to sing and dance to an audience of strange faces while an orchestra played her song? I had some work to do to grow in confidence, become more visible and achieve prosperity.

Lack of Closeness with One or Both Parents — While growing up, I had a conflicted, detached relationship with my mother and a loving, dependent relationship with my father. The cancer forced me to reexamine my childhood relationship with them. In doing so, I gained a deeper understanding of how my current health crisis was related to my past.

Many people do not consciously think the negative thoughts, and exhibit the negative mental patterns, that are commonly associated with their physical disease... I have come to the conclusion that there are other ways to carry this negativity besides in our conscious, thinking mind. There may be inner-child parts that are still carrying unexpressed, buried emotion that has never been released.

— Carol Tuttle, *Remembering Wholeness: A Personal Handbook for Thriving in the 21st Century* (2002, p. 67)

Mother Wound

From an energy perspective, the left side of the body is considered to be feminine, and the right side, masculine. This explanation of the body feels true to me. Therefore, the removal of my left breast cried out—mother wound. My relationship to my feminine nature needed attention, and this relationship begins with mother. The feminine aspects of life are associated with receiving, allowing, nurturing, nourishing, cooperating, connecting, unconditional love and intuition. Based on my mother wound, I found myself still trapped in the script: *"My needs and desires do not matter."* My emotional DNA screamed loud and clear: *"You are not good enough to have what you want. Even if you get what you want, it will be taken from you."* This ego-driven distorted inner message robbed me of the belief that the universe is abundant and I am entitled to have "the good life." My ability to receive and be sustained by life was constricted. While I was successful in my career, I did not receive the opportunities or support necessary to play a bigger game. I worked hard and contributed my greatest good, but could not break through to the next level of financial success.

My mother and I had a strained, conflicted relationship from toddler to teens. She was physically abusive to me as a preschooler and young child. Many kids were spanked in the 1940's, but her irrational screaming and hitting terrified me. I could not predict what would set her off. She had few skills to cope with raising two children. To protect myself, I stayed out of her way the best I could. I learned that it is safer to be invisible. I asked myself, *"How could I help more people and achieve financial independence if a part of me needed to be invisible?"* I began to see the internal conflict between being visible and feeling safe, which may have been contributing to my limited success. My inner child did not feel safe playing a bigger game.

Even though I learned to expect nothing from my mother at a very young age, I unconsciously sought her approval, as wounded children do, and rarely got it. She would say critical things about me that got in the way of my loving and backing myself, as well as valuing my accomplishments. She would find some way to take the wind out of my sails when I felt joyful about something. This continued until I reached my middle teens. At that time I was developing my own life outside of the family, and what she thought or said about me did not matter to me consciously. I connected to my own competence and power, and at the age of 17, I was planning my future. In the early 1960's, my personal options were to become a competent secretary, dutiful wife and devoted mother. Surprisingly, my mother's critical behavior toward me stopped at this time. She may have been changing too. (She turned out to be a superb grandmother to my two children.) But, the script of not being good enough was ingrained in my emotional DNA. It diminished my self-confidence and sense of entitlement. When I add the hidden need to be invisible in order to feel safe, I began to understand how I had trapped myself in limitation. A subtle anxiety at the core of my being still held me captive.

From a very young age, my body and I learned that life (the all giving mother) was not there to offer the nourishment and nurturing I needed to thrive. Survival became the norm instead, which is how life felt those few years before the cancer diagnosis. I believe growing up we need to experience the good mother, bad mother and absent mother. The good mother nourishes and nurtures us (in extremes, smothers us), the bad mother sets limits (in extremes, abuses us) and the absent mother allows us to do it ourselves (in extremes, neglects us).

I did not get enough good mothering from my own mother, but I did receive nurturing, praise and support from the eight maternal and paternal aunts who lived in the neighborhood. They treated me special. I think their attention and praise held that mother wound in check so it did not consume my entire being. How else could I get teased in my adulthood by my extended family for being a princess or debutant? Growing up, I definitely was a little princess to my father, his mother, and his unmarried brother and four sisters. They showered me with love, attention, food and gifts when I walked through their front door. From my perspective, the princess and debutant are not viewed as powerful women who run their own show. Hmmm? Was there more to this picture?

Father Wound

I had to acknowledge that my internalized relationship with my father was also preventing me from becoming a more successful businesswoman. This inner "glass ceiling" was not only related to my mother wound. Career success predominantly requires a highly developed masculine, which is associated with providing, protecting, analyzing, rational thinking, competing, risk taking, assertiveness and conditional love. My relationship with my father was complex because he provided the unconditional love I did not receive from my mother. He became a nurturer instead of the powerful father expecting me to claim my power and grow up into an independent woman. I was daddy's little girl and remained his little, sickly princess who needed her father to rescue her.

At the age of 18 months, my father left home to serve in World War II. He was gone for two years. His leaving felt like abandonment to the toddler, and the father wound went deep into my being. He was the nurturing force in my life, as well as the provider/protector, and he left me trapped with an overwhelmed mother, her new baby, an alcoholic grandfather and handicapped uncle. We all lived together in a two bedroom, cold water flat. I felt terrorized by all of it.

My powerful, nurturing father had abandoned me to the noise, abuse, cold and chaos of this setting. This early trauma sealed off a part of my heart and power. The part of me that needed what a mother gives and what a father provides gave up at a very young age. Instead, I learned I was on my own and had to take care of myself. This put me in conflict with the helpless little princess who needed rescuing. (This inner conflict continued to be a challenge until recently.) I survived the best I could, but by the age of three my body took a hit—it developed asthma.

In my elementary school years, I became the over responsible child in a moderately dysfunctional family. Unconsciously, I took on the job of keeping the conflict and yelling between my father, mother and grandfather to a minimum in our home. (My uncle was institutionalized when I was almost three years old.) I became sickly with asthma (many trips to the doctors) and had pneumonia twice by the age of twelve. This served as a diversion to restore order when the tension and noise in the home got to be too much. (Today I value peace and quiet above most things.) Of course, the dynamics in the household did not change because I had no real power to change anything. For all my efforts, I came away from my family of origin programmed to feel inadequate and powerless. At the same time, I learned to be aware of subtle cues, understand people and situations, and solve problems.

I finally woke up around the age of fourteen without being kissed by Prince Charming. The time had come to disconnect from my internal feelings of powerlessness and low self-esteem in order to align myself with the successful young woman I was becoming. Some part of me (I believe the adventurer) was ready to strike out on her own and take charge of her life. In high school I learned that I was a natural leader and very competent in the ways of the world. I finally took on a new identify when my fellow cheerleaders voted me to be "captain of the cheerleaders" and my senior classmates voted me "Best All Around Female" in our "hall of fame." The inspiration to be and do more is a part of my core truth. Being the best I could be in my teens replaced the sickly princess; she disappeared into the darkness of my subconscious mind.

Because of their personal limitations, my mother could not nurture me and my father could not protect me. I could have become a casualty in that family drama; instead, I became competent and wise in the ways of the world at a very young age. I left home as the wounded warrior fighting to control her own destiny and straining to soar to greater heights.

I can clearly see how my pattern of struggling to be successful with underlying feelings of inadequacy and impotency may have contributed to my cancer. No matter what I did or did not do in my family of origin as a child, I did not have the power to change anything. In addition, education and career were not valued so there were no expectations for me to achieve something extraordinary. I entered adulthood programmed with the limitations of my family of origin. (This is part of the human condition.) I made another attempt around the age of thirty to break free of family scripts. Again, something was calling me to be more.

Body-centered psychotherapy is a kind of clinical work that puts the body into action as a means of accessing repressed and fragmented parts of the self... This body speech often arises from our unconscious, or from parts of ourselves that have become fragmented and from which we have withdrawn.

— Christine Caldwell, PhD, *Getting Our Bodies Back: Recovery, Healing, and Transformation through Body-Centered Psychotherapy* (1996, p. 4)

My father died on November 29, 2010, the tenth anniversary of my mastectomy and a few weeks after his diagnosis. I know this has a special meaning, but I am not sure what it is yet. This deep loss is shaking the foundation of my being. The strong, loving presence of my father is no longer in this world. In my late sixties it really is time to stand on my own two feet and realize my potential. My father will take the journey with me in my heart. As a grieving daughter, I will carry him with me.

Beyond the Mother/Father Wound

At the age of 30 I decided to get a college education. A new part of me emerged as a result of teaching decision making skills to inmates within a county criminal justice program. Many of my clients achieved their goals and enjoyed working with me. The success I experienced with these men inspired me to become a professional counselor or social worker. Life gave me a second chance to follow my passion. This option was not available to me as a woman in a "blue collar family" in 1960. Becoming a psychologist was only a dream I did not share with anyone.

Going to college as an adult took me out of the roles of dutiful wife, devoted daughter and full-time mother. By choosing a career, I was doing something for me instead of for others, and my family did not encourage the change. I said goodbye to tradition and created a life that served me. During my college years, I became a single parent with two children. Leaving the security of marriage, I had to find my own way once again.

As a mature adult, I could get the support I needed to make this change from other women, as well as parent myself through the unknown and uncertain. Filled with disillusionment about marriage, I made a commitment to become my own provider and protector. Being financially dependent on a man lost its appeal. With help from the women's liberation movement in the 1970s and the fabulous women who led it, I became my own person.

My family of origin experiences prepared me to be responsible, follow the rules, not expect much and serve others. Sounds like Cinderella to me; however, no Prince Charming was about to rescue me. I chose to liberate myself instead. For many years after that first divorce, my life worked, but cancer showed up in my late fifties to remind me that I had more work to do on myself. The upside of my parenting: I became resourceful, courageous, creative, competent,

72

Provocative Questions that Lead to Golden Insights

by Sandra Miniere, Author of *A Lighter Side to Cancer: From Wake-Up Call to Radiant Wellness*

The questions listed here provide a way to discover the core issues obstructing health, happiness and abundance. Sample responses are also included.

Present

○ What life situation is making me feel trapped or burdened? (financial hardships)

○ What chronic negative emotions are draining my physical energy? (despair, resentment, anxiety or guilt)

○ What negative beliefs prevent me from feeling grateful and abundant? (I can't get what I want. Life isn't fair.)

○ In what situations or relationships am I *not* living my values? (Work prevents me from spending time with my children.)

○ In what situation or relationship am I struggling to get what I want? (I feel isolated and anxious in social situations.) When was the first time I recognized this limitation? (I could not connect with the kids in my high school.)

Past

○ What childhood experiences and messages still leave me feeling powerless? (I could not prevent my parents from fighting. My voice is still not being heard where it matters to me.)

○ What chronic negative feelings did not get expressed in my childhood? (sadness and anger) Are these feelings still stuck inside of me? Do these feelings have a message for me now?

○ What childhood experiences prevented me from feeling good about myself? (My mother repeatedly told me I was "bad.") Are these memories still affecting my esteem and confidence?

○ What parental messages are still contributing to feelings of lack and longing? (Money doesn't grow on trees; there is not enough to spend on you.)

Stressors

○ What were the stressful situations in my life two to three years before the cancer diagnosis? (death of my son, loss of a job or a move to a new place)

○ What current situation is making me feel stressed every day? (I do not have enough money to pay my bills each month, I am dealing with a divorce, or I am working 70 hours a week.)

adventuresome and self-sufficient. I was prepared to deal with any-thing. And, I developed the ability to love and connect with others and life in the process.

My mother died one year and one week after my father, the day after turning 92 years old. She wanted very little to do with doctors, medicines, hospitals and nursing homes. She did not want to leave her home after my father's death, and she almost died there. She slipped quietly away in the ambulance ride to the hospital. Her heart just stopped beating when it was her time to die. I am sure my father was helping her leave her body because he needed to take care of her right to the end. God bless both of them. For uneducated people, they lived a charmed life and had great deaths.

I Get It; Now What?

Cancer asked me to reexamine my relationship to myself, life and work. Like so many people, I worked out mother and father issues in psychotherapy and other healing modalities, and I could not believe that my parent wounds were still speaking to me through the cancer. The wounds of early parenting seem to chase us the rest of our lives. They seem to be triggered by life events, even though we think we have put them to rest. I was really getting tired of "the mother thing." By the time I got cancer, I did not have resentment or negative feelings toward my mother but it appears that my body and life were still tied up in the consequences of feeling unmothered. Being daddy's little disempowered girl was getting old too.

Reviewing the parent wound was not to blame my mother and father. They were doing the best they could based on their childhood experiences and scripts. My mother especially had a childhood filled with deprivation and who knows what else. All I wanted to do was understand what my body was trying to tell me. If I knew how the experiences of the past were limiting me, I could begin to clear this emotional coding, reprogram my distorted beliefs and change the things that needed changing. Most importantly, today I can review my past (the good, bad and ugly experiences) with gratitude for how it contributed to the person I have been and the one I am becoming.

The body my parents created could destroy itself through cancer, and I was not going to let that happen. I had a lot to live for in spite of the frustrations, setbacks and obstacles throughout the years. Determined to eradicate cancer from my body and soul, I took on the challenge to heal from the inside out. Whether the psychological and spiritual issues actually contributed to my getting cancer was less important than learning who I was in 2001, what I wanted and how I needed to change.

The cancer gave me another opportunity to become aware and take a few more steps toward self-mastery—to live my truth in harmony, peace and abundance. I believe healing occurs when a person achieves a deep sense of wholeness (internal unity and harmony) and inner peace. Curing occurs when the body is free of a specific disease.

My psychological blocks and limitations were getting clearer, but the insights alone were not enough to heal my body and life. I needed to back the insights with action. I tried a few healing modalities that enabled me to move through these specific limiting patterns and support some necessary changes. Determined to create a lifestyle that nourished and empowered me, I did what I had to do to get beyond cancer.

Chapter 5 Lessons Learned...

- Cancer offers an opportunity to reexamine the relationship with yourself, others, work, life and God.

- The body speaks in a child's language—simple words that can shatter illusions.

- Approach your body with an attitude of unconditional love; it will reveal its secrets.

- Allow your negative emotions to lead you to truthful insights without judging them or yourself.

- The right questions get to the core issues that may be contributing to your disease or sabotaging your healing.

- Early parenting affects your choices and actions until you eliminate the negative messages and emotions trapped within your body.

- Acknowledge the chronic stressors and personality traits that may be contributing to your illness; they provide the prescription for your healing.

- What is hidden within your soul can fester and play havoc within your body.

- Illness provides an opportunity for you to grow in love, personal power, wisdom and serenity.

...a time to know yourself better, ask soul searching questions, and grow in love, personal power, wisdom and serenity

Chapter 6
Choose Life!
(Strategies to Heal My Soul and Change My Life)

March through September 2001

The move to California forced me to change my lifestyle. Instead of serving others as a mental health counselor, my day-to-day activities revolved around me. Closing my private practice in New Jersey released me from the role of dedicated service provider. The original plan for the relocation placed Paul in the primary provider role for a short time while I searched for the next career opportunity. I still had a small income from intuitive and EFT consultations over the telephone. But, after the breast cancer diagnosis, my focus changed from reinventing myself to healing cancer.

In the spirit of a grand adventure, Paul and I took a huge risk moving across the country. But the cancer turned this exciting adventure into a very stressful ordeal. I seemed to be at the mercy of some universal plan and had to trust that everything would be OK. But, this wonderful "man of heart" gave his attention, time, energy and money generously to me, with no strings attached during my cancer crisis. He even gave when he lost his job five months after my mastectomy. He was a casualty of the "dot com crash" in 2001. I had little choice but to allow him to provide for me and help me heal my body and soul. He graciously carried this burden with me.

My career got put on a back burner during that first year after diagnosis. I quickly learned that receiving from Paul became a part of my healing, not an easy thing for me to do. The financial support I received from my first husband seemed appropriate. Raising our two children could be considered an unpaid job. However, receiving without giving a lot back was not in alignment with my identity. I could easily have slipped into feeling like a burden. Instead, I learned that life brought me the most generous person I had ever met. While I did not feel comfortable taking from him, I learned to accept it. Of course, I wanted to become financially independent again, but first I had to acknowledge and receive the good that was being given. This forced change put me at the top of the list—what a novelty for this helper. I had to go into receptive mode and love myself anyway; I hoped my body approved by getting well.

The cancer dictated that the time had come to change my beliefs and mend my ways. In addition to learning to receive, I reached for support from other women, applied Emotional Freedom Techniques (EFT), had healing touch sessions, addressed spiritual issues and took steps to change my future. I used all of these approaches to correct the psychological and spiritual issues associated with the dynamics of my cancer, as well as manage the life stressors at that time. I emerged from cancer more evolved on so many levels. Armed with a new perspective and better coping skills, I was ready to choose life and start over.

Cancer Support Group

Separated from the family and friends I left behind in New Jersey, I realized that I needed to create a support system locally. After the ten-day treatment program with Dr. Brodie, I went to a breast cancer support group at the local hospital. As the former executive director of a women's center, I understood the value of women supporting women. The most difficult thing about going to that first group: I had to face the fact that I had become a "breast cancer survivor." A part of me still could not believe it. I felt like I had failed at something even though rationally I knew that was not true.

When I went to my first group for separated and divorced women in the mid 1970's, I could hardly speak without crying. The cancer support group was different somehow. I did not shed a tear. When my turn came to share, I just gave a brief synopsis of my cancer story without much emotion. Perhaps, loss and disappointment in one form or another had become a part of my reality. I think the first divorce shattered my illusion of "happily ever after." The pain and vulnerability associated with that first big loss pierced my heart and shattered my innocence. It also prepared me to cope with crisis and thrive through change.

When I arrived and looked around the table in a large meeting room, I felt good being in the company of a dozen other women. But, I soon learned that many of these women were fighting for their lives and were filled with apprehension and powerlessness. They seemed overwhelmed with their cancer and treatment; thankfully, I was not at that time. My relationship with cancer included taking charge of my healing. Of course, it was easy for me to do that because I had stage I breast cancer with a 90% cure rate. When group members discussed anger, I reported that I was annoyed because I still could not get my legs over my head in the yoga plow pose. Thinking back, how ridiculous that must have sounded to women going through chemotherapy and radiation treatments.

Something did not feel right. The group felt heavy, not uplifting. I wanted a group that was going to give me hope and encouragement to take charge of my healing. My heart went out to these women. I wanted to tell the leader to do something different so we could focus on what was working in our lives and how we could participate in our own healing. But it was not my group to run, and that was not their agenda. I noticed a few members who sounded hopeful, positive and curious. I went to one more group and decided that talking about my cancer every week would not work for me. I think it was about that time that I got an intuitive message, *"Let the cancer move through you."* I interpreted this to mean that I was not to dwell on the cancer because it no longer was a part of my body and life. Six months after my mastectomy, I put being a cancer patient behind me and focused on achieving optimal health and wellbeing instead.

Emotional Freedom Techniques (EFT)

EFT is a meridian tapping technique for moving energy through the body, and it eliminates stress, as well as emotional and physical discomfort in minutes. It is based on the principles of acupuncture. After two years of using EFT with my clients, I began using it on myself to deal with all aspects of the cancer. I knew that focusing on the problem while tapping meridian points with my fingertips on my face, hands and upper body would help me clear current negative emotions, as well as energy blocks associated with past events and negative beliefs. The tapping would reduce stress, keep my meridians open to the flow of healing energy and promote my body's ability to heal itself.

EFT is also very effective because it uncovers the unresolved issues within the subconscious that sabotage successful completion of goals and objectives. These core beliefs are associated with the "writings on our walls" The writings come from the childhood messages we heard many times from others about who we are and how life works. The specific traumatic events from our past also influence the writings. These unconscious memories, emotions and beliefs are interfering with our health, wellbeing and success. I did not have the money to see an EFT practitioner on a regular basis, but I did work on myself frequently.

79

Meridian Tapping Reduces Stress

Cortisol levels were measured before and after treatment for 83 participants in a recent study conducted by Dawson Church, PhD, Garret Yount, PhD, and Audrey Brooks, PhD. The participants were assigned to one of three groups. The first group received an hour of meridian tapping ("talk" included), the second group received an hour of psychotherapy ("talk" therapy alone), and the third group (control group) received no treatment.

At the end of the hour, the first group who tapped produced a 24% decrease in cortisol. The second and third groups had no change in cortisol levels.

Tapping on acupuncture points (meridians) accesses the emotions and body simultaneously and provides powerful stress relief quickly.

This study was published in the *Journal of Nervous and Mental Disease*, 2012. (Cortisol is a steroid hormone produced by the adrenal glands, released in response to stress, and known to suppress the immune system.)

After my treatment in Reno, I began tapping to reduce the stress and negative emotions associated with having cancer, generating an income and Paul losing his job in April of 2001. I did not fear dying, but I did have some anxiety about what to do to earn money and prevent a recurrence. (The first cancer was a major hassle and cost me a lot of time and money.) The financial stress was intense with Paul out of work. It felt like another blow to my body. I had to figure out what I could do to increase my income. I did not have the credentials to counsel people in California, nor did I want to do that. A new beginning was calling to me while I was in free fall—nothing to hold on to. Apprehension set in, yet I remained open to the possibility of landing on my feet. Staying positive was a challenge. I did a lot of tapping. I chose to trust that something worthwhile was on its way to me. Without a destination in sight, I just kept going, like the Eveready Energizer Bunny®.

I tapped to eliminate some of the frustration I had about being powerless again. While tapping, I remembered feeling vulnerable when I had just given birth and was dependent on my husband to take care of me and our daughter. EFT helped me make peace with being vulnerable and dependent again. Just writing this, I realize more than ever that I had very little trust that my needs would be met by anyone but myself in life. It was natural for me to lead the charge of my healing journey. This is both a blessing and a curse. I would not change what happened because it all led to a positive

What Is EFT?

by Ruth Stern, MA, AAMET EFT Certified Trainer and Practitioner and Certified EMDR Clinician (www.taptotransform.com)

EFT (Emotional Freedom Techniques) helps to clear the blocks to healing from painful experiences, stress, physical pain, and more with remarkable speed and long lasting effects.

Traditional Chinese medicine believes there are 12 meridians that move throughout the body and bring energy to all the physical organs. In acupuncture, needles are used to unblock the energy and restore health. Using EFT, you stimulate certain energy/meridian points on your body by tapping on them with your fingertips while you tune into your particular issue. By restoring the balance of the energy system, you neutralize and reduce negative emotions and physical symptoms too.

The premise of EFT is "the cause of all negative emotions is a disruption or blockage in the energy system." These blocks include fear, anger, phobias, grief, trauma and other restricting emotions that can create physical problems as well. When you clear the disruption, you have **physical and emotional freedom**.

In the 1920s Einstein told us that everything (including our bodies) is composed of energy as described in his theory of relativity. EFT views the human body as an "energy configuration." Physicians use devices such as the EKG and EEG to measure the electrical activity of the heart and brain. So, it makes sense that we utilize energy sources in the healing process.

How I used EFT for my personal healing with breast cancer.

In 2006, I was diagnosed with stage 3 breast cancer, and for the first time in my life, I experienced periods of depression and anxiety as you would expect. EFT was really a gift for me to manage all my emotions. I tapped on the depression and the fears which gave me much more rapid relief. Then I started to tap for healing; seeing the chemo melt away the cancer cells, and visualizing my cells being lit up and healthy. I used all kinds of tapping phrases to assist in emotional and energetic healing. To my surprise, not only did I feel significantly less depressed, but the extreme dizziness from all the chemicals also reduced significantly.

EFT got me through so many different stages of my year of treatment. You can also tap on the emotions tied to your treatment and condition. You can tap on the negative physical symptoms you experience and the positive healing results you want. EFT was truly an unexpected gift for me in healing.

(See Appendix A of this book, "Basic Instructions on How to Do EFT," by Ruth Stern.)

outcome with maximum benefit to my body.

During this time of self-examination, I even tapped on any resentment I still had toward my parents for not being what I needed them to be when I was a child. I really wanted that issue to be cleared once and for all. (I question whether this is possible with our current clearing methods, but today I feel as though my internalized parents from childhood are standing behind me.) I think a major part of healing occurs when we can get on the other side of being a victim to our early parenting or the traumatic events from our past. I had stopped blaming my parents a long time ago, but I took this time to release more aspects and energy blocks associated with the "writing on my walls." I needed to feel entitled and confident instead of trapped and frustrated. I always end a round of tapping on the negative by tapping on a positive statement—how I want my thinking to be right now. One "choices set-up statement" (positive affirmation) regarding my parents was, *"Even though I still have unfinished business with my parents, I choose to release them in love. They were doing the best they could. I am free to be me."*

When necessary, I also tapped to clear away any negative emotions and thoughts that were preventing me from feeling connected to my Higher Power. In times of great stress, I turn to the spiritual to lift me beyond the doom-and-gloom messages my ego generates. EFT helped me stay connected to positive thoughts and beliefs instead of getting stuck in doubt and dread. The choices statement regarding my spiritual connection was *"Even though I have doubts about my future, I choose to know that Life is working with me and leading me toward my greater good. I trust the present moment will take me there."* EFT was an important part of my physical, emotional, mental and spiritual healing. I have been tapping everyday for thirteen years. It works!

Energy Work

My acupuncturist kept my energy pathways open, and my chiropractor kept my nervous system healthy. They did their part to promote my body's ability to heal itself. But I knew that I needed more help getting the vibration of cancer out of my body. It was time to make an appointment with my favorite energy worker. The next three times I went to New Jersey for a visit in 2001, I scheduled appointments with Diane.

Spinal Alignment Results in Optimal Health

**Dr. Wayne Rebarber, Chiropractor, Rebarber Family Chiropractic
Creating Health; Affirming Wellness
(www.rebarberchiro.com)**

We all are born with an innate, inborn intelligence. This intelligence is with us from the moment we are conceived until the moment we die. It is the organizing force that directs our cells from a single cell at conception to more than 80 trillion cells at birth. It helps us to stay healthy and to function at our optimum level throughout our lifetime. This Innate Intelligence guides the processes in our body that turn food into cells. It eliminates waste products, coordinates muscle contractions and communicates with or without our conscious thought with every cell, tissue and organ of our body by way of our nervous system.

As long as there is no interference, we have the ability to heal, to be healthy and to function at our highest potential throughout our life. If there is any interference in communication or the expression of this intelligence within our body, the result is disease. Interference can cause weakness, imbalances, and other types of health challenges. It can also lead to chronic conditions and deterioration of the spine, and it may set us up for many other types of illness, including cancer, down the road.

Physical, emotional and chemical stress can cause interference to our nervous system and wreak all types of havoc in our bodies. Poor health habits, environmental interference from toxicity in our air, food and water, and emotional stress that can cause our bodies to hold abnormal amounts of tension result in subluxations from overload to our nervous system. These interferences can cause pressure on our spine and nervous system, which affect our health and wellness on every level. Chiropractic adjustments help to remove these interferences so that you can quickly heal, stabilize, regenerate and regain optimal health.

Chiropractic care is helpful for many health challenges, including back pain, neck pain, headaches and other musculoskeletal conditions. It has also been shown to be helpful in correcting, slowing the progress of, or even alleviating many different conditions, including high blood pressure, ear infections, asthma, digestive disturbances, migraines, depression and, yes, even cancer.

How can chiropractic adjustments help a cancer patient you may be wondering? Stress and an improperly functioning immune system can weaken the body's natural healing ability and interfere with the central nervous system's ability to carry messages between the brain and the body. Chiropractic adjustments and other alternative and complimentary healing techniques can help the body to combat the various types of stress that result in poor health and help the body to heal from life-threatening diseases. *(Continued on the next page...)*

When spinal bones are even the slightest bit out of alignment, they can impinge on nerves as they exit the spinal column. Over time, this interference to the nervous system (subluxation) can affect any of the vital organs, joints, muscles, tendons, and even cells that lie along the affected neural pathway. Removing that interference and restoring integrity to the nervous system is the goal of chiropractic care. When a bone is moved so that it is no longer pressing on a nerve, the communication links between the brain and the body are properly restored and the body once again begins to function as it is intended.

While chiropractic care certainly cannot claim to be able to cure cancer, many cancer patients experience pain relief, a reduction in stress, and an increase in their strength and mobility, leading to increased feelings of wellbeing and a better quality of life. Reducing stress on the nervous system restores the body's innate ability to heal on its own and to function optimally.

As a Wellness Chiropractor, I am interested not only in the alignment of the spine, but other components that are essential to maintaining good health, including diet, exercise, proper nutrition, proper rest and adequate hydration. Maintaining healthy relationships is another vital component of our overall health. I also coach my practice members to focus on what they want instead of what they don't want and to watch their thoughts because their thoughts can dictate their reality.

Because of its overall effects on the entire body, Chiropractic should always be considered as part of an integrated approach to every patient's cancer treatment, and it's equally important that every person evaluate its efficacy as part of their individual health maintenance mix.

Most of us think nothing of having our teeth cleaned and examined on a regular basis; similarly, we need to have our spines and nervous systems examined, evaluated and corrected periodically throughout our life, so our bodies can function at their highest level of health and wellbeing.

Energy work (healing touch) clears out the negative emotions, memories and constricted energy that are stuck in my body and soul—my energy system. It is a great complement to EFT. When I performed body energy work, I observed the profound releases people had through healing touch. The release of negative symptoms by running energy through the body was often associated with some emotion, belief or event stored in the body. I believe the body is a memory and energy machine, and these events get stuck in the body and cells as energy blocks. These constrictions contribute to disease. With the proper intervention, the body is able to break up these energy blocks, release the stored memory and heal itself.

I have had many personal experiences with gifted healers in which my physical symptoms were eliminated once I had an energy release. The pain or constriction was released energetically from a specific part of my body or went right up and out the top of my head. I believe that our bodies are connected to energy pathways and chakras, and moving energy is a viable powerful healing modality.

Energy is the blueprint, the infrastructure, the invisible foundation for the health of your body. Your body is composed of energy pathways and energy centers that are in a dynamic interplay with your cells, organs, moods, and thoughts. If you can shift these energies, you can influence your health, emotions, and state of mind.
— David Feinstein, PhD, Donna Eden and Gary Craig, *The Promise of Energy Psychology: Revolutionary Tools for Dramatic Personal Change* (2005, p. 2)

During my first visit to New Jersey after the mastectomy, I contacted Diane Sherman-Levine in Princeton. She would offer her perspective on what the cancer was trying to tell me. I needed to hear it from another person. When it feels appropriate, I seek the opinions of others who can agree or disagree with the messages I get. She would also put her healing hands on my body to remove the energy blocks that may have contributed to the cancer or might be interfering with my healing. The information she obtained through her intuition would help me know how to change my thinking and behaviors. I also wanted my body to know that I was honoring the

85

cancer and working with it to change me and my life. I made a commitment to bring harmony to my body and soul.

With little surprise to both of us, Diane uncovered grief and despair. My spiritual optimism could not sugar coat the disappointments I had experienced several years before I received a cancer diagnosis. A deep secret grief was eating away at my connection to life even though I was walking around with a smile on my face. And, underneath the grief was some anger associated with feeling disempowered. I did not feel this anger consciously, but my body was holding on to it. The dense energy associated with the despair and anger appeared to be squeezing the life out of my cells. It is just amazing to me that at one level I look like a success and many people value working with me, and at another level I need to work on empowering myself. Diane and I laughed because we had worked together for many years, and these patterns were getting very, very old. Enough was enough. I wanted every part of me (all of my selves and archetypes) to move beyond the limitations of my past.

While lying on the massage table, Diane used toning (healing with sound) to get a deep release. I felt a dense, heavy energy collecting throughout my entire body. It began moving up from my back and out the front of my body toward the ceiling. I felt it being lifted out of my whole body. I hoped that a major obstacle to my body healing itself was being removed. I do not think we got an insight associated with this murky energy release, but when it was over, my body felt lighter and clearer. Something of significance had happened, because I felt optimistic again. I no longer felt the heaviness associated with the cancer trauma. I did not even need to understand what my body was trying to say. It did not matter. I just gave thanks. Diane and spirit had worked their magic.

Energy work reconnected me to my resourceful, optimistic center. I realized that the time to change my life for the better was now, and living 3,000 miles away from my old life seemed a good place to do just that. If I took a closer look, life appeared to be repeating itself: I was about to do what my grandparents did when they left Italy in search of a better life in America.

Almost one year after my cancer diagnosis, I felt determined to live courageously and leave those old energy blocks in New Jersey. Emotionally, mentally and spiritually I could connect to the potential of the new life awaiting me in California. The San Francisco area was bursting at the seams with a creative and entrepreneurial spirit. I wanted a little of this high energy to rub off on me. I came away

Reiki: Radiant Energy

by Rev. Maria Antonieta Riveros-Revello
Reiki Shrine: Classes for Healthy Living
(www.reikishrine.org)

Reiki is a vibrational or subtle energy therapy, facilitated by light touch or no physical contact. It can be done at a distance with equal effectiveness.

The World Health Organization, (WH0), has recognized Reiki as a complementary therapeutic modality. The National Institute of Health's Center for Complementary and Alternative Medicine (NCCAM) has classified Reiki as a biofield modality, affecting the energy fields that surround and penetrate the human body.

Reiki restores energetic balance, harmonizing the biofield. The proper energy frequency is re-established by stimulating the repair of tissues and communication between cells. The biophoton communication is reconnected through subtle energy. We scramble our energetic field through pollution, life style, trauma, emotional distress, and mental conditions. Reiki repairs and returns us to the energy system of Universal Divine Order.

Scientists found Extreme Low Frequencies (ELF) produced by the hands of Reiki and other energy practitioners. Non-practitioners do not produce these pulsing field signals. These frequencies are very weak in intensity although very powerful in their effectiveness. They also found that the pulsing field varies from moment to moment according to the needs of the person. Medical research found that these subtle energy fields are very effective to start the healing process.

Reiki complements any form of therapy. Some benefits are: recuperation time is faster from surgery or other treatments; side effects lessen; and hospitalization time is shortened, avoiding infections as well as other unnecessary expenses. For this reason, Reiki is used in most hospitals around the world. In Europe, Reiki treatments are reimbursed by health insurance providers.

Reiki is good for animals and plants as well. There are Reiki practitioners that specialize in horses, dogs and work with veterinarians. Since it is subtle energy, it works with living and nonliving things—machines, batteries, etc.

How is Reiki done?

A person can receive a Reiki treatment while sitting in a chair or lying on a massage table fully dressed. He or she can also receive Reiki from a distance. People usually experience feelings of bliss, deep relaxation, release, and a sensation of feeling lighter. Reiki is an experience in which everyone has a different outcome according to their needs.

from my few energy sessions with more clarity, feelings of empowerment and hope.

Spiritual Work

The deep disappointment I experienced around not being able to launch my co-creating model reminded me that I had more work to do on myself spiritually. Self-acceptance and living in abundance were up for review. Financial issues are real stressors that must be managed; however, the attachment I had to that perceived career failure was ego driven. Although I did not realize it at the time, I had more work to do to get my ego out of the driver's seat, live in the present moment, and work more effectively with the Law of Attraction. This perceived failure was an inside job, and it was blocking my co-creative flow. Lynn Grabhorn's book, *Excuse Me, Your Life Is Waiting*, reminded me to stay focused on the positive in a state of positive emotions and high energy.

Looking back at the situation, I can hardly believe I succumbed to my own ego manipulations. I thought I was so evolved. What a blind spot! Being attached to the outcome took me into the judgments of not being good enough. My subconscious mind did the rest and kept me stuck in the script of lack, struggle and limitation.

Today I understand that when the time is right, I will serve life in my unique way with the support of spirit; whatever it is, it will be good enough. Cancer gave me a jump start to the next level of awareness and truth. If I had achieved prosperity ten years ago, I might still be feeding my ego instead of just being a creative channel. I forgot that my job is to "show up, do my best and allow the universe to do the rest." Living this mantra will enable me to live as a co-creator with the Great Creator without trying to control outcomes to feed a fragile ego.

Several years before the cancer, my connection to the divine felt like a roller coaster ride. One day I was in bliss and expansion and the next in constriction and turmoil. The financial stress in New Jersey must have been testing my metal. I could not find a way to live my spiritual truths consistently even though I spent a lot of time reading self-help books, meditating and doing yoga.

Cancer was one of my greatest teachers. It forced me to bring more acceptance to myself, others and life; stay focused on the positive; and feel abundant in the present moment.

Acceptance: My spiritual healing around the time of cancer required that I feel at one with myself, others, life and a Higher Power. To honor this connection, I had to eliminate the negative, critical judgments that separated me from living in harmony with my life. I released more of my ideal expectations about how things "should" be. Instead, I learned to bring love and acceptance to what was happening. Acceptance created the fertile ground for my unity consciousness to grow.

Positive Thinking: By staying focused on the positive more consistently, I became a problem solver rather a problem dweller. The cancer challenged me to visualize positive treatment solutions and outcomes for my life. I allowed myself to be real with the negative thoughts and feelings that came up, but I quickly turned my gaze toward the possibilities that would protect my body and enhance my life. Visualizing optimal health and wellbeing kept me on a path of optimism and high energy.

Present Moment: Present moment awareness prevented me from striving toward the future. I made peace with not knowing where I was headed because I trusted that my future was on its way to me in divine right order. The next steps of my healing journey came into focus because I did not resist what was happening and did not strive toward the right destination. By letting go of the need to control the process and the outcome, a destination that felt right came to me.

Integration: Growing in acceptance, positive thinking and present moment awareness seems to be an on-going endeavor. These three personal growth approaches served me well through a time of crisis and upheaval. I am much more grounded in these principles than I was eleven years ago, but I still have work to do. I know I am making progress because I am filled with more trust, serenity and feelings of abundance.

For me, a part of self-mastery includes living spiritual principles that I have learned from others and experienced for myself. Today I feel whole because I have integrated my human nature with my spiritual nature. I am not striving to be some perfect spiritual being; I am just holding myself accountable in a loving way to live my truth. Every day I choose peace on the inside. Recently, I received an intuitive message after meditating: *"Focus on the One until this world becomes the dream."* Whatever happens in the physical world, I remind myself of the Divine Presence that exists deep within me— a source of stillness, unity and love. Expressing it to the best of my ability every day is my intention.

Radiation Prayer

by Judith Ansara
(www.sacredunion.com)

This prayer came to me right before I started my radiation treatments for breast cancer. It helped me stay positive and vital during treatment. While silently repeating this prayer I actually felt happy, peaceful and full of life. May this prayer serve you in your own radiant healing.

Radiation treatments are composed of electromagnetic waves similar to light. These waves of energy penetrate our bodies and alter our physiology. It is normal to feel some anxiety about the process and its possible side effects. You have no way of knowing if your treatment will be successful. And cancer by its very nature is frightening to most of us.

By using this prayer and visualization, you can help direct your radiation treatment to help heal and prevent further disease. It can also help you to remain positive and "in charge" in a way that promotes healing physically, mentally, emotionally and spiritually.

Our minds are tremendously powerful. What we think or imagine influences our experience and outcomes. When you align your mind and heart with positive thoughts and imagery, you are giving yourself the best possible chance to go through your treatment with ease. You are aligning yourself with the healing modality you have chosen. You become an active partner in your own healing. As you do this, fear and helplessness can dissolve.

As you lie on the table, close your eyes and breathe slowly, focusing on the gentle rising and falling of your belly. Remember you are here to live! As you say the prayer in your mind and heart, imagine the waves of radiation entering your body and eradicating any remaining cancer cells. See your body as radiant and whole, glowing with positive healing light.

Please adjust the words of this prayer to reflect your own spiritual beliefs and orientation. Prayer has been shown to have measurable, positive impact on health and wellbeing.

> *I dedicate myself to my complete and total healing.*
>
> *I welcome this gift of radiation as a daily dose of divine healing light.*
>
> *As I receive this light, my energy, wellbeing and peace of mind increase.*
>
> *My body, mind and spirit gratefully receive this gift and healing on every level of my being.*

Many blessings to you. Judith

This contact with our spiritual self gives us an expanded perspective on our lives, both as individuals and as part of humanity. Rather than just being caught up in the daily frustrations and struggles of our personality, we are able to see things from the perspective of the soul. We're able to look at the bigger picture of life on earth, which helps us to understand a lot more about why we're here and what we're doing. It helps to make our daily problems seem not quite so huge, and makes our lives feel more meaningful.

— Shakti Gawain, *The Path of Transformation: How Healing Ourselves Can Change the World* (1993, 2000, p. 77)

Getting on with It!

Nine months after diagnosis, my time of introspection was running out. With Paul not working, I had a sense of urgency. Instead of focusing on my past, the time had come to mobilize and design my future. Discovering the next step in my career and establishing financial stability became a top priority. I needed something to get my attention and guide me out of my healing retreat mode. A part of me wanted to play a bigger game; and I needed to give that part a chance to succeed. In the past I had helped a lot of people accomplish some amazing things. I wanted an opportunity to help even more people. As I began exploring what to do next, I was being challenged to trust life more and control the process less. A greater plan appeared to be unfolding.

That summer, a friend visited Paul and me from the East Coast. While we were walking around Jack London Square in Oakland, CA, she encouraged me to explore becoming a life coach. Coaching seemed like the natural thing for me to do after being a psychotherapist for twenty years. The possibility began to wrap itself around me. For a couple of months I explored the Internet for coach training programs. As I approached the one-year anniversary of my cancer diagnosis, I began to feel energized and empowered by the thought of becoming a coach. I became filled with hope about my future. When I sent the Institute for Life Coach Training my deposit, it felt right. I had a path upon which to place my feet. Free fall was coming to an end. Yes!

As a coach, I would inspire people to accomplish what they wanted instead of helping them heal from their wounds of the past. Coaching offered me a new way to help others. It felt exciting and positive, so I assumed my body would like this new approach too. Again, I felt myself being guided to follow the path being placed before me.

The vision of becoming a success coach felt like the turning point Dr. LeShan discussed in his work with cancer patients. I could see myself feeling happy and alive as I inspired people to take themselves, their lives or their businesses to the next level of success. Instead of carrying their pain and suffering, I could carry their hopes and dreams. This possibility gave me a sense of joy. Reinventing myself as a life coach rekindled the spark of creative fire in my belly. Having a vision gave purpose and meaning to my life again.

One year after the cancer diagnosis, I felt relieved to have a new career path and prepared to implement the final phase of my treatment plan.

The year of healing my cancer through a variety of modalities would culminate with a detoxification cleanse in Hawaii. Through an intense ten-day liver and colon cleansing program, I would detoxify my body and give my immune system the additional boost it needed to keep me healthy—a major step toward achieving optimal health. This took me WAY out of my comfort zone. I had no idea what to expect. Apprehensive, but optimistic, I just knew I had to do it.

Living a Purposeful Life

Excerpts from *Live Your Life's Purpose: A guidebook for creating and living a purposeful life* by Dorothy Ratusny, PhD

Individual & Couple Psychotherapy, Workshops & Retreats
(www.dorothyratusny.com)

The secret to authentic happiness is in knowing our self intimately. Self-knowledge precedes inner work and the discovery of our life's passions. Nurturing our innate talents and gifts, we begin to define a purposeful existence for our life.

With conscious awareness comes the realization that there are many more possibilities to your life than the stereotypical ideals that society deems as important. Service of others and being loving and kind go a long way to feeling a sense of fulfillment in who you are.

Your life's purpose is, to a large degree, shaped by the innate abilities and talents you already possess. When you contribute to the world and its people, you feel a profound sense of purpose and meaning. Each of us has unique and specific "gifts" that we might share with others in order to help in service. Your gifts are uncomplicated, often requiring little effort at best. They are not determined by intelligence, wealth, privilege, or physical attractiveness. While your gifts are pre-destined, you use your free will to decide how you share your gifts with others.

To help you get started, ask yourself the following questions, noting what common themes and ideas emerge: What are the things that you are naturally good at? What do others come to you for help with? In moments when you feel a deep sense of inner happiness and fulfillment, what are you doing? As a kid, what did you dream about becoming? What do you most enjoy doing in your free time right now? If money were plentiful, what would you be doing with your life?

Take the first step toward figuring out what you would most enjoy doing with your life. Act on this love or passion by finding a means (right now) of sharing it with those around you. Notice what feelings you experience as you consciously seek out ways to share your gifts with others.

To create a life that has meaning and purpose requires that you rely on yourself for answers and guidance for what's best for you. Be true to yourself, and to what gives you the greatest source of inner happiness and fulfillment.

Chapter 6 Lessons Learned...

- When you are down, it could get worse; choose life anyway!

- Find the support that is right for you; say no to what doesn't uplift you.

- Energy healing techniques can reveal and clear the unfinished business from childhood.

- Change what is within your power to change about yourself and your life; create a life that supports you.

- Reinventing yourself after cancer helps you live with more passion and purpose.

- Positive thinking and purposeful action generate extraordinary outcomes in the real world.

- Failure is an illusion created by the ego; the authentic self has nothing to prove.

- Being accountable and responsible is empowering when you stay out of self-blame.

- The healing journey is leading you where your authentic self wants you to be.

- Your perception of the real world changes as the spiritual realm becomes more real.

- You are alive today; live each day to its fullest.

...a time to clear the negative, connect to spirit, and create a life that serves your true self

Chapter 7
The Proof Is in the Poop
(Ten-Day Internal Cleansing Program)

October 2001

Yes, the word is poop. After participating in a ten-day internal cleansing program in Hawaii, I have a new appreciation for and connection with elimination. Sitting on the removable plastic toilet seat on top of my private bucket in a plastic draped stall gave new meaning to the term out-house. Depositing my specimen and carrying it out to be shared with others on inspection days erased any potty training trauma I had brought with me. I followed instructions without judging them as gross (maybe once or twice I slipped). I surrendered to this protocol to detoxify my body, and in the final hour I was given a gift.

As a result of Nicole's intuitive reading about a Hawaiian woman healer, I set out on a quest to locate Auntie Margaret on the Kona coast of the big island in Hawaii. I wanted to explore the possibility of participating in her internal cleansing program. Finding her proved another matter! Twelve years before my cancer diagnosis, I had tried to connect with her. After reading an article about her program with cancer patients in a holistic health magazine, I was curious to know more. I wanted to share the information with some of my clients with cancer. However, when I called the magazine to obtain her contact information, a staff member told me they could not release it. Consequently, I only had the name, Auntie Margaret, and her general location when I tried to find her for my cancer treatment in 2001. Even though an Internet search revealed nothing in 2001, I continued the pursuit to find her. After my work with vitamin infusion treatment in Reno, Paul and I started asking anyone we met in the holistic health community if they knew about Auntie Margaret.

During the summer of 2001, Paul began going to a woman in Berkeley for Trager sessions, a form of energy bodywork. When he learned that she had spent time in Hawaii, he asked her whether she knew about Auntie Margaret. She did know about her, and she had a friend who had the contact information. Bingo! The universe delivered again. I was becoming more of a believer in this process. A divine order to things kept showing up. When I called the number

I was given, I discovered that Auntie Margaret Machado no longer ran the cleanse. Instead, a Dr. Glenna Wilde, the naturopathic physician who studied with her, had taken over the work. After speaking with Dr. Glenna, I decided to participate in this ten-day intensive and managed to get into the October 2001 program. I would be spending my birthday with four other pilgrims in search of optimal health. After asking a few questions to verify that I could handle what was about to happen to me, I took the plunge. I do have a habit of biting off more than I can chew, but I was in—and it felt right. The world of detoxification was about to become a part of my reality.

Sniffing Things Out

One year after my cancer diagnosis, and ten months after surgery, I arrived in Kona, Hawaii. As I rode in the van from the airport to the countryside, I felt alone heading into unchartered territory. I had no idea what to expect on this trust walk. The peace, beauty and culture I associate with Hawaii made the whole thing feel doable. I could not think of a better place to stretch myself. After getting out of the van, I cautiously walked up to a small house that faced a beautiful bay and noticed a huge plastic green tent located in the yard. Feeling a little nervous, I climbed a few steps and knocked on the side door of the house. A soft-spoken woman with a big welcoming smile greeted me and I felt more at ease. However, when I was shown to my bedroom, a draped corner of the great room (living room and kitchen) my optimism quickly deflated. The previous warm welcome chilled when I realized there would be no bedroom for my stuff and me. Later, I learned that two women friends and a married couple would have the two bedrooms.

Looking very quickly past this glitch, I decided to stay positive and make the best of what was about to happen to me. As the other participants arrived and introductions were made, the cleanse came to life. That evening we had a delicious organic vegetarian dinner and met all of the amazing people who would help us with the process—the staff, cook, and the massage therapist, who was also a talented Hawaiian dancer. Best of all, I met Auntie Margaret, her husband Daniel and her daughter. What an honor to be in their presence! The first evening felt like a party with a group of strangers, but I was beginning to feel connected and my initial apprehension began to diminish. The staff was very friendly. *"These are good people,"* I reassured myself.

Detoxification: Pathway to a Healthy Body

by Beth Poindexter ND, MPH
Creative Health Professionals
(www.naturalmedicinetucson.com)

Toxins are ubiquitous in modern life and have detrimental effects on cell function or structure. The body is burdened with five main categories of toxins: heavy metals, chemicals, microbial compounds, breakdown products of protein metabolism, and personal relationships. Physiologic elimination of toxins happens either by direct neutralization, urination, excretion (fecal elimination), and to a lesser extent via mucous membranes, lungs, and skin. The primary organs of elimination are the liver, intestines, and kidneys. The inability to eliminate toxins results in their accumulation in body tissues or the creation of a toxic body burden.

Effective detoxification depends on appropriate assessment of the toxic burden. All toxic burden assessment requires an exhaustive and detailed history of exposure and physical examination. To gain an understanding of the toxins you've been exposed to in your life visit www.scorecard.org and enter your zip code.

Heavy metal burden can be measured using hair mineral analysis or urine sample collected after a challenge chelator is ingested or injected. When appropriate, chemical burden can involve the measuring of blood and fat for the suspected chemical exposure. Several methods are used to determine the presence of microbial compounds including the measurement of abnormal microbial concentrations and disease-causing agents in the stool, microbial byproducts (urine indicant test),bacterial overgrowth in the small intestine (culture of bacteria from the small intestine or hydrogen breath test) in addition to standard blood work. The breakdown of proteins results in metabolic end-products such as ammonia and urea. Most of these toxic metabolites are eliminated by the kidneys.

Many people underestimate the contribution of toxic personal relationships to their overall toxic burden. Toxic relationships can be as insidious and detrimental as any environmental toxicity.

Detoxification should target an individual's body burden. However, all detoxification supports and enhances the body's inherent detoxification pathways with nutrition. In addition to improving the body's detoxification pathways, efforts are made to "open the emunctories" with the use of constitutional hydrotherapy, colon hydrotherapy, and sauna. The removal of heavy metals requires the use of oral and/or intravenous chelators.

(Continued on the next page...)

The time that it takes to detoxify the body depends on the total burden as well as a person's willingness to engage in the work of the offloading of the toxins. Professionals who are trained in methods for detoxification include licensed Naturopathic physicians (ND or NMD — www.naturopathic.org) and Medical doctors (MD — who specialize in environmental medicine — www.aaemonline.org). There is a host of other alternative practitioners who may have formal training in detoxification who may or may not be licensed in your state.

The first rule of environmental medicine is to avoid exposure. In order to limit your exposure to harmful metals and chemicals I recommend you visit www.goodguide.com to aid in the selection of many products. Also, the Environmental Working Group publishes a food list identifying the top twelve most pesticide laden crops, fondly referred to as the "Dirty Dozen," and the foods lowest in pesticide measurement, the "Clean 15" (www.ewg.org/foodnews/summary/). The choices are yours.

Besides the cleanse itself, a few other things took me out of my comfort zone. People in this wooded area apparently lived with their doors open. Any critter could enter the house, and they did. Geckos scurried along the ceiling beams, yet no one seemed to care. When Dr. Glenna and her assistant got ready to leave that first evening to go to their home, the geckos were making a lot of noise. I also heard scratching against the kitchen windows and was informed that the scratching came from the rats living in the trees. *"Great!"* I thought, but neither Dr. Glenna nor her assistant seemed to be concerned.

I made a comment about the geckos making noise as Dr. Glenna closed the side door to leave. She looked at me and said, *"Don't worry, they won't bother you."* Easy for her to say, but I was freaking out. How was I going to sleep with the rats and geckos? As I lay awake, I realized the sliding glass doors to the porch stood wide open. That would not do. I closed them, leaving a one-inch opening for some air, since the house did not have air conditioning. Of course, this action was not rational. Any rat or gecko could get through the opening. But, it gave this woman from the suburbs of New Jersey a false sense of security. We do not make it easy for critters to get into our homes where I come from! This was over the top for me. Somehow I did fall asleep that night in my cozy corner of the great room. On the bright side, I had the largest bedroom in the house.

Determined to stop resisting the geckos because they were not going away and would be interacting with me every day for the next ten days, I decided their presence might teach me some valuable life lesson. I discovered it during the next few days when I noticed spots on my clothes that lay around the curtained bedroom. Those geckos were pooping on my clothes! Then one day I was sitting in the living room reading a book when I felt something land on my shorts. Again, I saw a small brown spot. One actually had the nerve to poop on me! When I complained to Dr. Glenna, she informed me that geckos often take a liking to someone. *"Me?!"* By this point, all I could do was laugh. This whole thing blew the lid off my reality. I had to accept living with the geckos and in the process learned an important spiritual truth: *"Do not resist what is happening now."* I expected to go to the head of the class after this cleanse.

Cleanse Overview

The ten-day program focused on cleaning out the intestinal tract and the liver. My day began at 6:00 a.m. with my drinking two

99

quarts of seawater solution with lemon juice and as much cayenne pepper as I could stand.

During the first three days of the cleanse, I drank large doses of grape juice with Perfect 7, a colon cleansing formula, three times a day. Dinner consisted of vegetable juice and wheat grass. The middle three days boasted superb organic vegetarian meals including pro-biotic fruit, and I had no food or Perfect 7 mixture for the seventh, eighth, and ninth days. Instead, I had tea three times a day made from a local, handpicked herb and continued drinking the seawater solution each morning. I was expected to drink a gallon of regular water daily. Every day for nine days I also went for steam treatments, swam in the bay, and reclined on slanted boards with legs held higher than my head. The final three days of herbal tea and fasting were intended to clean out the organs of the body, especially the liver and large intestine. Tape worms, parasites, gallstones, polyps, yeast and more would find their way into the specimen buckets after ten days of this detoxification program.

The Spirit Is Willing, but the Flesh Is Weak

As we sat around the kitchen table drinking the seawater solution on the second morning, I shed some tears. Dr. Glena announced that I had to go swimming in the bay because it was an important part of the cleansing process. Unable to swim the crawl stroke due to the limited range of motion of my left shoulder, I dreaded the idea of trying to swim. Plunging into cool or cold water, I would experience pain and even more restricted motion because the left chest wall muscle would constrict over the implant.

A compromised body and an intimidating bay both pushed me beyond my comfort zone. I guess I was having a little pity party of one, but she was having none of it. Once I explained my situation, the staff found a way for me to get into the water with a swim board. While a decent swimmer, I am not a strong swimmer, and the bay had strong currents. However, I managed to swim awkwardly with the board.

To my astonishment, after one trigger point massage with Dr. Glenna, I was able to swim the crawl stroke. By pressing certain points in my shoulder, upper chest and back, she managed to improve my range of motion in one massage session. Life felt magical; I had gone from being constricted one minute to being freed up the next. Dr. Glenna gave me the massage on the large porch of the house, and I can still hear her voice say to me, *"You need to choose life."*

Colon and Detoxification Cleanse the Hawaiian Way

by Mimi George, PhD, Director of the Hawaiian Cleanse Program
(www.hawaiiancleanseprogram.com)

Me ke Aloha pau'ole

The Hawaiian Cleanse Program uses the proven methods of our late teacher, Auntie Margaret Machado, as she requested. Auntie Margaret embodied the spirit of aloha and the power of prayer and love. Her ways have been known to yield miracles. Her healing tradition continues in her faithful students.

The Hawaiian Cleanse is a residential program emphasizing ohana (family style). The staff have all taken the Cleanse themselves and have studied Lomilomi massage in Auntie Margaret's school. Staff lovingly lead and support cleansers through the ten-day process of spiritual, mental, and physical cleansing. Staff aid cleansers in doing daily ho'oponopono (traditional release of toxic emotions and realization of forgiveness) throughout the Cleanse.

Cleansers are served fresh, local, fully organic, pro-biotic and herbal cleansing foods. Formulas are served every two or three hours, every day for ten days. Cleansers experience daily hydrotherapy (between the steam house and ocean), use slant boards, have "opu lomi" (belly treatments and massages), and do breathing exercises/yoga and skin brushing. Educational presentations are given, and a research library about cleansing and nutrition is available. They also create art and music.

The first three days frequent formulas and enzyme drinks are served. The second three days include fully organic and pro-biotic fruit and vegetable meals in addition to all the ongoing daily formulas. Days seven, eight, and (usually) nine, a Hawaiian organ-cleansing herb named "koali" is made into a tea that is taken. Koali offers gentle and thorough organ cleansing, and supports ho'oponopono (spiritual process) and rest. On the tenth day cleansers again have pro-biotic and solid food meals in addition to seawater formula.

Our bodies automatically switch into cleansing and healing mode when we fast from solid foods AND REST. Liquid formulas and alternating rest and light exercise (not any type of work) support the process. Daily bathing in the ocean, hydrotherapy, skin brushing, and lomi massage treatments keep the body comfortable during the very intensive process of flushing out toxins that have accumulated over a lifetime. This Cleanse results in a huge boost to the immune system and brings a tremendous sense of wellbeing and energy. People often say they feel ten years younger...or more.

Apparently, my body and soul spoke to her while she worked on me. She gave voice to the part of me that had given up on myself and life. Signing up for this experience proved to be one small step toward getting my health back and claiming my life. I am so grateful to have had the opportunity to work with her and will always hold her in my heart. The other good news? I still swim using the crawl stroke for short distances.

My second crying spell came when all my coping mechanisms felt stretched to the max. On the third morning of the cleanse, I asked a question of one of the women in the group, and she gave me a caustic answer in front of everyone. It was a simple, innocent question, which was not really personal in nature.

After being with this person a few more days, I noticed that she did have an edge. At the time of her critical remark, I just let it go right through me. I had done enough work on myself not to take her comment personally, but that morning I walked down the road trying to find a spot to get a cell phone signal so I could call my daughter. When I started to speak to her, I began crying about this person who was "being mean to me."

The situation made me feel vulnerable and sorry for myself. After speaking with my daughter, I began to question what I was doing there. If I were a quitter, I would have jumped on a plane and not looked back. Clearly, I needed to be there for some reason, so I just made the best of a challenging situation. I was sure that my personhood was also being tested. I hoped to be a different person once this ordeal ended because more than my body was being detoxified and healed.

Walking on that country road, I felt really alone but committed to seeing this through. I liked Dr. Glenna, and her staff seemed very special. Besides, specimen day was about to happen and I was curious.

You Want Me to Do What?

After the first three days, it was time to produce a specimen for inspection. Each of us had to poop in a white plastic bucket sitting on a plastic toilet seat. We all did our business in our private green plastic draped stall. It was hysterical to say the least. We each carried our bucket to Dr. Glenna and her staff when it was our turn. Our first specimen would reflect a mold of how open or constricted our colons were and how much yeast or other things were in us. It was quite something to see a long mold of my intestine. Thank goodness mine was pretty healthy, and I did not have too much yeast. It confirmed that I had been living a healthy lifestyle both before and after the cancer diagnosis.

All I could think about was how the staff had to deal with our waste as part of their job. The five of us supported each other while each of us got our poop analyzed. As strange as it may sound, we bonded over this intimate experience. The next three days of the cleanse would include some healthy organic vegetarian meals by an extraordinary cook. Life was looking up.

After three days of food, we went on the special brewed herbal tea to clean out the organs of the body from toxins and more. For those three days, the grape juice, Perfect 7 and vegetable juice were eliminated. By the eighth day we were eliminating black liquid and sludge. On the ninth day, Dr. Glenna examined our sludge and gave us feedback about how our body was functioning. Mine revealed no major problems.

Going Within

Throughout the ordeal I was astounded by the depth to which the cleanse had taken me. It had been designed by Auntie Margaret to eliminate a lifetime of toxins stored in the organs of the body. She incorporated a spiritual component too. During the final days without food, I was still swimming and having steam treatments. Interestingly, I did not feel hungry or anxious. I discovered that getting silent and still on the inside took the hunger away. I focused less on the daily activities and allowed a deep calm to wrap itself around me. It seemed like things slowed down—almost like the herb had been a sacred tonic going deep into my organs while taking me deep into my soul. From this meditative state of awareness, all looked well with the world on that ninth day. I had actually made it and lived to tell about it. Nevertheless, the reason I needed to take this cleanse was about to be revealed.

Pooped My Way to Health

Before I went to sleep on the evening of the ninth day, I eliminated what looked like soot and looked into the toilet bowl. As I was about to flush the toilet, I became shocked by the activity I saw there. Three different kinds of small organisms were swimming around and interacting with each other. Some looked like dark lentils, others like a small jellyfish and some like translucent worms. I spoke to one of my fellow cleansers, who was still walking around the house, and she came to look into the toilet. Before long, five of us were looking into the toilet trying to figure out how to capture a specimen to show the doctor in the morning.

My companions went from complaining about not having any food for dinner to shrieking about the creatures in the toilet. At one point I bent over to look into the toilet. A one-inch long translucent worm, which looked like Casper the Friendly Ghost, swam up to the top of the water and looked directly at me. It seemed innocent enough. We stared at each other, and I spoke to it: *"Oh my God, you have been living in me for a very long time."* Of course, it did not answer me, but for some strange reason, calm and peace filled me. Perhaps another clue was being revealed as to how cancer invaded my body. Our group excitement over the parasites turned my trauma into laughter...until it was time to fall asleep. The full impact of what had been swimming around in my body, and might still be there, kept me awake for a long time.

More parasites came out of me the next morning, and Dr. Glenna saw them for herself. She diagnosed them as liver flukes. I may have gotten them in Egypt fifteen years before the cleanse or in Mexico ten years before the cleanse. During my long healing journey with other health care providers, my stool specimens were analyzed a few times. Parasites were never diagnosed. My search for improved health prior to cancer was becoming clearer. The doctors and health practitioners throughout the years had not been able to uncover the cause of what I intuitively knew: I had something wrong with my liver and digestion. In their defense, I did not present with symptoms that would indicate parasites. Once the parasites were eliminated, the puffiness in my abdominal area decreased a little— my only recognizable symptom. However, if left untreated, these parasites would have continued to erode my health and lifeforce— a very frightening thought.

When I left the cleanse that afternoon, I wondered whether the parasites were returning home with me. Still in a state of shock, I felt calm at the same time. Even though Dr. Glenna assured me that the parasites were gone, I knew I would have to confirm this for myself once I got home. As I left the place, the people and process, gratitude overwhelmed me. I hugged people goodbye and acknowledged the difference these gifted healers and good people had made

Parasites — The Silent Health Epidemic

Excerpts from *Guess What Came to Dinner?*
Parasites and Your Health (pp. 1-3)
by Ann Louise Gittleman, PhD
Dr. Ann Louise™ First Lady of Nutrition
(www.annlouise.com)

Do you feel tired most of the time? Are you experiencing digestive problems that come and go but never really clear up? Do you suffer from food sensitivities and environmental intolerances? Have you developed allergic-like reactions and can't understand why? Do you have difficulty gaining or losing weight no matter what you do? Do you sense something is not quite right with you but just can't figure out the cause—and, for that matter, neither can your doctor?

You may be an unsuspecting victim of the parasite epidemic that is affecting millions of Americans. It is an epidemic that knows no territorial, economic, or sexual boundaries. It is a silent epidemic of which most doctors in this country are not even aware.

The idea of harboring a living organism inside our bodies is repulsive and unpleasant to dwell upon, but learning all we can about our unwelcome boarders is the only way we can discover enough to evict them and rid ourselves once and for all of their presence. This is one situation in which ignorance is definitely not bliss. Worms —from the microscopic amoeba to the feet-long tapeworm—are a fundamental but unrecognized and therefore undetected root cause of disease and are associated with health problems that go far beyond gastrointestinal-tract disturbances.

The first part of *Guess What Came to Dinner?* will introduce you to the major reasons parasites are found in America today, what they are, how they do their damage, and how to recognize their symptoms and effects on the body. Then there will be discussions of the most common methods of transmission, from food and water to pets and daycare centers. The final chapters deal with ways to diagnose, treat, and prevent parasites.

Over the years, I have seen a multitude of patients with symptoms as diverse as overweight or severely underweight, fibromyalgia, chronic fatigue, sleep disorders, attention deficit hyperactivity disorder (ADHD), Type 1 and Type 2 diabetes, hypoglycemia, food and environmental sensitivity, constipation, diarrhea, irritable bowel syndrome, Crohn's disease and respiratory disorders get well when parasites were eradicated from their systems.

in my life. I had survived an unbelievable experience. Thanks to Nicole, I had been guided to the late Auntie Margaret Machado and Dr. Glenna Wilde. Both of their deaths are a great loss to the healing community. These very wise people—an incredible Hawaiian healer and gifted doctor of naturopathy—may have saved my life.

The universe in its infinite wisdom must have wanted me to have this experience—three days of diarrhea and all. Something good had come from something difficult. The magic had touched me again, and I had received another installment toward my healing. I am glad that I was able to take myself out of my comfort zone and do what needed to be done. I put the princess and debutante aside and showed up with guts and grace. I believe it truly saved my life. I cannot imagine how I would have discovered the parasites without the cleanse. I did return for another cleanse one and one-half years later to make certain the parasites were totally gone. And, they were. I survived that one too!

After learning so much about nutrition and elimination from Dr. Glenna, I made a commitment to change my lifestyle even more. With raised awareness, I embarked on a mission. I wanted to honor my body by staying clean on the inside. I gained a deeper understanding of how detoxification contributes to a strong immune system. I also learned how a healthy biological terrain prevents parasites from taking up residence in the body. I felt inspired to do more to clean up my nutrition.

Chapter 7 Lessons Learned...

◆ When you are open minded, positive and focused, your desired outcome is brought to you.

◆ "Letting go and letting God" takes you to higher levels of personal empowerment, spirituality and healing.

◆ Life works in mysterious ways. Be aware, and you may see grace, the Law of Attraction and synchronicity working with you.

◆ Caring people are available to help you. Trust that Life will bring you together.

◆ Taking risks and stepping outside your comfort zone is part of the cancer recovery process.

◆ Stretching yourself may have the occasional meltdown; keep going anyway, especially when it feels right.

◆ Going to the still place of peace within will get you through almost anything.

◆ Something extraordinary may come from something difficult.

◆ What is hidden within your body can be harming you; curiosity, openness and grace will help you uncover the truth.

◆ Healing happens through installments. Act now!

...a time to step outside your comfort zone, let God lead and allow the extraordinary to come to you

Chapter 8
My Body Knows What Works
(Wellness Through Nutrition, Supplements and Exercise)

October 2000 through October 2002

My holistic healing journey began with a visit to the Association for Research and Enlightenment in Virginia Beach, Virginia, twenty-five years before I received a breast cancer diagnosis. Edgar Cayce was known as the sleeping profit who gave hundreds of readings on how to heal health conditions and more while in a sleeping trance. In the foundation library, I looked up treatments for asthma. Based on the Cayce readings and recommendations, I eliminated dairy and red meat from my diet and reduced refined sugar. I began going to a local chiropractor listed in a practitioner directory at the foundation. Several months after I made those dietary changes and worked with that chiropractor, my sinus allergies cleared up—a confirmation that I was on the right track.

Throughout the twenty-five years before cancer, I went to many doctors and alternative health care providers as well as attended workshops with some of the best healers and shamans in the country. I made dietary changes and spent many thousands of dollars on supplements to support my health. Many of those supplements were thrown in the garbage or given away because most of them gave me negative side effects. If something made my asthma symptoms worse, it had to go. It was so frustrating. One liquid supplement made me very sick (flu like symptoms), and I lost a week of work as a result of taking it. Worse, I did not feel any better after what the manufacturer called "the healing crisis." I learned the hard way that I must honor my body when taking a supplement or herbal remedy. When a new product is making my body feel worse, I move on or find a different way to take it. I learned to start taking all supplements at less than the recommended dosage and build up to the full dose, or not.

The ongoing quest to get off asthma medicine, have more energy, and look and feel good inspired me to explore ways to heal my body naturally. I told my body that it could not age beyond 40 years old. As I move into the senior citizen category, I may bump that up to 50. More important than looking young, I am committed to not letting the age factor slow me down too much. With all my so-called "healthy living" and positive attitude, a cancer diagnosis came as a shock. I may have been doing a lot of things right to honor my body. But, it appears I was only scratching the surface.

This chapter will highlight the changes I made to my diet, supplements and exercise routine after my cancer diagnosis. I thought I had a healthy food plan going into cancer; however, Dr. Brodie convinced me it was not good enough. I was not getting enough good nutrition from my food. Dr. Wilde and Joan Kasich, an herb specialist, raised my awareness about nutrition and detoxification even more. Instead of going on Tamoxifen or Evista for breast cancer prevention, I used food, supplements and exercise to prevent a recurrence. These drugs were avoided because of their toxic side effects to the body.

Cancer Prevention Diet

While working with Dr. Brodie, I explored the cancer prevention diet and discovered that alcohol, sugar, caffeine, white flour, tobacco and unhealthy fats are the top six things to avoid if a person has cancer or wants to prevent it. I eliminated wheat from my diet several years before I developed cancer. In addition, my sugar, caffeine and alcohol intake were minimal.

Sugar

Glucose plays a role in encouraging the growth and metastasis of cancer. In 1931, Dr. Otto Warburg, PhD, discovered that rapidly dividing cancer cells consume as much as four to five times more glucose than normal, healthy cells. When the source of this fuel is reduced; the rate cancer cells multiply slows down. Therefore, the cancer prevention diet includes eliminating all refined sugars—fructose, sucrose, sorbitol and maltodextrin.

Sugar was and will continue to be my biggest challenge. I have made some progress over the years compared to most people, but put an exceptional dessert in front of me—Gelato or good dark chocolate, and I will have some. Therefore, I only bring processed sugar desserts into my home for special occasions and only sample the confectionary, not eat a large piece. By the time I got cancer, my refined sugar intake was greatly reduced because I knew it was not good for my health. If I ate too much sugar, the next day I felt tired.

After the cancer diagnosis, I cleaned up my sugar intake even more. As I got off the processed and more natural sugars like honey, fructuous, maple syrup and molasses, I could not tolerate anything too sweet. Most sweets tasted disgusting to me. It seems like my taste buds for sugar have changed. Even today, I can't eat most gluten free cookies and other snacks because they taste much too sweet and leave an aftertaste in my mouth. To be honest, desserts that appeal to me continue to call to me. It just feels good to have something sweet once in a while. Because I no longer have active cancer, I indulge myself on a limited basis.

Alcohol

Research supports the link between alcohol consumption and certain types of cancer. Current wisdom suggests that it could increase hormone levels or is carcinogenic because of the way it is metabolized. This metabolic process makes cells more vulnerable to cancer. The liver's ability to metabolize some carcinogenic substances into harmless compounds or to eliminate existing carcinogens is altered with alcohol consumption.

Ten years before the cancer struck me, I had stopped drinking alcoholic beverages. I was a social drinker before that. Two or three drinks at a party were my limit. I did not consume alcoholic beverages on a daily basis. I think the energetic changes in my body from all of the yoga and meditation influenced my decision to let it go. I would feel awful and lethargic the day after having a couple of drinks. One time I drank too much Champagne. The next day I felt really depressed. I decided to stop. With the grace of God, I was able to stop and not even miss it! I imagined the glass of wine as a glass of chemicals and it lost its appeal. Grace carried me the rest of the way. I think I gave it up after a five-day yoga workshop. It just felt right to put the alcohol partying side of myself aside. It was no longer congruent with who I was becoming.

When I no longer drank alcohol, I began carrying my own healthy drinks to social gatherings because I did not drink sweet sodas either. I would carry some natural fruit juice and seltzer with me wherever I went. I would mix them to make a pleasant tasting drink. Some of my friends made fun of my new ways, but that did not stop me. Today I primarily drink water and green tea. Even with cancer, I still allowed myself to drink champagne a few times a year on special occasions. A few years ago I went off daily asthma spray. At that time I decided I could have a glass of wine about once or twice a month. And, this decision could change, if I notice any negative side effects to my body.

Caffeine

Several studies have found connections between caffeine and breast and ovarian cancers. Caffeine may increase the risk of certain cancers because it affects the fluctuation of sex hormone levels.

Coffee drinking was not a significant part of my day, so switching to drinking naturally decaffeinated coffee wasn't a big deal. I rarely had more than one or two cups of coffee a week. And, while I love chocolate, my reduction in sugar reduced the amount of chocolate I ate. After learning about the health benefits of dark chocolate, I allowed myself to sample dark chocolate desserts with low sugar content once every couple of months. Post cancer diagnosis, I increased my decaffeinated herbal green tea consumption.

Tobacco

According to the National Cancer Institute, among the 250 known harmful chemicals in tobacco smoke, more than 50 have been found to cause cancer—hydrogen cyanide, carbon monoxide, ammonia, Benzene and Beryllum, to name a few. And, we now know that tobacco smoke can be harmful to both smokers and nonsmokers.

I never smoked habitually because I had asthma. In my youth, I smoked occasionally but rarely bought a pack of cigarettes for myself. However, I grew up in a smoke filled house. One day while having a hands-on energy session on a massage table, I could smell and taste the smoke being released from my lungs. And, I can only imagine the other chemicals trapped in my cells and body as a result of smoking myself and living with smokers. When I had asthma attacks as a child, no one thought to question the smoke in the environment. (This reminds me how dangerous ignorance can be, especially when it comes to health.) I was, however, sleeping in a dust free bedroom. I slept on a foam mattress and pillow with a special covering, and the room contained no curtains, bedspread or rugs.

White Flour

Several research studies, including one in the *Journal of Cancer Epidemiology*, are linking the consumption of refined carbohydrates and cancer. Carbohydrates more quickly raise blood sugar levels in the human body and accelerate the growth of cancer cells and tumors. Glycemic Index food lists are a guide to help people choose foods that prevent sugar levels from spiking.

My early research about how certain foods react in the body kept me away from white flour products like bread and pasta, even white rice. However, it was not until I went off all wheat that I lost ten pounds in a couple of weeks and had a lot more energy. When I got cancer, I already had a wheat free diet. Today, I have a mostly gluten free diet. I do think the gluten free diet is helping me stay cancer free because my body is able to assimilate nutrients more efficiently. Research studies on nutrition are promoting the health benefits of a gluten free diet. Without gluten clogging up the wall of my small intestine, the nutrients from the food I eat are able to feed and fuel the cells in my body. The digestive enzymes are helping the assimilation process too.

Hydrogenated Fats

Eating a diet high in certain fats increases the risk for many types of cancer. The unhealthy fats that increase cancer risk are: 1) saturated fats found in red meat, whole milk dairy products and eggs; and 2) trans fats (partially hydrogenated oils that are created by adding hydrogen to liquid vegetable oils to make them solid and prevent spoiling). Trans fats are found primarily in margarine, shortenings, salad dressing and most processed foods.

I stopped eating too much of the unhealthy fats when I began my holistic health journey. After going to the Association for Research and Enlightenment, I avoided red meat and fried foods, including fried snacks. Besides, a high fat diet made my asthma worse and affected my gall bladder. If I ate too many fats, I would get a sharp pain in my right upper back. My gall bladder also bothered me when I ate too many nuts. After my two internal cleanses, I no longer experience gall bladder discomfort, even when I eat nuts.

Post cancer, I incorporated more of the good fats into my diet. I began to cook using the unsaturated fats found in olive oil and eat more salmon. For some reason, fish oil supplements, whether capsule or liquid, made my asthma worse. Fish oil is a good source of omega-3 fatty acids and is important to combat inflammation and support brain and heart health. (I can now take krill oil capsules.) Right after the cancer, I could not find a way to take flax seeds either. Eating them gave me stomach pain. (About one year ago, I discovered that I could take them mixed with cottage cheese and flax seed oil, once I had some food in my stomach.)

Evidently, all my efforts to heal my body during the many years before cancer were just not good enough to keep my immune system strong. HRT, the parasites, asthma and financial stress did not help either. As my own health detective, I had to constantly

Understand Good Fats and Bad Fats

Excerpts from *Natural Strategies for Cancer Patients* (pp. 136-139)
by Russell L. Blaylock, MD
(www.russellblaylockmd.com)

Many people have to be convinced that favored foods truly are bad before they are willing to give them up, especially when virtually every processed food we buy contains these fats.

The Bad Fats

Diets high in the omega-6 fats, which are bad fats:

- Depress immunity
- Increase inflammation
- Increase coagulation
- Increase the 15-alpha hydroxyestrone levels
- Increase depression
- Increase tumor growth and spread

To improve your diet, there are a number of things you can do. Most important is to avoid all commercially prepared foods containing omega-6 fats: safflower oil, sunflower oil, corn oil, peanut oil, soybean oil and canola oil.

The Good Fats

Unfortunately, the consumption of the omega-3 type fats is at an all-time low. During the process of preparing foods for market, the manufacturers remove these oils and replace them with the procarcinogenic omega-6-type fats. In the past, we could obtain some omega-3 oils from animal products. This is because animals that graze obtain some omega-3 fats from the grasses they consume. With today's corporate farming methods, however, food animals are fed grains, which contain little or no omega-3 oils.

Vegetables contain some omega-3 oils, but it is impossible to eat enough to meet your needs. Most of these beneficial oils come from seafood, flaxseed oil, and nutritional supplements.

Even though I refer to the omega-6 oils as bad, they are essential oils—that is, they are essential for life and must be supplied by the diet. Problems arise when we consume too many of these oils.

A common mistake people make when they learn of the beneficial effects of the omega-3 oils is to start taking a lot of fish oil supplements without cutting back on their omega-6 fat intake. While the ratio of good fats to bad fats is important, it is also vital to cut down on the total amount of bad oils you consume. This is because ingesting large amounts of the omega-6 type oils can suppress the entry of the omega-3 oils into the cancer cells' membranes. Cancer cells that have a lot of omega-6 fats in their membranes are resistant to immune attack and are more likely to metastasize.

check in with my body to find out what it could tolerate in terms of food and supplements. It did not feel easy at times, and I had a few tantrums and pity parties. Cancer forced me to pay closer attention to my nutrition and make the adjustments necessary to get healthier and save my life.

Food as Medicine

Alternative health care providers all seem to focus on diet and supplements as critical components to healing disease naturally. Becoming more aware of the role food plays in healing and preventing cancer became my focus. The content listed on packaging labels would determine what I put in my shopping cart. I put many products back on the shelf once I read the amount of sugar and fat they contained, as well as the sources of these ingredients. The book *Anti Cancer: A New Way of Life* by David Servan-Schreiber, MD, PhD, elaborates on the role food plays in causing, preventing and healing cancer. He describes the Glycemic Index, omega-3/omega-6 and alkaline/acidic issues in great detail. Unfortunately, this book was not available eleven years ago when I needed it. I learned through direct experience and awareness what foods gave me energy as a result of good digestion and what foods made me feel tired and/or bloated, or increased the mucous in my lungs.

Switching to organic foods was easy when I lived in California. I had three stores from which to buy organic produce and healthier processed foods, as well as good sources of fish and natural poultry. I shopped at two different Whole Foods Markets. While money was an issue after Paul lost his job, I did the best I could to eat organic.

Healthy processed foods can be more expensive than regular processed foods. I draw the line at $19.00 for a jar of organic raw almond butter. For the most part, the choice of fresh foods in California was amazing, and I still miss seeing the beautiful fruits and vegetables in the stores. My lunch consisted of a salad with some protein. Healthy eating for me, at that time, revolved around eating vegetarian four days a week and adding chicken and fish the rest of the week. However, cooking and preparing fancy meals no longer held any interest for me. The homemaking phase of my life was over, so I kept our meals simple but healthy. We continued to eat out a few times a week at modestly priced cafes and restaurants. I gave up eating at fast-food places after going to the Association for Research and Enlightenment. They were not a part of my lifestyle

10 Tips to Lower Your Risk of Breast Cancer

by Christine Horner, MD, Author of
Waking the Warrior Goddess: Dr. Christine Horner's Program
to Protect Against and Fight Breast Cancer,
Speaker and Champion for Women's Health
(www.drchristinehorner.com)

As a plastic surgeon, I witnessed the horrors of breast cancer almost every day while taking care of my breast reconstruction patients. Then, this disease became too personal—it claimed the life of my own mother in 1994. At that moment I vowed to go after her killer.

My goal was to see if this disease could be stopped before it ever started. What caused it to start growing and threw fuel on its flames? So, I searched through the collection of medical research—and found the answers. There, I discovered thousands of studies that pointed out exactly why we have a breast cancer epidemic—what we are doing and not doing that contributes to birthing and feeding it.

Here are a few tips from my book, *Waking the Warrior Goddess: Dr. Christine Horner's Program to Protect Against and Fight Breast Cancer.*

Tip #1: Eat fresh, organically grown fruits and vegetables — especially cruciferous vegetables—every day.

These plants—particularly those in the cruciferous family (broccoli, cauliflower, cabbage, kale)—are filled with a variety of nutrients, vitamins, and plant chemicals that act as powerful natural medicines against breast cancer.

Tip #2: Eat organic whole grains every day.

Whole grains are rich in cancer-fighting antioxidants, vitamins, trace minerals, fiber, and lignans.

Tip #3: Avoid all health-destroying fats. Consume health-promoting fats every day.

Saturated animal fats, trans fats, partially hydrogenated fats, and hydrogenated fats fuel breast cancer, whereas healthy fats—especially omega-3 fatty acids found in flaxseeds—offer protection.

Tip #4: **Eat 2–3 tablespoons of ground flaxseeds every day.**

Flaxseeds are the richest plant source of omega-3 fatty acids, are high fiber, and contain one hundred times more cancer-fighting lignans than any other known edible plant.

Tip #5: **Eat soy-based whole-food products several times a week.**

Women who eat the most whole soy foods, such as tofu, tempeh and miso have a 30% to 50% lower risk of breast cancer.

Tip #6: **Embrace thirty minutes of aerobic activity every day.**

Just thirty minutes of aerobic activity three to five times a week can lower your risk of breast cancer by 30% to 50%.

Tip #7: **Drink green tea every day or take it as a supplement.**

Women who drink green tea have a much lower risk of breast cancer— and if they get breast cancer, their chances of surviving are much greater.

Tip #8: **Consume turmeric every day.**

Turmeric, a potent antioxidant and anti-inflammatory, is considered the #1 anticancer spice.

Tip #9: **Keep your home as toxin-free as possible.**

Toxins are everywhere—in your water, clothing, furnishings, construction materials, dry cleaning, personal-care products, lawn and garden products, insect repellant, flea collars, paints, wallpaper, carpet, tile, particleboard. Assume that everything is toxic unless it is labeled otherwise and choose its nontoxic solution instead.

Tip #10: **Go to bed by 10:00 PM and get up before 6:00 AM.**

Melatonin, the sleep hormone, is a powerful antioxidant that arrests and deters breast cancer in many ways. Staying up past 10:00 PM, alcohol and electromagnetic fields (EMFs) cause melatonin levels to drop.

for a very long time.

I really did try to get into juicing, but doing it was difficult. I bought a $250.00 juicer and gave it my best shot. But, I just could not make myself juice even three times a week. Cleaning the vegetables, cutting them, and cleaning the juicer took more time than I was willing to spend for one glass of vegetable juice. I kept renewing my commitment to get back to regular juicing, but I just could not keep it up. By the end of the first year, I was lucky if I was juicing once a week. The carrots I bought sat in my refrigerator growing white strands. Juicing continued to elude me, but I began eating less processed foods and more fresh and raw foods. I made three different bean soups from dried beans and froze them in my freezer. I would eat them several times a week. Cancer got my attention. It forced me to make better choices in food and beverages. I went to the refrigerator instead of the pantry for my food—a sign I was eating fresh.

By the time I went to the Hawaiian Cleanse (eight months after treatment in Reno), my new food plan was doing some good. According to the few darkfield live blood analyses I had in Reno, my immune system was improving; however, it was not great. After I worked with Dr. Glenna and finally Joan Kasich, I took my nutrition to another level. Best of all, I was beginning to understand how food and supplements were affecting my body and promoting its health.

Naturopathic Doctor

Dr. Glenna Wilde spoke about nutrition in terms of its effect on digestion, assimilation and elimination. She emphasized the importance of bowel health and liver function. Both affect the immune system. Many prominent health care providers support the belief that 80% of the immune system is located in the gut; therefore, digestive health is essential to a strong immune system. Dr. Glenna promoted a detoxification diet, which included more things to avoid than the cancer prevention diet. She suggested that I avoid processed cereals, dairy and eggs (excluding homemade yogurt), sulfured or canned foods and juices, all meats, fermented foods, roasted and salted nuts, and more. This diet was designed to rid the body of the toxins and promote healthy digestion, which ultimately would lead to a strong, healthy body.

When I returned from Hawaii, I made a commitment to eat right and honor my gut. After the three days of herbal tea, at the end of the cleanse, we were served a wonderful yogurt smoothie to replace healthy flora in the intestines. Dr. Glenna emphasized the importance of lactobacillus in our overall health. As soon as I arrived in my own kitchen, I dove into making yogurt in the oven using soy milk. Watching the lactobacillus mixture turn to yogurt in my oven gave me a thrill. I had a huge glass jar of homemade yogurt in my refrigerator. I began grinding seeds, cooking organic vegetarian meals and began using liquid Bragg Aminos (amino acids) to flavor my food. Needless to say, this healthy cooking frenzy lasted about six months. Once I started feeling better and felt secure about my health, I wanted to get out of the kitchen, spend my time on other things, and wished for a cook to make me the nutritious, delicious meals I had in Hawaii. (That is still on my wish list.) I could not sustain the time commitment delicious vegetarian cooking required. Spending a lot of time in the kitchen to prepare meals had lost it appeal to me. I did, however, become a more conscious eater. Having a healthy digestive system became a priority; it continues to be a priority today.

The Herb Specialist

Approximately one and one-half years after the mastectomy, I met Joan Kasich at my first women's business-networking group. She described herself as an herb specialist. After hearing her explain what she did, I felt as though she could help me regain my health through nutrition and herbs. Knowing that I could not take many herbs and supplements, I approached the opportunity with cautious optimism. Joan became the perfect follow-up to my work with Dr. GIenna and Dr. Brodie. I began seeing her on a regular basis, and we became friends.

Joan gave me periodic alkaline/acidic biological terrain assessments using my urine and saliva. She assessed the oxidative stress and toxicity within my body. She could also tell how effectively my cells were receiving nutrients and letting go of toxicity. (This issue is highlighted in *Never Fear Cancer Again*.) Digestion, assimilation and elimination once again were the focus of my getting healthy. We worked to get my biological terrain within a healthy alkaline range of 6.35 to 7.00. A slightly alkaline terrain promotes health, while an acidic terrain is a breeding ground for disease. Chronic stress and acid forming foods contribute to an acidic biological terrain. Acidic fluids within and outside cell tissues carry less oxygen than alkaline fluid, and research is demonstrating that cancer cells thrive in a low

119

oxygen biological terrain. Creating an optimal alkaline/acidic environment in which the cells of the body are able to perform properly is a constant balancing act. The pH food chart began influencing my eating habits and still does. High alkaline foods turn alkaline in the body after consumption. They include most vegetables and fruits, alfalfa grass, lemons and limes, avocado, olive and flaxseed oils, green tea, seaweed, soybeans, almonds, just to name a few. A pH food chart is listed in Appendix B.

Through nutrition and supplements I tried to create a healthy alkaline terrain. A healthy terrain would ensure that pathogens, parasites and fungus would not compromise my health. Joan would check my pH levels from my urine and saliva during each visit and look at my live and dry blood cells through the darkfield microscope occasionally. As a result of the feedback of these two approaches, I could assess whether my diet and supplements were working. I liked this approach because, through my urine, saliva and blood, I received feedback that my health was improving. Looking at my blood with Joan and Dr. Brodie, I felt as though my body was speaking to me. My blood did not lie. It revealed whether I was making progress in improving my immune system and detoxifying my body, or not.

After a six-week series of Aqua-Chi detoxification ionic foot baths, my blood looked great! And, after one of the foot baths, a foot massage felt painless which is unusual for me. I dislike having anyone work on my feet. The Aqua-Chi machine is a water-energizing system that creates healing electromagnetic frequencies in the foot bath. The frequencies recharge the body's energy and allow toxins and foreign matter to be released through the pores of the skin. The water in the basin changes color from slightly murky orange to dark brown. I could not afford to continue these treatments, but I knew they could help me if I needed them again.

While I worked with Dr. Brodie and Joan, my progress was an up and down thing. One time the feedback would look good, another time the numbers and pictures would be lacking. But, as a result of working with these two gifted health care professionals, my body appeared to be healing itself, and I began to look healthier and have more energy. My treatment approaches were getting me on the other side of the darkness called cancer.

Balance Your pH; Balance Your Life

by Joan Kasich, Certified Natural Health Professional —
The Herb Specialist
(www.herbspecialist.com)

What is the pH? PH stands for "potential for Hydrogen," but I like to think of it as the "potential for health." PH measures the acidity or alkalinity of a solution. On a scale of 5.0-9.0, with 7.0 being neutral, the higher numbers indicate alkalinity. A healthy body ranges in pH from about 6.3-7.3, and these ranges fluctuate throughout the day.

Maintaining a perfect pH can be difficult. For example, you may eat perfectly healthy organic food. But, if you are extremely stressed for one reason or another, your body will process that healthy alkalizing food as acidic. Your mental, spiritual and emotional state is as important as the healthy food you put in your body. That's why, when a person is extremely ill with a life threatening diagnosis like cancer, you can bet they are very stressed. So to balance their pH, taking care of their adrenals and nervous system is just as important as building up their immunity. Without those adrenals in great shape, their body cannot process and distribute minerals. It's those minerals that help to keep the body balanced.

If your pH shows **high** alkaline numbers, that is NOT an indicator that you are alkaline. It means you are SO acidic your body is using calcium and minerals from your bones to buffer the acids. When that runs out, the body produces ammonia to alkalize the inner fluids, which is eliminated in urine.

To have a healthy pH level requires that people have a ratio of 65% alkalizing forming foods and 35% acid forming foods. If you ate 6 veggies, 2 fruits, 1 protein source, and 1 starch, you would have a ratio that alkalizes your body. Vegetables do a great job alkalizing the body; eat them often.

Eating healthy live foods from nature (not processed and empty foods) as well as eliminating stress appears to be a great combination for staying healthy. I have found over the years that "happiness is health." The best pH results I ever got from clients occurred when they had just returned from a restful vacation. So my advice to clients is—find out what brings joy to your life and stick to it!

Supplements

Controversy abounds around the issue of whether vitamins and minerals can cure or prevent cancer. Unfortunately, I do not think researchers from the conventional medical field understand the sources, complexity, diversity and dosages alternative doctors recommend. The issue of natural versus synthetic must also be addressed. As a result of my journey through cancer, I learned that the supplements prescribed by alternative health professionals were often different than the vitamins and minerals purchased in a store.

I thought I was spending an exorbitant amount of money on supplements before cancer, but that seemed inconsequential compared to the price tags on the supplements prescribed by integrative doctors. A large bottle of Univase Forte digestive enzymes (400 count) cost $130.00 and lasted about six weeks. I committed to spending what I considered to be a reasonable amount of money on supplements to heal the cancer and achieve optimal health. Taking charge of my own healing process meant putting my hands deep into my bank account. Today, I continue to make the financial commitment optimal health requires. With curiosity and commitment, anyone can improve their health using supplements because effective healing strategies exist for every budget. I invest in my health before I invest in my wardrobe.

Immune System

Dr. Brodie prescribed ten digestive enzymes between meals. They would break down the protective protein coating surrounding cancer cells, which prevented the white blood cells of the immune system from recognizing and destroying them. Ten tablets gave me a headache, so I had to lower that dosage to six. My on-going inability to take many supplements got in my way often. I could not take everything that was recommended because of my sensitivities. Dr. Brodie and I were both frustrated, but I took what I could tolerate. To boost the immune system, I also took Amygdalin (Laetrile), 6,000 mg of vitamin C and a thymus extract every day.

Estrogen Dominance

Three different estrogens are created by the body: estradiol, estrone and estriol. The body can also take in chemical estrogens called xenoestrogens. These synthetic chemicals found in plastics, pesticides and many manufactured products mimic estrogen, and both types of estrogen stimulate cell growth. Too much estrogen within the cells increases the risk of estrogen related cancer and interferes with treatment. Oral supplements were prescribed to block the estrogen receptors of the cells from taking in too much estrogen. I also rubbed a small amount of progesterone cream on my inner thigh and arm and a little directly on my right breast and over the scar on the left breast. According to Dr. John Lee, author of *What Your Doctor May Not Tell You About Menopause*, the hormone progesterone inhibits estrogen dominance within the cells. These supplements and cream were used instead of Tamoxifen or Evista to protect my body from producing another estrogen related cancer.

A soy powdered drink was recommended for its phytoestrogen activity. Phytoestrogens are plant based estrogen-like chemicals used to reduce breast cancer risk. (Today, there is controversy as to whether soy increases or decreases the risk of breast cancer.) The soy drink made my breathing worse, so it had to go. (I learned later that I might be allergic to soy.)

Thyroid

My thyroid functioned on the slightly low side (hypothyroidism), which is known to raise the risk for breast cancer. Dr. Brodie put me on thyroid medicine. However, I began feeling a tingling sensation in my brain, and no matter what dosage or form I took, my body did not like those medications. I avoided foods like kale, chard and cabbage that negatively affected the thyroid's function, but because my symptoms were not clinically noticeable, this condition did not receive the attention it deserved at the time. Adrenal support supplements also helped reduce the effects of stress on my body and improve the endocrine system. Healthy adrenal glands are necessary for the thyroid to function properly.

Lymphatic System

Once I began working with Joan, I took an herbal remedy by Nature Sunshine labeled Lymphatic Drainage to cleanse the lymphatic system. It is designed to disperse fluid efficiently, improve nutrient absorption and enhance the immune system. Bouncing on a small trampoline is known to be a great way to cleanse the lymphatic system, so I bought a rebounder. I could not afford to get lymphatic drainage massages, and I did not like scrubbing my body with a dry brush. My efforts to cleanse my lymphatic system fell short too.

The Basics of Estrogen Dominance

by **Michael Lam, MD, MPH, ABAAM**
Author of *Beating Cancer with Natural Medicine* and
How to Stay Young and Live Longer
Adrenal Fatigue Center
(www.drlam.com)

Estrogen and progesterone work in synchronization with each other as checks and balances to achieve hormonal harmony in both sexes. It is not only the absolute deficiency of estrogen or progesterone but rather the relative dominance of estrogen and relative deficiency of progesterone that is the main cause of the majority of hormonal based health problems. The continuum of hormonal imbalance conditions include PMS, fibrocystic breast disease, endometriosis, PCOS, fibroids, and even cancer.

While sex hormones such as estrogen and progesterone decline with age gradually, there is a drastic change in the rate of decline during the perimenopausal and menopausal years for women in these two hormones. With the gradual drop in estrogen but severe drop in progesterone, there is insufficient progesterone to counteract the amount of estrogen in our body. This state is called estrogen dominance. According to the late Dr. John Lee, the world's authority on natural hormone therapy, the key to hormonal balance is the modulation of progesterone to estrogen ratio. For optimum health, the progesterone to estrogen ration should be between 200 and 300 to 1.

In the west, the prevalence of estrogen dominance syndrome approaches 50% in woman over 35 years old. Natural progesterone (not synthetic forms called progestins) acts as an antagonist of estrogen. For example, estrogen stimulates breast cysts while progesterone protects again breast cysts. Estrogen enhances salt and water retention while progesterone is a natural diuretic. Estrogen has been associated with breast and endometrial cancers, while progesterone has a cancer preventive effect. Studies have shown that pre-menopausal women deficient in progesterone had 5.4 times the risk of breast cancer compared to healthy women. Using natural progesterone to offset estrogen dominance should be considered when clinically indicated.

Our body normally functions in perfect homeostasis. In the past 70 years, our body has been subjected to unprecedented insults from estrogen overload. Sources of estrogen come from within the body as well as outside. In our body, estrogen is made in the adrenal glands, fat tissues, and ovaries. Those who are under mental stress or overweight are particularly vulnerable.

Environmental contribution to estrogen load in our body includes the presence of estrogen-like compounds called xenoestrogens. These compounds behave like estrogen once inside our body. They are found commonly in petroleum based household products including shampoo and nail polish. Not to be forgotten are hormonal laced food we ingest from animals fed with growth hormones and the like. We have managed to turn our diet from whole fruits and whole foods to fast, genetic modified, and processed food. In the past, cattle were raised on grass and natural organic feed and chickens were allowed to run free. Worse yet, feeds laced with pesticides and hormones, both of which have estrogen-like activities, are routinely given to animals, which in turn is passed to humans and contributes to estrogen dominance.

Women in non-industrialized cultures whose diets are whole food based and are untainted with modern processed foods and pesticides seldom suffer a deficiency in progesterone and the signs of estrogen dominance manifested as menopausal symptoms. Keeping estrogen dominance at bay is an important tool in cancer prevention and anti-aging.

Estrogen dominance is also part of the body's response to stress from a neuroendocrine perspective, involving the thyroid and adrenal glands, leading to Adrenal Fatigue Syndrome. In addition to symptoms of estrogen dominance, dry skin, low body temperature, fatigue, lack of energy, hypoglycemia, low blood pressure, anxiety and insomnia are commonly exhibited. Always consider adrenal fatigue syndrome and estrogen dominance if you are on thyroid medications but still don't feel good.

The 12 most common reasons for estrogen dominance are listed in my full article called Estrogen Dominance, with additional articles covering natural cancer prevention, Adrenal fatigue syndrome and hypothyroidism. All are available free at www.DrLam.com

Digestion/Elimination

Lactobacilli had been a part of my daily supplement regime for many years before cancer. However, I tried to improve the quality of the lactobacilli after cancer. But, most of the varieties I tried did not work for my body because of one side effect or another. Although I could not keep up the momentum of making my own yogurt, I did find a few supplements that worked for me. I also took digestive enzymes after meals in addition to between meals. As a result of participating in the Hawaiian Cleanse, I believe in Perfect 7 for cleansing my colon; I continue using it twice a week.

Nutrition and supplements have played an important part in my healing process. Trying new things was frustrating at times because of my sensitivities and limitations. However, I did manage to find products and foods that contributed to my getting beyond cancer and improving my health. I know there is much more I could have done those first few years regarding my diet, but I did the best I could at that time. If I had stage IV cancer, instead of stage I, my food plan would have been much stricter, and juicing would have been a must. I can choose to criticize myself for what I did not do, or I can acknowledge myself for what I did. I have decided to accept my efforts eleven years ago as good enough. I recognize that I am a work in progress.

Exercise

Once my body recuperated from the mastectomy, I returned to walking several times a week for 30 to 40 minutes. Walking the hill near my home got my heart rate up. The climb was difficult for me, but over time I could do it with relative ease. Walking became a form of exercise when I moved to California. (In New Jersey, Paul and I took ballroom dancing once a week.) I hiked Mission Peak several times a month, although getting to the top eluded me. I put a modest exercise plan in place to keep my body moving because I understood the importance of movement to relieve stress, as well as oxygenate and detoxify my body.

As I said earlier, I bought a Cellerciser (rebounder). I started bouncing up and down on this small trampoline several times a week. I would do several minutes of just simple bouncing; then I would run in place on the rebounder for up to 20 minutes. Rebounding turns out to be a great way to cleanse the lymphatic system, a very important component for healing and preventing

Your Gut Is Your Lifeline to Health and Happiness!

by Barb M. Mahlmeister RD, LD/N
Natural Choice Nutrition, Nutrition and Functional Medicine
(www.naturalchoicenutrition.com)

Why is it so important to keep your gut healthy? The gastrointestinal tract has many functions and is host to over 80% of your immune system. Your gastrointestinal tract starts at your esophagus and ends at your rectum.

Many of my clients have dysbiosis; that is, their gastrointestinal tract is not working efficiently. They have irritable bowel syndrome (IBS), which includes diarrhea, constipation, gas and bloating. Other symptoms include reflux, heartburn, burping, belching, headaches, migraines, depression, and changes in mood, inability to focus, bone disease, iron-deficiency (anemia), thyroid dysfunction, mouth sores and dental issues. Symptoms may also include outward signs such as eczema, psoriasis, acne and/or rheumatoid arthritis.

The connection between your gut and your immune system is as long as the intestinal tract itself. It starts by chewing with your teeth, down the esophagus into the stomach, through the small intestine where 95% of nutrients are absorbed, then to the large intestine (colon) where waste material is eliminated. If you are unable to properly digest your food, malabsorption occurs (inability to absorb nutrients from food), along with damage to the lining of your intestine. In other words, when your colon is not functioning at maximum capacity, your immune health is at jeopardy. For instance, if you have constipation (less than two or three bowel movements daily), food builds up in the colon and is unable to pass. This causes the colon's tight junctions to loosen, which allows toxins to leak out into your blood stream. This is called "leaky gut." Diarrhea or lose stools immediately after consuming food also lead to nutrients not being absorbed. If food is either stuck in your colon or zips on by, your brain is not receiving the nutrients it needs to function.

Food sensitivities or allergies are a major player in dysbiosis. Many people react to a variety of food groups. A few of the more prominent ones are dairy (casein/whey), gluten (wheat-durum, semolina, spelt, malt, couscous, bulgur), barley, rye, soy, egg, shellfish, tree nuts and peanuts. Food allergies are easy to identify, as they tend to elicit an immediate reaction (think Howard Wallowitz in *The Big Bang Theory* when he eats peanuts) or gluten if you have Celiac Disease. On the other hand, symptoms from food sensitivities can take up to two days to appear, making it difficult to determine which foods are the culprit.

(Continued on the next page...)

The first defense is to know who your enemies are. There are several labs that offer food sensitivity testing. Once you determine which foods are causing one of the above issues, eliminate those foods. Make sure you examine all food labels, as there are often hidden ingredients.

Supplementing your diet with pre- and probiotics is another important step to take in protecting your gastrointestinal tract. Probiotics are carbohydrate fibers called oligosaccharides. Oligosaccharides are indigestible and remain in the digestive tract where they stimulate the growth of beneficial bacteria that help defend against illness. Sources include fruits, legumes, soybeans, inulin, chicory root, Jerusalem artichoke, oats, dandelion greens, garlic and yacon, and whole grains. Probiotics help improve digestion and mineral absorption, thereby boosting the immune system. Yogurt and fermented foods (natto, kimchi, meso, tempeh, sauerkraut and kefir) are probiotics. Taking a daily probiotic supplement will also help aid digestion and eliminate symptoms.

The bottom line is a healthy, functioning gastrointestinal tract is key for almost every function in your body. So the next time you are experiencing any of the above mentioned symptoms, pay attention to your gut's beneficial bacteria.

cancer. Rebounding actually improved a weakness in my left knee—a total surprise.

Someone referred me to Qi Gong, an oriental form of exercise and moving energy. I bought videotapes and worked with the tapes several times—and never got back to it. Sound familiar! (They are still sitting on a shelf in my home.) I could stretch almost every day, but I did not have the interest, energy and commitment to tackle something new. My excuse: I was doing all I could to stay positive and cope every day with cancer recovery, finances and my unknown future. I could not take on one more thing, even though it would help me.

Move More

The "Move More" report by Macmillan Cancer Support, one of the largest British charities, reviewed 60 studies and surveyed 400 health professionals who deal with cancer patients. Their findings confirm the benefits of physical activity in recovery and long term health care for cancer patients.

The report states that recommended levels of exercise for 2.5 hours per week could reduce a breast cancer patient's risk of recurrence or dying by 40% and a prostate cancer patient's risk of dying by 30%. The report also indicates that exercise decreases effects like fatigue, depression, osteoporosis, and heart disease for all cancer patients, as well as reduces the risk of colon cancer by as much as 50%.

The American Cancer Society Recommends:

◆ Maintaining an active lifestyle to reduce cancer risk for adults.

◆ Getting at least 30 to 60 minutes of moderate to vigorous activity five times a week.

— Moderate activity is anything that makes you breathe as hard as you do during a brisk walk. During moderate activities, you'll notice a slight increase in heart rate and breathing, but you may not break a sweat.

— Vigorous activities are performed at a higher intensity and generally engage large muscle groups. They cause a noticeable increase in heart rate, faster breathing, and sweating.

— Weight lifting and stretching improve physical strength and flexibility.

Physical Fitness and Optimal Health Go Hand in Hand

**Excerpts from *Fit Moms for Life: How to Have Endless Energy to Outplay Your Kids*
by Dustin Maher, Fitness Professional for Moms and
Creator of Fit Fun Bootcamps
(www.dustinmaherfitness.com)**

Having the big picture in mind is necessary when you go from starting an exercise program to making it a lifestyle. If you have a big enough "why" in your life, the "how" becomes a lot easier. The people you surround yourself with will play a crucial role in lasting success. If you make initial changes but remain in the same environment, that environment will likely bring you right back to where you started.

Creating a Fitness Plan that Is Right for You

Rather than spend hours exercising and burning a low number of calories, you need to redirect your focus to more intense exercise that will raise the heart rate, burn a lot of calories, and generate a good after-burn. The burst training I'm recommending is supported by the research in the last five years, which shows that training more like a sprinter, instead of steady-state cardio, is more effective.

Any kind of exercise can be considered burst. It could be climbing stairs, swimming, biking, squat jumps, running in place. All that is necessary is for the HR to reach 90% plus of max within a 60 second period of time. The beauty of burst training is that instead of doing an hour of cardio, you only have to do about 15 minutes. Plus, it's going to be more effective because you're burning more calories and more fat, and you're raising your metabolism for a longer period with the more intense workout. So as you go on with the rest of your day your metabolism is still elevated and burning extra calories.

To stay fit and healthy and lose weight, I recommend you strength train your whole body three days every week, and do burst training at least two or three days a week. You have two options. You can commit roughly an hour a day for three or four days a week or about 30 minutes for five or six days a week. I believe that shorter workouts more days of the week are more effective, but of course, that doesn't work for everyone's schedule.

Hour-long exercise, three to four days per week. You want to include strength training on three of your exercise days, working both your upper and lower body each time. To let your muscles rest and recover, I recommend you exercise every other day and try not to do the strength training on two consecutive days. I prefer to start with a dynamic workout for a few minutes and then go into 30 minutes of strength training. Then do ten to15 minutes of burst training and five to ten minutes of core work before you stretch. My *Fit Moms for Life* DVDs follow this structure, and it takes about an hour to do a whole DVD.

Shorter exercise five to six days per week. If you're going to exercise five to six days a week, there are a couple different ways you can structure your workouts. The first is to alternate lower-body and upper-body workouts for a shorter strength-training portion. That way, your lower-body muscles are recovering the day you're working your upper body, and vice versa. That might take about 20 minutes, and then you can alternate whether you use the remaining time for burst training or core work. (Of course, you need to warm up before your workout and stretch afterward, no matter how you structure it.)

The other way to set up shorter, more frequent workouts is to do 30 minutes of full-body strength training one day and do core work and burst training for about 30 minutes the next. If you want to do something extra or different like yoga, that's fine. Just make sure you get three days' worth of strength training in for both upper and lower body.

Eating right and exercise are the nuts and bolts of any training program for strength, health and weight loss. The other pillars of fitness are a positive mindset and supportive environment. All of these aspects of training determine whether you will truly be able to transform your body, health and life, and maintain those positive changes over time. Just start telling yourself that you will succeed, even if you don't believe it right away.

Yoga, rebounding and walking were cost-free ways for me to contribute to my healing. 2001 and 2002 were two of the most difficult and stressful years of my life. I had to heal my body of cancer while our money was being depleted, and we did not know how to stop it. The grand California adventure was turning into a dead end. Exercise became one of my stress reducers, but I only gave it a half-hearted commitment. I rarely broke a sweat when I exercised. I told myself that I don't sweat. How were those toxins going to leave my body? At that time I did not really understand the importance of detoxifying my body and boosting my metabolism through aerobic and muscle building exercise.

Onward and Upward!

Around the two-year anniversary of the cancer diagnosis, my new career as a personal life coach came to life. My spiritual outlook and nutrition had improved significantly. I worked at staying positive and trusting that God was in charge of my future. I had become wiser about the kinds of foods and supplements my body needed to thrive. Unfortunately, the push to exercise more vigorously was missing. But, based on my live blood cell analyses, my immune system looked good most of the time, even if not great.

Because I could not take all of the recommended supplements prescribed by Dr. Brodie and Joan Kasich, I had gaps in my healing program. And, I could not tolerate the recommended doses for some of the supplements either. For the most part, my health seemed to be improving. However, I was walking around with a false sense of security. Several months after celebrating two years of being cancer free, the universe, in its infinite wisdom, sent me a message I could not ignore.

Chapter 8 Lessons Learned...

- Nutrition, supplements and exercise require an investment of your attention, time and money.

- Good nutrition happens as a result of proper digestion, assimilation and elimination.

- The cancer prevention diet promotes great health.

- Eighty percent of the immune system is located in the gut. Keep your intestines healthy.

- Eat organic when possible and avoid foods that have the most pesticides.

- An optimal alkaline/acidic balance in your body contributes to having a healthy body.

- Work with professionals who understand the impact nutrition and supplements have at the cellular level.

- Nutrition, supplements and exercise require a disciplined lifestyle that evolves over time. If you have stage IV cancer, be disciplined now!

- Exercise is a critical part of healing. Find what feels right for you and do it regularly.

- Become your own health detective; you are in charge!

...a time to understand how nutrition, supplements and exercise impact your cells—and be committed to having a healthy body

Chapter 9
Relapse Is Not an Option!
(Elevated Two–Year Cancer Markers)

Winter 2003

After my two-week treatment in Reno, I appointed Dr. Brodie as my cancer specialist. He agreed and became my trusted healing advisor. During the first year after my mastectomy, I saw him on a quarterly basis and then every six months during the following two years. Traditional oncologists would not understand what I was trying to achieve without Tamoxifin or Evista, and I did not want to explain myself to them. And, traditional cancer tests could not tell me how my body was functioning to prevent a recurrence. I wanted to have a warning sign before another tumor showed up.

The live darkfield blood cell analysis, AMAS test results and breast thermography became my cancer prevention indicators. Thermal imaging captures the natural infrared emissions from the human body, showing thermal patterns that reflect underlying neurovascular physiology. These images can identify abnormal patterns in the area of breast tissue based on body temperature. The thermogram interested me because it examined both breasts. Not only would it give me information about the right breast; it would indicate cancer activity near the site of the scar on my left breast where two tumors were removed.

Most of my darkfield blood analyses looked OK during the years I went to Reno. Once in a while, my blood looked great. Several times the white blood cells (leukocytes) were sparkling with a lot of energy. I could see the difference when the immune system was strong and when it had challenges. My diet, exercise and the supplements were still somewhat lacking. The financial stress of Paul not earning enough money to pay our bills and my starting a new career was taking its toll on my health too. We were going through our savings fast and living on credit. Even though I found myself in this stressful situation, I generally felt better and had more energy. My cancer indicators did not give me or Dr. Brodie cause for alarm.

On November 29, 2002, I felt a weight lifted from my body and soul. This two-year marker held within it the "all-clear sign" I patiently waited to receive after my mastectomy. On that date, I felt confident that the original cancer no longer threatened my life.

Thermography: Another Breast Screening Option

by Maria E. Belluccio, DOM, AP, RN, CCT, Doctor of Oriental Medicine
and Certified Clinical Thermographer, Physician/Owner of
Lotus Path Wellness Center
(www.lotuspathwellness.com)

The current screening tool that is used to assess our breast cancer risk is actually increasing our exposure to cancer causing ionizing radiation. In 2005, the National Toxicology Program at the National Institute of Health released its Eleventh Report on Carcinogens in which ionizing radiation, including the 15% that occurs during medical procedures, was identified as a known human carcinogen. In light of this knowledge, there is an increasing demand for safer and more accurate screening tools.

What are our options?

There is another option that offers no radiation or breast compression. It is called digital infrared thermal imaging. It is based on the principle that angiogenesis or new vascular growth is essential for pre-cancerous and cancer cells to grow. Our vascular patterns are generally symmetrical in our bodies and have similar temperatures bilaterally. A thermographic image of the breast can determine suspicious vascular patterns as well as pin point inflammation. Temperature differentials assessed by a highly sensitive digital infrared camera can visualize "hot spots" that can alert us to an area of concern.

A suspicious area can be detected possibly 5 to 10 years prior to it being seen on a mammogram or through self-breast examination. Not all lesions grow at the same rate, which makes it challenging for any screening tool to be 100% accurate. Thermography carries a 95-97% accuracy rate. This is superior to any current screening tool available at this time. Often times combining it with ultrasound technology can increase our chances of seeing a true picture without the exposure to ionizing radiation or tissue compression.

Is thermography a standalone procedure?

The current screening tools—mammography, thermography and ultrasound are not diagnostic. Accuracy of any one test increases when combined with another. Thermography is set apart from the others due to its ability to see the earliest changes in breast vasculature and temperature. These two criteria are important when tracking progression of a suspicious area.

Monitoring women starting in their twenties for stability in breast vascular and temperature patterns would offer the opportunity to see changes and move toward a safe holistic treatment approach.

However, that jubilation was short lived. Whether my intuition took over or I was having some symptoms, I do not remember. It may have been that I had too much yellow mucous in my lungs again or felt tired. But, several months after the two-year mark, a bizarre incident magically pointed me in the right direction and saved me again.

Ignorance Is Not Bliss

A friend of ours, who lived in an apartment complex, invited us for dinner at her home. We parked in a spot with a number. There were no signs or other indicators not to park there, so we did not give it any thought and just parked our car. That evening when we returned to our car to leave, we were in shock. The car was gone. We could not believe our eyes. After much turmoil and a few phone calls, we discovered it had been towed. Around 11:00 p.m. my friend drove us to the towing establishment to pick up our car. This kind of thing has never happened to me, and I knew the universe was giving me a message. If I interpreted this incident as a dream, I would say the car is the vehicle that takes me through life—my body. Because of ignorance, it was taken from me. This gave me cause for concern about my health, habits and lifestyle. I did not know the specific message associated within the event, but it got my attention. I just tucked it away in my mind as a warning sign of something.

During my next visit to Dr. Brodie about a month later, I told him that I wanted another AMAS test. On each visit, I would have an IV drip, get my blood analyzed and see him for a consultation. He said it was not necessary. Personally, I did not need to spend the hundreds of dollars for the test, but I knew the missing car was telling me to be vigilant. With my insistence that something was not right, he agreed to do the test. A few days later, I received a call from him, and he informed me that my cancer markers were elevated. This meant I had too many cancer antibodies in my bloodstream and could be at risk of developing cancer somewhere in my body. He was amazed. With a chuckle, he told me to keep listening to my intuition because it was doing a great job. He recommended that I go on the peptides, which cost $430.00. Money was an issue, and I asked whether I could use something less expensive. He said yes, but in cases like mine the peptides bring the numbers to normal 100% of the time. It did not take me long to decide to go with the peptides, and they were sent to me overnight in a refrigerated container.

Intuition

Intuition is an inner sense of knowing when you do not know how you know. It may take the form of a hunch, a gut instinct, a feeling, a symbol, an insight or an epiphany. An immediate whole message drops into your awareness and connects you to truth. The knowing comes from a place beyond the rational mind (sometimes called a sixth sense). Your intuition becomes important when you are facing the unknown, have a decision to make, need to solve a problem or understand a message. It has even been known to save lives and could be the creative leap that turns thinkers into geniuses. — Sandra Miniere, Author of *A Lighter Side to Cancer: From Wake-Up call to Radiant Wellness*

After my initial two-week IV treatment in Reno in 2001, the staff sent me home with my first bottle of peptides in a refrigerated pack. (They must always be refrigerated.) While traveling for a week during that first round of peptides, I did not take this liquid gold with me and resumed taking it when I returned home. The total protocol took about three months. Without realizing what I was doing, I did not follow the directions to the "letter of the law." When I took them the second time, I followed directions carefully. When I traveled to the East Coast, I carried these liquid peptides with me in a small brown bottle within a small, soft insulated case. I treated them like they were an elixir of life. This time I would do exactly what needed to be done. I was becoming my own health care *enforcer*. My next AMAS test was normal.

After the car incident, I decided my health and life were in a precarious state so I asked Dr. Brodie to put me on the drug Evista as a preventive measure against breast cancer. He agreed to do that. Because I could not take all of his recommended supplements and because I was living with tremendous financial stress, Evista seemed the wisest thing to do at that time. It gave me a stronger sense of security against cancer.

After the incident of the elevated cancer markers, I remained curious about what other people were doing to stay cancer free. While taking Evista, I tried supplements people recommended and continued working with my acupuncturist, chiropractor, and nutritionist. I was determined to do my part and allow my body to heal itself naturally. The insight came to me that the cancer issue would not just go away and be forgotten. Right then, I made a lifetime commitment to monitor my body and health so I could remain cancer free. I believed then, and believe now, that cancer can be cured or

Four Steps to Listening to Your "Intuitive Voice"

by Sandra Miniere
Author of *A Lighter Side to Cancer:*
From Wake-Up Call to Radiant Wellness

Step 1: Get centered.

A mind free of mental chatter and a body free of disturbing emotions prepare you to listen with every cell of your mind, body and soul. This state of calm awareness allows your "intuitive voice" (inner knowing) to share its wisdom through inspirational insights and messages with few distortions.

Challenge: To be open and receptive, you must create a quiet inner space, even if it is only for a few seconds. You do this by being willing to hear the truth, letting go of attachment to an outcome; having a heart filled with gratitude; and accepting, rather than resisting, what is happening now.

Step 2: Ask for what you want.

Once you are clear about what you want, design an open or close ended question that will give you a valid answer.

An effective open-ended question can be answered in a simple phrase or two: "What is preventing me from getting healthy?"

A close-ended question might be: "Will this person contribute to a positive result for me?" For questions requiring a yes or no response, you must develop a process you can trust. It might be using a pendulum, noticing a specific physical sensation, doing a muscle test or just hearing a yes or no.

Challenge: When forming your questions, you may need to break a global issue down into specific, smaller parts. Focus on getting answers for the next steps rather than the big goal if something does not feel right.

Step 3: Receive the answer.

Your intuition communicates in words, symbols, sense of knowing, and physical sensations. Know how truth feels in your body. If you "listen" with your gut and your heart as well as your mind, you will recognize truth on many levels. *(Continued on the next page...)*

An epiphany can feel like one of Zeus's thunderbolts, shattering an old limiting belief while leaving a feeling of ease, expansion and freedom in your body.

Challenge: Intuitive messages need to be interpreted accurately. Mental clarity (no ego distortions or attachment to outcome), feelings (positive or negative) and energy (heavy or light; constricted or expansive) are a part of the receiving process. They help you interrupt the message. You must learn to discriminate between ego driven messages (what your intellect wants to hear) and intuitive guidance (what Universal Intelligence wants you to know for your greatest good).

Do not judge the message; just receive it. If you do not understand the meaning, ask another question about that.

If you do not get an answer right away, Universal Intelligence may send you the message from another source—a person, movie, book, article or TV program. Be aware.

Step 4: Take action.

Once the message feels right, take the action steps necessary to support it. When you act upon what you have learned, you are encouraging your "inner knowing" to continue sharing.

Challenge: Be patient with the process. Trust develops over time. Begin by taking actions on low-risk situations. As you play with the process and experience success, you strengthen your "intuitive voice" until it becomes a part of your decision making process and internal guidance system.

Listen and act; but also check things out in the real world. Proceed with the curiosity of the child and wisdom of the wizard.

contained with the right interventions. Awareness, discipline, action and optimism go a long way to beat the cancer odds.

Three Things We Can Do to Protect Ourselves Against Cancer

◆ *Reduce the consumption of refined sugar and white flour.*

◆ *Reduce the omega-6 fats found in margarine, vegetable oils and animal fats.*

◆ *Limit our exposure to chemical contaminants found in the environment since 1940 including electromagnetic fields.*

— David Servan-Schreiber, MD, *AntiCancer: A New Way of Life* (2009, p. 94}

I do not worry about my cancer returning. I just accept that monitoring my body is a part of life, not a frantic search to stay alive. I am not afraid to die, and I do not fear my body. My job is to work with it and assist it in its journey toward optimal health and longevity. I am tuned in to the subtle signs that it gives me when something isn't right. When I get into my car to drive, I also recognize when something isn't right with the engine, steering and braking. There is an ease to the process of this mindfulness. My job is to just pay attention. When I do that, I seem to be in a flow that keeps me out of trouble and brings me everything and everyone I need to heal.

I stayed on Evista for three years until I began having slight dizzy spells as well as leg cramps. After I read these side effects in the Evista literature, I decided to stop the drug. The symptoms disappeared. I had to take charge again and trust that all of the natural things I was doing to heal my body and prevent a recurrence were in place. Most important, when I got off Evista, Paul and I were living in Tampa and my life stressors were much less. Paul loved his teaching position at a state university, and my revenue was improving. We were actually having fun again. Better still, our finances were in control, and this contributed to intense feelings of gratitude every day.

Eleven years post cancer, my health is better than most people my age. Even though I am eleven years older, my level of energy and physical activity are greater than before cancer. I now monitor my cancer markers through Dr. Schandl's Cancer Profile. I also rely on my lifestyle, which includes an anti-inflammatory food plan, high quality supplements, regular exercise, positive attitude, daily meditation and EFT to keep me cancer free.

Chapter 9 Lessons Learned...

- Staying cancer free is a lifetime commitment.

- When you work with a doctor you trust, the burden of cancer feels lighter.

- Sometimes following instructions exactly is the only way to get the results you want.

- Develop a working relationship with your intuition; your life may depend upon it.

- Analyzing the facts and trusting your intuition will help you choose what is right for you.

- Mindfulness allows you to be aware of the signs the universe provides. Listen carefully and take appropriate action.

...a time to notice the subtle signs, trust your intuition, and do your part to stay cancer free

Chapter 10
Wellness Is My Reality Now!
(Current Health and Life Update)

2012 Health Update

Eleven years after breast cancer, I still work diligently on healing my body and uplifting my soul. Preventing cancer continues to be a priority in my life, including the financial commitment it requires. For the most part, my daily habits support my vision to achieve optimal health. However, I know that I can do better. Staying healthy, young and vibrant continues to be a challenge as I approach my seventies. My time and money are stretched, but I am doing the best I can for now. With awareness about products and services in the marketplace, I will continue to explore options and make choices that take me to greater aliveness. I do notice that something is different within me: Cancer no longer scares me.

As a result of learning about genes and cells and what influences them, I have taken the mystery out of cancer. The research and experts tell me that the terrain within the body turns the cancer process on or off. Our thoughts and emotions influence physical terrain, as well as nutrition, supplements and drugs, exercise, and environment. This feels like truth to me, and I now believe cancer is controllable and preventable with the right interventions.

The information age has exploded. Experts like David Servan-Schreiber, MD, PhD, Russell L. Blaylock, MD, Bernie Siegel, MD, Christiane Northrup, MD, Tanya Harter Pierce, MA, Raymond Francis, MSc, Suzanne Somers, and Brian Luke Seaward, PhD, just to name a few, are sharing valuable health and healing wisdom with the world. The options for treating disease and living longer are expanding. Energy medicine and the mind-body therapies are moving toward center stage in the healing matrix. The experts in the integrative health arena are beginning to get the attention they deserve. Cyberspace has more information than I can possibly investigate, and much of it is free. (I do need to be cautious regarding the sources and validity of this information.) I recently listened to free radio interviews on *The Aware Show* hosted by Lisa Garr. She had experts speaking about issues related to health, personal growth and spirituality. While I sat in front of my computer screen, experts from all over the globe came into my home and raised my awareness with their timely wisdom. And, I made changes to my diet based on what I learned. This is awesome!

Six Basic Strategies

Greg Anderson, author of *Cancer: 50 Essential Things To Do* (1999) describes six basic strategies cancer patients are using to "enhance their health and enrich their lives." The strategies emerged as a result of thousands of survivor interviews. They include:

◆ **Medical Treatment** (standard of care)

◆ **Nutrition** (diet and supplements)

◆ **Exercise** (regular physical activities)

◆ **Attitude** (empowering beliefs)

◆ **Support** (nurturing relationships)

◆ **Spirituality** (deep spiritual transformation)

Most cancer survivors associated with the Cancer Recovery Foundation International agree that a comprehensive integrated approach to healing plays an important role in beating cancer. This book is designed to help cancer patients participate in their recovery process through actions that may save their lives.

My life and wellbeing depend on learning because I believe that once my body has produced a cancer, it could happen again. I want to avoid that unexpected surprise. With a sense of ease, not dread, I do what I must do every day to remain cancer free. I only had stage I cancer, but I have made a lifelong commitment to my health. My healing goals include boosting my immune system, improving my digestion and breathing, and having a body filled with high energy. Living each day with a positive attitude, serenity and abundance is part of my master plan too. The physical decline of old age is not a part of my reality. I do not see myself in a nursing home and will do my part to stay out of one. Spirit is eternal, and I want my body to live that message until the time of my death. The investments toward wellness that I make now will keep me vibrantly healthy into my nineties and beyond.

Every single thought you have generates a physiological change in your body. You are a product of all of the thoughts you have thought, feelings you have felt, and actions you have taken up until now. And...the thoughts you think today, feelings you feel today, and actions you take today will determine your experiences tomorrow.

— Jack Canfield, *Jack Canfield's Key to Living the Law of Attraction* (2007, p. 15)

Finding My Stride in Florida

Most days I wake up with a sense of gratitude. When I look out my kitchen window and see the water flowing in the pond 50 feet from our house, dense trees draped with moss and our beautiful palm tree, I acknowledge how blessed I feel to be living in this environment. A peace and tranquility exist in the Tampa Bay area of Florida that even the summer storms cannot shatter. I am not sure whether the outside affects my insides, or my insides affect how I see the outside. But, I will take it, whatever it is, because I am thriving here. Of course, I still have stressors in my life, including a health crisis with my husband and the recent deaths of my parents. But, an ease has settled into my life, and it is also showing up in my body and soul.

It took some courageous decisions to get to this inner contentment and outer place of beauty, but the payoff has been worth it. With minimal income, my husband and I took the risk to move ourselves from California to Florida. Both of us were working for ourselves and did not need to live in California to run our businesses. We traded the most expensive San Francisco area for the inexpensive Tampa area. We bought a small house we could easily afford and shipped our two older cars rather than buy a new car. The move reduced our housing expense by two-thirds. My cousin welcomed us; he and his wife lived a few miles from our new home. We had no idea what awaited us in Wesley Chapel, but it felt right based on my intuition. The thought of living in a modern Florida style house with a big master bathroom, high ceilings and quiet neighborhood inspired me to keep going during this stressful transition.

Inner Wisdom Contributes to Health

Excerpts from *Women's Bodies, Women's Wisdom:*
***Creating Physical and Emotional Health and Healing* (pp. 514-519)**
by Christiane Northrup, MD, copyright © 1994, 1998, 2006, 2010
New York Times Best-Selling Author and Visionary Pioneer
(www.drnorthrup.com)

Our bodies are permeated and nourished by spiritual energy and guidance. Having faith and trust in this reality is an important part of creating health. When a woman has faith in something greater than her intellect or her present circumstances, she is in touch with her inner source of power. Each of us has within us a divine spark. We are inherently a part of God/Goddess/Source. Jesus said that the kingdom of heaven is within, and we can make this spiritual connection through our inner guidance. We need go no further than ourselves to find it.

Learning to connect with our inner wisdom, our spirituality, is not difficult, but neither our intellect nor our ego can control either the connection or the results. The first step is to hold the intent to connect with divine guidance. The second step is to release our expectations of what will happen as a result. The third step is to wait for a response by being open to noticing the patterns of our lives that relate to the original intent.

Guidance is always available, but we have to be open to receiving it. Seeing the patterns that connect is a way of looking at life. Understanding the big picture doesn't mean getting stuck in the particular moment. Gaining access to spiritual guidance means looking at the pattern of our lives over time.

Though each of us is part of a greater whole, we are also individuals. The unique part of this whole that we each embody must be expressed fully in order to create health, happiness, and spiritual growth for ourselves and others. The way to best express this divine part of ourselves is by becoming all of who we are. Our bodies direct us toward full personal expression by letting us know what feels good and "right" and what doesn't.

When we invite the sacred into our lives sincerely asking our inner wisdom, or higher power, or God for guidance in our lives, we're invoking great power. Being in tune with our spiritual resources is a vital healing force. Committing to remember our spiritual selves and receive guidance for our lives is part of creating health.

Used by permission of Bantam Books, a division of Random House, Inc.

Preparing for the move, I remembered the view from the glass doors and windows at the back of our new home. The vision filled me at a time when I was running on empty. The house pulled me to it, and it has been a blessing ever since. Someone or something was watching out for me. I felt guided at a time when I could not see.

Physical health is a reflection of the stressors in people's lives and the way they cope with those stressors. As I review where I have been and analyze the lives of people I have helped, this is crystal clear to me. Major life stressors, like death of a loved one or loss of a job, as well as chronic conflictual situations, like a dysfunctional relationship or negative work environment, play havoc on the body. People must manage the stressors in healthy ways, as well as make wise choices about their lifestyles. Looking back at the first few years after cancer invaded my body and life, I am amazed that I kept going and stayed positive while feeling the heavy weight of financial instability and career uncertainty. Most important, with no road map, I found a path that led me to my current lifestyle and state of health. I know that God was around somewhere because I could not have done it without the courage and empowerment grace provides.

Almost every major illness that people acquire has been linked to chronic stress.
— Bruce Lipton, PhD, *Biology of Belief* (2005. p. 121)

My life is now filled with passion and purpose because I love helping others become all they can be and eliminate what is getting in their way. As a life and leadership coach and Emotional Freedom Techniques practitioner, I am making a difference in people's lives, connecting them to their inner truths, and having fun doing it. Work is my best medicine because serving others and taking them to new heights of authenticity, success and wellness fuels me. In return, I get to live my values and purpose, and also reap financial rewards. While my office is not the large suite of rooms I had in New Jersey overlooking a park like setting with a lake, it has a large window that often allows the morning sunlight to bathe me in bright light. My work contributes to my feeling alive, and I can do it into old age! Through positive thinking, inspiration and wise choices, I found my way into a lifestyle that serves me well.

A Mind-Body-Spirit Approach to Managing Stress

Excerpts from *Achieving The Mind-Body-Spirit Connection:*
A Stress Management Workbook (pp. 4-5)
by Brian Luke Seaward, PhD,
Inspiration Unlimited & The Paramount Wellness Institute
(www.brianlukeseaward.net)

Holistic stress management promotes the integration, balance, and harmony of one's mind, body, spirit, and emotions for optimal health and well-being. Indeed, stress affects all aspects of the wellness paradigm. To appreciate the dynamics of the whole, sometimes it's best to understand the pieces that make up the whole.

○ **Emotional well-being:** The ability to feel and express the entire range of human emotions and to control them, not be controlled by them.

○ **Physical well-being:** The optimal functioning of the body's physiological systems.

○ **Mental well-being**: The ability of the mind to gather, process, recall, and communicate information.

○ **Spiritual well-being:** The maturation of higher consciousness as represented through the dynamic integration of three facets, relationships, values and a meaningful purpose in life.

The Nature of Holistic Stress Management

With the appreciation that the whole is always greater than the sum of the parts, here are some insights that collectively shine light on the timeless wisdom of holistic stress management:

○ Holistic stress management conveys the essence of uniting the powers of the conscious and unconscious minds to work in unison (rather than opposition) for one's highest potential. Additionally, a holistic approach to effectively coping with stress unites the functions of both right and left hemispheres of the brain.

○ Holistic stress management suggests a dynamic approach to restore one's personal energy in which one lives consciously in the present moment rather than feeling guilty about things done in the past or worrying about things that may occur in the future.

○ Holistic stress management uses a combination of effective coping skills to resolve issues that can cause perceptions of stress to linger and sound relaxation techniques to reduce or eliminate the symptoms of stress and return the body to homeostasis. This is different from the standard practice of merely focusing on symptomatic relief.

○ Holistic stress management is achieving a balance between the role of the ego to protect and the purpose of the soul to observe and learn life's lessons. More often than not, the ego perpetuates personal stress through control and manipulation. With a holistic perspective, one responds rather than reacts.

○ Holistic stress management is often described as moving from a motivation of fear to a place of unconditional love.

When all of these aspects are taken into consideration, the process of integrating, balancing and bringing harmony to mind, body, spirit, and emotions becomes much easier, and arriving at the place of inner peace is easier to achieve.

Living close to Walt Disney World, Busch Gardens, performing art theaters and more have added an element of fun to my life. This lifestyle is a welcomed change after the stress filled years of cancer and financial struggle. Florida residents get discounts to the Disney theme parks, and we took advantage of their offer the second year we moved here. I return from Disney feeling happy. It has a magical effect on me. Just watching the kids is so uplifting and saying hello to Mickey and Mini when I drive under the archway to the Magic Kingdom puts a smile on my face. We go several times a year with our granddaughter, friends or by ourselves. Taking our five-year-old granddaughter to have lunch with the princesses at Epcot gave me such a high that I am sure my body chemistry and immune system were reaching new levels of optimal health. Taking the Segway tour around Epcot's World Showcase early in the morning brought out the joyful seven-year-old in me. After all the years of stress and uncertainty, we have made fun a part of our lifestyle, and it is working.

Cancer Prevention Is Still on My Radar

After moving to Florida, I no longer had Dr. Brodie to analyze my AMAS tests to see whether I was at risk of developing another breast tumor or some other type of cancer. I took two AMAS tests on my own and had my primary care physician get the results. The second one came back with the numbers slightly elevated. I took charge and worked with a naturopathic physician for about one year. My blood eventually looked normal under his microscope regarding cancer activity. But, I decided I needed more information to get the kind of cancer prevention screening that would put me at ease. I wanted to know when I was headed toward cancer, not in it—a reasonable request of the medical community from my perspective. Four years ago, I learned about Dr. Schandl.

When I read the conference program from the Cancer Control Society Doctor's Symposium, I was drawn to "The Cancer Profile" for early detection and monitoring therapy success. It read, "Tumor markers can be detected in the blood several years prior to the time when a diagnosis can be made. The Cancer Profile will detect metabolic changes leading to or indicating cancer." This sounded too good to be true. Could this be exactly what I was looking for to monitor cancer activity in my body? With a simple blood and urine test, I could know in advance whether I had to be concerned with cancer again. And, I got more than I ever imagined.

Dr. Schandl did what no health care provider could do. He got me off the daily use of asthma spray by suggesting specific supplements and rigorous exercise. The search had only taken 30 years; yet, I always knew it was possible. As I got healthier after cancer, I intuitively felt as though my body just needed the right chemistry. The natural strategies I used for many years to bring the asthma under control should have worked, to my way of thinking. But, they did not. He took me the rest of the way. I cannot thank him enough. Cancer prevention would be a bonus.

In three and one-half years, I have had four cancer screenings with Dr. Schandl. My last test had very good news. The hormone markers that were elevated were beginning to come down, the right direction for me to get out of the "cancer caution zone." The supplements I am now taking and the exercise I am doing are working for the asthma and the cancer. Reduced inflammation is not only clearing up the mucous in my lungs, it is reducing my risk factors for cancer. Something is making a difference because my health is improving. We still do not actually know what got me off the asthma spray, but I am fine with that because I have been off daily medicine for over three years. I went to Dr. Schandl to prevent a cancer recurrence, and he is helping me heal my body. What a gift in finding him. Grace was leading me again.

Dr. Schandl suggested that I take various supplements, but I think the ones that made the biggest difference were the digestive enzymes. I cannot take most digestive enzymes because of their negative side effects. To my surprise, I could take the enzyme tablets he suggested; however, I was taking them wrong. Instead of taking ten tablets before a meal, I took three or four with my meals three times a day. This protocol may not have been helping the cancer markers; however, they did their magic to get the asthma under control. I did not take the minerals as he suggested either because I got a headache if I took all three pills before bedtime. When he told me I was taking the supplements wrong, I told him it was OK because I got off the asthma medicine. He laughed and made some derogatory comment about me. His comment went right through me because I felt ecstatic about the victory over the asthma spray.

After 30 years of searching and experimenting, my lungs cooperated—a monumental achievement. But, the time had come to listen more closely and follow directions, if there were no negative side effects of course. I changed how I took the enzyme tablets: I took five approximately 45 minutes before breakfast (not ten because they gave me a headache) and three with my other meals. After ten months, my hormone markers on the Cancer Profile came down 50%. Currently I am taking eight on an empty stomach approximately two hours before one meal a day. My body did not like ten. I expect my hormone markers to be in the normal range soon.

Dr. Schandl recommended taking high doses of special minerals as well as iodine and L-Tyrosine for my thyroid, higher doses of vitamin D than I was taking, and small doses of DHEA because my levels were low. He had me exercising more rigorously than I have ever done. He wanted my heart rate up for twenty minutes three times a week. (He was part of the reason I trained and walked in the Disney 5K race in 2011.) Today, I am walking 15-minute miles for two miles about four times a week. Getting my thyroid and metabolism working normally seems to be making a difference in my overall health. The breast cancer tumor markers also came down ten points from the previous test. It is still in the normal range, but the numbers are lower. Yeah! I am so lucky to have found Dr. Schandl. He really understands the body and how to keep it healthy. He also does longevity testing and consultations.

Food Continues to Be My Medicine

My food plan is better than it was eleven years ago. It is mostly gluten and dairy free, as well as low in sugar, grains, red meat, fats, caffeine and alcohol. I do eat mostly organic fresh foods, specific types of fish, and organic poultry. The air chilled organic chicken from Whole Foods Market is exceptional. Several times a month I eat organic grass fed beef, which I also buy from Whole Foods Market. I make every effort to buy organic, especially for the foods with the most pesticides according to the Environmental Working Group. The "Dirty Dozen" list includes apples, celery, strawberries, peaches, spinach, imported nectarines, and imported grapes, sweet bell peppers, white potatoes, domestic blueberries, lettuce, and kale/collard greens. I have introduced organic kefir, a thin yogurt from dairy or coconut, to improve the flora in my intestines and drink small amounts of Kombucha several times a week. I am only eating about 30% raw food each day. I would like to get that to 50%. My food plan is designed to bring nutrients into my cells, reduce inflammation in my body and increase my level of energy.

What the Expert Says...

Optimal Health Benefits from a Raw Food Diet

**Excerpts from *Raw Fusion Living* by LindaJoy Rose, PhD,
Life Makeover Therapist, Wellness Chef
and Pioneer of the Raw Fusion Movement
(www.drljrose.com and www.rawfusionliving.com)**

There are many documented cases of physical conditions and chronic diseases that have been improved or entirely cured through adhering to a mainly raw foods diet. Eating a diet high in raw foods can also reverse or stop the advance of life-threatening conditions, such as heart disease and cancer.

Eating high-energy foods that have not been denatured by processing or over-cooking also boosts the immune system. A stronger immune system also helps you overcome the toxic overload that is not only derived from the food that you eat, but also from environmental conditions beyond your control.

Raw foods are generally much easier for the body to digest. Committing to a high raw lifestyle has made me very conscious of what I am eating. As a result, I have learned to "listen" to what my body is telling me—by reactions, symptoms, energy shifts, mood changes or subsequent digestive discomfort, things that I would have ignored in the past.

A healthy and balanced raw foods diet provides you with an intense infusion of phytonutrients and antioxidants, especially when you stick to organic and naturally (as opposed to artificially) ripened fruits and vegetables. Like a powerful defense team working in your favor, these nutrients battle the free radicals that oxidize your bloodstream and vital organs, helping to neutralize and reverse the effects of aging. Vegetable juices are also very alkalizing to your system, helping defray the acidic residues created from stress, toxicity and certain foods. Eating and drinking more alkaline foods actually relaxes you, ultimately leading to a younger and more radiant visage.

When your body is burdened with the task of having to metabolize food without the benefit of the natural enzymes in living foods, it becomes progressively more drained and fatigued. This process is naturally inverted when you switch to a diet composed of more wholesome foods. You begin to feel surges of energy and can accomplish more in less time. Raw foods are loaded with enzymes that help break down the food to release the beneficial nutrients that support a clearer mind, a more positive mental outlook, less need for sleep and a strong healthy immune system.

(See Appendix C of this book, "Raw Fusion Recipes," for recipes provided by Dr. Rose from her book, *Raw Fusion Living*.)

Raw Fusion is a hybrid of the best of the raw foods world, intermingled with an informed and conscious mainstream lifestyle. Individuals who find a high raw diet too limiting can find ways to integrate more variety into their meals without compromising nutrition. High raw foodists seeking healthy ways to add cooked foods into their diets will enjoy the versatility and variety of these tips. Families or individuals accustomed to more mainstream meals, but searching for tasty and convenient ways to increase their nutritional intake, will be surprised at how effortlessly one can fuse more raw ingredients into meals.
— LindaJoy Rose, PhD, *Raw Fusion Living* (2010)

The book, *Anticancer: A New Way of Life*, influences the foods I eat. Dr. Servan-Schreiber produced an amazing book about the prominence of food and lifestyle in the cancer causing equation. Because chronic inflammation within the body has demonstrated a close link to cancer, I am committed to an anti-inflammatory nutritional program. Even the American Cancer Society, which has a traditional view of cancer, states that one-third of cancer deaths are linked to poor diet, physical inactivity, and excess weight.

Of course, when eating in restaurants or traveling, I eat as healthy as I can with the choices available. My beverage of choice is purified water, and I do not miss the other types of drinks. The sugar in juices and sodas is not worth putting into my body. When I have sugar, it needs to be in some awesome dessert, according to my taste buds. I try to eat foods that contribute to a more alkaline terrain. On my salads each day, I use Bariani Olive Oil, fresh squeezed lemon juice, turmeric (anti-inflammatory spice) and Bragg Liquid Aminos. Drinking at least three cups of green tea daily detoxifies my body and contributes to my blood and urine being more alkaline. My food plan is not for everyone and still needs improvement because my health is not where I want it to be. I am not as disciplined as I could be when it comes to the foods I eat. I do not like spending time in the kitchen. But, I am doing the best I can right now, which feels good enough because I am only preventing cancer, not treating it.

The Role of Inflammation in Disease

**Excerpts from *The Inflammation Syndrome: Your Nutrition Plan for Great Health, Weight Loss, and Pain-Free Living* (pp. 3-6)
by Jack Challem, "The Nutrition Reporter"
(www.jackchallem.com)**

Inflammation is now recognized as an undercurrent in all disease processes. Inflammation (not cholesterol) is now understood to be the primary determining factor in coronary heart disease...Inflammatory disorders—for example, allergies, arthritis, heart disease, and inflammatory bowel disease, to name but a few — share common causes and also increase the risk of developing other inflammatory diseases.

Medical thinking about the role of inflammation in disease began to broaden in the late 1990s, following the development and increased use of the high-sensitivity C-reactive protein (hsCRP) test. The test was revolutionary in that it could measure subtle, low-grade inflammation—the type of inflammation that is not always obvious but that slowly breaks body fat. High-sugar and high-carbohydrate foods also tend to be short on fiber, protein, omega-3 fatty acids and vitamins and minerals that either buffer the absorption of carbohydrates or aid in the body's metabolism of them.

Your body is a remarkable biological machine, designed to make an assortment of pro- and anti-inflammation substances. What you eat—proteins, carbohydrates, fats, vitamins and vitamin like nutrients and minerals—provides the nutritional building blocks of these substances. Some nutrients help form your body's inflammation-promoting compounds, which normally help fight infections. Others help produce your body's anti-inflammatory substances, which moderate and turn off inflammation.

Until recently, people ate a relative balance of pro- and anti-inflammatory nutrients. Today, because of extensive food processing, our diet has become seriously unbalanced. The typical Western diet now contains at least thirty times more of some pro-inflammatory nutrients than just a century ago. As a result, people have become nutritionally and bio-chemically primed for powerful, out-of-control inflammatory reactions.

The Inflammation Syndrome explains how and why inflammation eats away at your health. You will also learn plenty of practical information about how to prevent and reverse inflammation. Ultimately, you alone are responsible for your own health. This book provides a plan for you to empower yourself to safely prevent and overcome inflammatory disorders. You will discover how easy it is to take charge of your diet and your health—and to feel better than you ever imagined.

From my perspective, people need to eat what makes them feel good whether it is for their blood, metabolism or nutritional type, or not. I do not adhere to a specific program. I believe in what works. My body is always giving me feedback about what constitutes "high quality" foods. My breathing, digestion and energy give me superb warnings that I am eating or drinking the wrong things. I still use that asthma spray if I am around pets, in a toxic environment, or eating too much of the wrong things (mostly gluten and sugar).

For the past two and one-half years, I have actually been juicing. I now juice three to four times a week, but about two years ago, I was juicing almost every day. I probably would not juice for myself; however, my husband needs to do it for his health, so together we get the job done. We work as a team to wash and cut vegetables, run the juicer and clean it. We bought a new Omega single gear juicer, which is still a nuisance to clean and assemble after each use. But, it is easier to use than our old centrifugal juicer and does a better job with leafy greens.

When we were juicing every day, I had to drive one hour twice a week to buy fresh organic greens and vegetables. Add this time to preparing vegetables and juicing, and I was feeling very STRESSED. After six months of this, I did not know how I would be able to keep it up. Then, another miracle happened. About two years ago, one of the health food stores located 25 miles from my home opened a new store five minutes from my house. They opened just before Christmas—my greatest Christmas present ever! Nutrition S'Mart saved me from myself! I am in there three or four times a week.

Is life supporting my efforts? I like to think so. As my body gets healthier at the cellular level through good nutrition and a life affirming lifestyle, the healing energy flowing through my body will increase. I trust that cancer cannot invade a body filled with oxygen, nutrients and high energy. Food matters!

Supplements that Make a Difference

Chia Seeds

Another supplement that I think contributed to my getting off asthma spray is chia seeds. Keeping my lungs mucous free is a major contributor to my remaining cancer free. Therefore, breathing without medicine is a priority. My lungs are the greatest indicator that something isn't right. I think they are the red flag reminder that

I have too much inflammation in my body, a definite cancer risk factor.

Several years ago I read an article about chia seeds. The seeds looked promising as a way to protect my bones naturally. In the past I could not take fish oil because of side effects, and I needed a way to get Omega 3 into me. (The omega-3 and omega-6 imbalance is covered in Dr. Servan-Schreiber's and Dr. Russell Blaylock's books.) The chia seed is a dry food, not oil, so I thought I would give it a try. The seeds are mixed with water to make a gel, which can be refrigerated for up to two weeks. I started out with one teaspoon a day.

In about two months, I noticed that I had less mucous in my lungs and my breathing was better. In three months, I noticed that the lines in my face were disappearing. Evidently, the seeds do something to the moisture in the body, and my skin was beginning to reflect this. I started telling other people about chia seeds, and the women I shared it with also discovered that it put moisture in their faces, which is exactly where we want it. But, I can only imagine what it is doing for the organs and joints within the body.

I am sold on chia seeds as a supplement that has worked wonders for my health. Organic chia seeds are inexpensive and easy to use. I now take one heaping tablespoon of the chia seed gel with a little Pom Wonderful juice and water every day.

Cancer Prevention Supplements

I continue taking oral supplements and cream to protect my body against breast cancer, and I take L-Tyrosine, Xymogen T-150, and liquid iodine to boost my thyroid gland. For my general health, I take 8,000 mg of vitamin C per day, CoQ10 (Ubiquinol), high doses of B vitamins and vitamin D, Glutathione, digestive enzymes, minerals, curcumin, broccoli extract, flax seeds and flax seed oil, a magnesium and calcium drink, probiotics, and Perfect 7 Intestinal Cleanser. (I find that Perfect 7 also contributes to less mucous in my lungs.) My body is even allowing me to take krill oil in place of fish oil, a great way to boost my omega-3s. Most of the supplements I take have been recommended by health care providers. Of course, a few of them I found on my own, but when dealing with something like cancer, I feel more secure working with someone who really understands how nutrition and supplements affect the cellular activity within the body. Many of the pharmaceutical grade supplements cannot be found in a retail store.

The Search Goes On

The search for supplements that will improve my health and prevent cancer is ongoing. I am always willing to try something new if I think it will benefit my body in some way. Recently I learned about a new supplement while placing a telephone order for other supplements. After hearing a description of natural astaxanthin, I wanted to try this powerful antioxidant. I got more than I could have imagined. While vacationing on a seven-day Caribbean cruise, I pushed my luck and ate small amounts of gluten and sugar every day. Based on what I stated earlier, I expected to use the asthma spray by the third day. To my amazement, my lungs remained clear; so I just kept eating these forbidden foods for the entire seven days. And, I never had to use the asthma medication. I am convinced that this supplement and the clean ocean air made this possible. I hope my body continues to allow me to indulge once in a while. (If I had active cancer, I would have been more disciplined.)

I cannot understand how "the researches" report that supplements do not make a difference. My experience tells me that supplements work and then some. Of course, I returned to my restricted diet once I got home because I know that gluten and sugar compromise my health and immune system. However, this latest experience tells me that my body is getting healthier.

Many supplements have anti-aging as well as health benefits. The anti-aging health movement is discovering the specific natural supplements that keep our cells healthy and strong. Anti-aging medicine appears to be contributing to the treatment and prevention of cancer too. I am sold on supplements in conjunction with diet and exercise to keep my cells functioning in ways that promote great health and longevity.

Energy Work for the Body, Mind and Soul

Emotional Freedom Techniques (EFT)

EFT continues to be one of the most important tools I use for self-healing. My belief is that by changing my energy, I am changing my symptoms. As I eliminate negative emotional, mental and physical symptoms, I will change my life. As more and more unresolved traumatic events and core limiting beliefs are cleared from my body and energy system, my health and wellbeing will improve. I will attract more abundance into my life on so many levels—love, health, serenity, creativity, fun, opportunities, money and more.

Tapping into Abundance

by Carol Look, Author of *Attracting Abundance with EFT: Emotional Freedom Techniques* and EFT Founding Master (www.attractingabundance.com)

Abundance consciousness is a critical ingredient to have in our lives if we are to enjoy thriving health and emotional well-being. Using EFT/ Meridian Tapping is the most exceptional tool I have found in over 20 years in the mental health field for clearing all of our blocks to enjoying our lives by living from the place of abundance consciousness. EFT/ Tapping allows us to access and release any negative energy blocks in our body and mind—this improves our mood, our immune system, and our mindset.

Tapping into abundance is made simple when we redefine "abundance"—***abundance is a vibration, not a dollar amount***. Abundance is the feeling of joy, optimism, and passion for your work, your hobbies and your family. Abundance is feeling excitement about any level of success in any part of your life. When we come from a place of abundance consciousness, we allow abundance manifestations to show up for us, and we easily meet with success personally, professionally, financially, and spiritually.

So why aren't we more "abundant" in our attitudes, mood, and feelings? Because we have emotional and energetic blocks that keep us playing small...Most of us have a fear of being successful—some of us want to stay under the radar, some of us would prefer to stay invisible, and still others of us would rather not "shine" or stand out because we fear other people's reactions. If we had any experiences as a child of being punished or criticized for standing out, we will naturally block our success in our adult life as a way to protect ourselves from being hurt or attacked again.

Below is a classic tapping exercise to release your fear of being successful:

First, choose a "target" for tapping. A target can be an emotion, a symptom, a memory or an event. For the purposes of this exercise, let's choose an emotion as our target—*the fear of success*.

Once we choose our target, we need to measure how upset it makes us on the 0-10 point intensity scale. When you think of getting the big success you want, how high is your fear on the 0-10 point scale?

Then start tapping on the designated tapping points:

(Continued on the next page...)

What the Expert Says Continued...

- ○ **Karate chop point:**
  - *Even though I'm afraid of being successful, I accept who I am anyway...*
  - *Even though I'm afraid of being successful and standing out, I accept who I am and how I feel.*
  - *Even though I have this fear of being successful—what if they criticize me—I deeply and completely love and accept myself anyway.*

  Then start tapping on the stress relief points on the face and body as follows:
- ○ **Eyebrow:**
  - *I'm afraid of being successful.*
- ○ **Side of Eye:**
  - *I don't want to be successful because they might judge me.*
- ○ **Under Eye:**
  - *I'm afraid of standing out.*
- ○ **Under Nose:**
  - *I don't want to shine.*
- ○ **Chin:**
  - *What if they criticize me?*
- ○ **Collarbone:**
  - *What if they judge me?*
- ○ **Under Arm:**
  - *I'm so afraid of being successful...*
- ○ **Top of Head:**
  - *I'm surprised that I'm so afraid of being successful.*

Then repeat the chosen target phrase out loud: "I'm afraid of being successful" and measure the level of your fear again on the 0-10 point scale.

Continue tapping on this original phrase or make an adjustment to the statement that more accurately reflects what you're feeling and going through around the topic of success. You will soon enjoy being as successful as you can imagine!

As you continue to tap on clearing any additional fears or conflicts you have to being successful, you will develop a deep consciousness of abundance in your life, allowing you to attract exceptional health, more satisfying relationships, tranquility and overall wellbeing.

Life continues to lead me into situations that trigger the unresolved issues from my past. For example, completing and promoting this book triggered feelings of fear and helplessness. Recognizing the old script, *"It won't happen for me because I don't get the support I need,"* gave me an opportunity to eliminate more fear, self-doubt and sense of lack associated with this negative thinking. This "writing on my walls" prevented me from completing this book project with an attitude of abundance. The right belief would allow me to understand that the Universe is supporting the book and me, and it will bring me everything I need to get the job done. Using EFT, I cleared the negative emotions, thoughts and physical constrictions with this set-up phrase, *"Even though my needs do not matter, I deeply and completely love and accept myself."* Once I cleared the negative, I came up with the positive belief of how I wanted it to be and tapped on, *"Life supports me as I support myself."* By eliminating the negative and increasing the positive, the outcomes I want are inevitable.

Positive thoughts held in a state of high energy create positive outcomes in the real world—the power of positive thinking and universal Law of Attraction. EFT is a great tool to enhance peak performance and create optimal health and wealth. It eliminates the internal emotional and mental patterns that interfere with accomplishing the outcomes we want. These days, my tapping focuses on inner peace, a healthy body and abundance. As far as I am concerned, they all go together. On a daily basis I tap on *"I am one with the One."* This mantra allows peace, love and harmony to flow through my body, mind and soul. Abundance is a natural consequence of this alignment and connection with Source. EFT used consistently increases my ability to heal my body, perform my best, and accomplish extraordinary outcomes.

Energy Healing

Diane Sherman-Levine and I continue to do energy work over the telephone on an as-needs basis. This energy work helps me eliminate any energy blocks and self-limiting emotional and mental patterns that prevent me from achieving optimal health, confidence and inner peace. My subconscious speaks through dream images. I take these symbols and feelings to Diane for her additional insight. As we speak over the phone, she gets to the core issues that my soul and body are trying to reveal in my dreams, or through some physical or emotional symptom. Once the truth is uncovered and Diane channels energy through me (from a distance), my body is able to release the constriction. I leave her consultations feeling uplifted, lighter and clearer. Energy work also aligns me with my personal truth. Interestingly, I find that as my connection to a divine Presence becomes stronger, I contact Diane less and less.

Energy Bodywork

I was in China recently and had an amazing massage called "head to toe massage." Two young men worked on me at the same time—one at my feet and one at my shoulders and head (fully clothed). When I left the massage center, I felt really light walking back to the hotel. However, the next night while I was walking through the lobby of the hotel, I felt a severe constriction across my chest, and I felt weak. My first thoughts were *"Could this be a heart attack?"* I quickly found a chair, sat down and assessed the situation. My breathing was OK, and my heart felt fine. Then I thought of what it could be like to go to a hospital in Beijing. That terrified me for 30 seconds. But my vital signs seemed to be OK, so I told my companions to just let me sit there for a few minutes.

In about five minutes, the constriction began to move up into my shoulders. It eventually moved into my neck and out the top of my head. Within fifteen minutes, I could walk to the hotel room. I felt fine but a little shaken emotionally. I asked myself, *"What just happened to me?"* My best explanation: I released blocked energy as a result of the massage the previous day. Energy blocks that get stuck in the physical body are real, and I just witnessed one example of how they can be released. If an emotion or traumatic event was associated with this release, I have no idea because I never received an insight. Something significant happened, and I let the "why of it" go. I am just glad I had my wits about me and did not rush to call for an ambulance. The healing process reminds me that my body is constantly taking me closer to optimal wellness, one energy release at a time.

Recently I had an experience with CranioSacral bodywork for a lower back injury from a fall on ice and snow. And, I also experienced epigenetic programming during the session, which greatly contributed to the ease I felt in my body. Because of the profound experience I had, I intend to make CranioSacral bodywork and epigenetic programming a part of the on-going health protocols I use to align my bones, maintain my flexibility and keep my energy flowing.

> *What I found was that some of the greatest scientific minds of our times—Nobel Prize winners, people with doctorates in various fields, medical doctors, authors, inventors—have said when they spoke about health issues, that the root of all health and illness is always an energy issue in the body. They also said that someday we're going to find a way to fix the energy problem that underlies every health issue, and on the day that happens, the health world will change forever.*
>
> — Alexander Loyd, PhD, NK (with Ben Johnson, MD, DO, NMD), *The Healing Code: Six Minutes to Heal the Source of Your Health, Success, or Relationship Issues* (2010, p. 63)

As the Chinese know through the thousand-year-old practice of acupuncture, the body thrives on the flow of Chi (lifeforce) through it. The physical body is a powerful energy machine that promotes longevity. I intend to find innovative ways to harness this subtle energy in order to remain cancer free. I want healing lifeforce to penetrate every meridian, organ, gland, muscle, bone and cell of my body.

Spiritual Practice Is a Priority

During my "almost daily" stretching, I can hear little snaps and crackles throughout my spine, especially in the neck, shoulders, upper back and hips. This was not always the case. For the past five years I have noticed a big difference in my ability to adjust my spine while stretching. If I did not do this habitual stretching and meditation, my body and mind would be filled with energy constrictions. Spiritual enlightenment and the spine are connected in some way. My body is finally reaping the rewards of twenty-five years of mild yoga practice.

Based on my experiences, I have come to understand that my body is very much a part of my mental and spiritual transformation. After stretching and deep breathing in the morning, my mind goes right into a focused trance, as the spiritual eye (third eye) looks inward. In this meditative state a spiritual presence seems to descend and fill every cell of my body until my body feels alive with a pulsing energy and a feeling of wellbeing.

CranioSacral Therapy and Epigenetic Programming

by Molly Snow, LMT, Neos Massage
(www.neosmassage.com)

CranioSacral Therapy is a gentle, hands on therapy that releases restrictions in the bones of the spine, cranium and tissues deep within the body. The result is a sense of balance, calm and pain relief. CranioSacral Therapy helps with chronic fatigue, fibromyalgia, migraines, ADHD, anxiety, depression, autism, MS, TMJ, bulging disks and more.

One of the techniques used is decompression of the sacrum and cranium via gentle tractioning, which relieves the tension in the bones. This releases impinged nerves and alleviates tight muscles. Muscles follow bones, so when a bone is given the correct space, the muscles start to relax automatically. This is a process that usually takes 24-48 hours to be fully realized depending on the individual. After a CST session, it is a good idea to allow the body time to adjust in this process before adding any other bodywork therapies.

CST is also part energy medicine. It moves energy like acupuncture, but uses the hands instead of needles. Where acupuncture focuses on specific points on the body that follow an energetic line, CST focuses energy into specific regions of the body. This helps open the blocked energy to that region and to facilitate the movement of burdening toxins out of the body. Drinking lots of water after a session will encourage this process.

Emotions play a role in our health and healing as well. Emotions have their own energetic signature. Most people think we feel with our mind, but we really feel with our body. The energy of those emotions are stored in the body. CST will also help to facilitate movement of "stuck" emotional patterns by releasing those emotions out of the tissues. When appropriate, combining counseling with CST offers great benefit to the client.

Everyone's healing journey is unique. Seeing the response of the person's body after one session will help to determine how many sessions a person may need. A therapy plan typically is 3-9 one-hour sessions one day a week. Determining factors to the therapy plan are the severity of the issue, the age of the client, how long the issue has been in the body and a few other factors. There are no rules to the therapy plan! It really is so completely individual to the person. Because this therapy is not like a traditional massage and is partly energy work, clients stay fully clothed in a session.

Epigenetic Programming is energy medicine on a cellular level. This therapy looks at the details, right to the energy of the DNA. The new science has found that the function of our genes is determined by the shape of the gene. The shape of the gene is triggered from outside of the gene or the Epigenome. The Epigenome is the place outside the gene where all the triggers are located. These triggers or switches can be chemical or energetic. Epigenetic Programming finds the energetic switches according to the need the body has and applies the necessary energy charge.

Positive or negative charges act like switches that switch on or off a particular gene. Much like tuning a guitar, Epigenetic Programming gives a positive or negative charge and "tunes" an organ, gland, nerve, system or cell to the right frequency.

Sometimes the immune switch gets turned off in the body and needs to be turned back on. When this happens, the body stays in fight or flight mode. The proper charge given during an energy session allows the immune switch to be turned back on, and the body can return to the parasympathetic mode or the resting/healing mode.

Epigenetic therapy plans are different than CST plans. Where CranioSacral sessions are generally one day a week (there are exceptions), Epigenetic sessions can be scheduled five days a week. This therapy works quickly and with a quick response time. This is a powerful new therapy, and I am proud to be a pioneer in this healing work.

For more information on CranioSacral Therapy and Epigenic Programming, please go to www.neosmassage.com.

The oldest discipline of inner awareness is yoga. In Sanskrit, the term "yoga" designates a set of practices aiming at the merging of body and mind for the sake of unity and inner peace.

What seems essential to the mobilization of the body's forces is to renew contact every day—with sincerity, benevolence, and calm—with the life force that vibrates constantly within our bodies. And to bow to it.

— David Servan-Schreiber, MD, PhD,
AntiCancer: A New Way of Life (2009, pp. 174 and 175)

To my way of thinking, self-mastery involves the body, as well as the mind and spirit. Yoga practice brings them together. One without all three is only part of the truth. My goal is to integrate all three. (I thrive on getting to the whole truth.) I begin each day with a quiet mind, energized body, and abundant spirit. However, holding that state of bliss throughout the stresses and strains of the day can be a challenge. I still hear limiting words coming out of my mouth too often and feel myself striving at times. Enlightenment is a work in progress.

I do not know whether inner peace or a flexible body came first. My body once reflected back to me the rigidity with which I lived my life. As I learned to let go of having things my way, my body and spine responded. Of course, twenty years of monthly visits to the chiropractor made a difference too. Stretching and meditation will be a part of my health and wellbeing for the rest of my life, and so will chiropractic adjustments. My goal is to get my feet over my head in the plow pose into my nineties.

All Is Well!

After 30 years of meditating and doing the inner work, I am mastering the ability to control outcomes less and accept "what is" more, including myself and others. I trust that all is evolving toward some greater good. I choose to focus on peace over conflict, love over hatred, personal wisdom over ignorance, and trust over fear. I still doubt and judge myself at times when I think I am not doing enough, but I work at replacing internal critical messages with words of acceptance and encouragement.

Grace is available to everyone who invites it into his/her life. It came to me because I was willing to grow in unconditional love, keep an open mind and connect to a "knowing" that is beyond doubt and fear. (I am far from mastery, but making progress.) With all that I am doing to heal my body, mind and soul, I am evolving spiritually.

Each time new wisdom takes root in my being, I make higher level choices that reflect deeper and deeper personal and universal truths. Best of all, my body reflects this deeper connection through more vibrant health. My mind is becoming more disciplined in its ability to be still and allow inspiration and imagination to speak to me. From my way of thinking, the spiritual, physical, emotional and mental are ultimately one path. These aspects of healing are woven intimately together and influence the actions I take to live well longer.

Chapter 10 Lessons Learned...

- Sometimes you get more benefit than you ever imagined.

- Healing is a journey; value what is working and be open to what is next.

- Persistence pays off.

- Having fun can be the best medicine.

- Managing and reducing stress lays the foundation for wellness.

- High quality food protects the body against cancer and other diseases.

- Miracles happen consistently when you believe they are possible.

- Acceptance and gratitude allow grace to carry you.

- The body is an energy machine. Releasing energy blocks is a part of the healing process.

- Dreams provide clues to the deeper issues sabotaging your sense of self, health and wealth.

- The lifestyle choices you make today will keep you healthy into your 90s and beyond.

...a time to do your best, live in abundance, welcome grace, and have fun

Chapter 11
I Did It My Way!
(Important Life Lessons)

People may think that I made my journey through cancer more difficult than it needed to be because I did it my way rather than follow the pack. However, difficult is a matter of perspective. Everything I did felt right, saved my life and got me closer to optimal health. From a body-mind-spirit perspective, optimal health includes a body filled with radiant energy, a mind filled with peace and stillness and a heart filled with love and acceptance. Add to that, living each day with passion and purpose, and life is at its best.

Even though I did not realize it at the time, cancer led me down a path that would become a gift for my body and soul. My body is healthier than it has been since my thirties, my view of myself and the world is positive, and my spiritual connection to Source is stronger than ever. I have learned to quiet my mind, listen to my inner voice, and trust that life is working with me. Feeling more secure in general, I allow life to flow through me. When I receive an inspired message from the place of deep inner knowing, I take it seriously. I act on it after checking things out in the real world. By integrating inner knowing with analytical thinking, I use the best of both worlds—intuition and reason—to create a life that works for me.

Living from this place of authenticity and faith, I see magic working in my life. In small things and big things, the universe guides me and speaks to me. For example, an article about chia seeds resulted in improved breathing, and a conference flyer led me to the doctor who got me off daily asthma medicine. I remember the evening beautiful Snow White came over to this 60+-year-old woman at a Disney parade. I was sitting on the curb with the other kids waving and calling to her. (I think now that I may have been the only one waving and yelling, "Snow White, Snow White, over here, over here.") She walked right over to me, took both of my hands, looked into my eyes with a big smile and touched my inner child. It felt like the wounded child within me received a healing that day. Life feels miraculous as blessings flow to me in unexpected ways.

When I review the time surrounding the cancer diagnosis and treatment, I am struck with the intensity of all that was happening in my life. In a span of one and one-half years, I closed my business, left my family and friends in New Jersey to move to California, was diagnosed with breast cancer, had a mastectomy, received alternative treatment in Nevada, suffered a financial setback, pooped my way to health and changed my career. That I landed on my feet is truly amazing!

Miracles

In *A Book of Miracles: Inspiring True Stories of Healing, Gratitude, and Love* by Dr. Bernie Siegel (2011), we are reminded that miracles are an important part of life and occur on a regular basis. The personal stories in the book provide hope and inspiration on so many levels. If we know how to change our perceptions, we will recognize the magic when it happens to us and others. As always, Dr. Siegel reminds us to love unconditionally, live with gratitude and turn our challenges into opportunities for deep personal transformation. With a sense of harmony and inner peace, we all will attract the miraculous.

A near drowning experience in my teens comes to mind as I recall the events that occurred in my life eleven years ago. Those life stressors were relentless, like the waves in the stormy ocean that nearly took me out. Two of my teenage friends and I went swimming in the turbulent ocean at the Jersey shore and got pulled out with the undertow and caught in a rip tide. One tried to swim for shore and one was struggling next to me. Waves were breaking so fast and hard that I could hardly catch my breath. With arms pinned to my side by the swirling ocean, I could not raise my hand to call in the lifeguards. They did not see us clearly because we were far from the shore. If they did see us, they seemed unconcerned. Struggling to free my arm, I got very sleepy and began to relax. I told myself: *"Drowning won't be so bad; I'll just go to sleep and my life will be over."* For a brief moment the waves and churning stopped. In that moment I found the strength to raise my arm and signal the lifeguards to come in and get us. All three of us were rescued.

During the year and one-half after the cancer diagnosis, I found myself fighting for my life again. In a short amount of time, I was bombarded by many stressful events, some of my choosing and others thrust upon me. I could hardly come up for air. Once again, my own hand and the assistance of others rescued me, including a power greater than myself.

As I review the choices and changes I have made since the breast cancer, I am filled with gratitude because I have accomplished my objective—my body is healthy and my new life works. I did my best to turn things around. I created a path, took action and the rest was given. I am still reminded how there was a plan even when I could not see or feel one. I wish I could live each day with the assurance that my future is secure 100% of the time. Knowing this truth intellectually is different from living it emotionally and spiritually, but I am working on it. The good news is that I am much better at trusting life than I was eleven years ago.

Breast cancer has influenced my transformation as a human being and helper. It allowed me to put into action spiritual and psychological principles that matter to me. I walked the talk eleven years ago, but now I am living these truths on a daily basis. Perfect, no, but good enough so that I stay connected to "who I am" (a spiritual being having a physical experience). Without this tumultuous journey, my inner growth and outer healing may not have happened. Life brought me to my knees, and I was not defeated. Instead, I evolved.

Now the external no longer defines me, and most of the time, I no longer struggle against what is happening. Let something happen to my loved ones, especially my children, and I go down for the count in fear, powerlessness and dread. At those times I ask for the strength to show up in ways that are helpful and the courage to keep going. The death of my beloved father on the tenth anniversary of my mastectomy took the wind out of my sails. When I learned he had lung cancer and months to live, my knees went weak. I wanted to collapse; instead, I mobilized, stood tall and helped him die with dignity. He died a few weeks after the diagnosis. My grieving came later. When my mother died a year later, I was more prepared to let her go because I knew she was ready to die; her quality of life had deteriorated without my father. Her peaceful, easy death made me accept that she died her way. I feel very sad that my parents are gone, but I also accept that they left us when it was their time, not ours.

I have learned not to judge what finds its way into my life; I just show up and deal with it. I understand that the events in my life are opportunities to grow in love, power and wisdom. I do not have to like these challenges; I just have to live them. Even when I am caught in struggle and turmoil, I do not judge or blame myself. Trying to live up to some state of perfection cuts me off from grace, and I will not go there. I allow the despair or temper tantrum to move through me as quickly as possible. No matter what happens, I accept that I am doing my best each day. Seeing myself through the "eyes of love" feels so much better than beating myself up for not being good enough.

Love has been described as the physician of the universe—as the medicine that heals all disease. Love can heal all ills because love is more than emotion or even a spiritual quality. Love is also a mind power. This mind power of love is located in the region of the heart, which is the center of love in the body.

— *The Healing Secrets of the Ages* by Catherine Ponder |
9780875165509 DeVorss Publications www.devorss.com
(1966, p. 69)

Today my life is filled with ease, my mind is awake, and my body feels alive. One part of me has jumped into the ever-flowing river of life, and I am not holding on to anything. I just flow with the current, trusting that I will be taken where I need to go. The other part of me is sitting in my little boat steering the course with a rudder, making sure I have a sense of control over where I am headed. I am not sure which one is more real and relevant to the final outcome. Being in the flow, I trust the bigger plan. Steering my own boat, I stay in action and take control of the small things. One viewpoint is based on trusting whatever outcome shows up for me and the other is based on taking charge of what is within my power to control. Both strategies have served me. Moving forward, I do not know any other way to be.

In *Leveraging the Universe: 7 Steps to Engaging Life's Magic* (2011), Mike Dooley reminds us that creating the lives we want lies somewhere between action and surrender. We need to discriminate between what we can, should and must do for ourselves and what we can, should and must turn over to universal, timeless principles.

Fertilizer for My Growth

I have learned a few important life lessons since breast cancer became my teacher ten years ago. The seeds that have taken root in me are these:

Acceptance, gratitude and positive thinking attract grace.

To judge and blame myself, others, life, or God distorts my perception of truth and takes me out of alignment with grace. This wisdom is written in so many books like *The Course in Miracles* and *The Tao*, but living it is another matter. It takes commitment and discipline to count your blessings every day, focus on positive solutions, and offer unconditional love. By acknowledging and praising what I do have, I stay closely connected to the abundance life offers. Thinking positively, I attract more positive outcomes to me and my loved ones. As I accept myself and life more, peace, harmony and grace follow me. When negative events occur in the lives of family, friends and strangers, I feel empathy toward others, but I do not get stuck in their pain and suffering. I cannot change what is happening in other people's lives or the world, but I can bring positive energy to negative situations. If I am able to do so, I take some action, like sending a donation to victims of a disaster, writing a politician or visiting a friend in need. Staying positive keeps my soul uplifted. My body chemistry likes it too.

Let us realize that we should so live in body and mind that we may be channels through which the Creative Forces may flow...Let us give more attention to our thoughts, for thoughts are deeds and are children of the union of the mind and the soul. What we think continually we become. What we cherish in our minds is built into our own physical bodies, becoming not only food for our souls, but also the soul's heritage in realms of other experiences.

— Edgar Cayce, *A Search for God—Book1* (1982, p. 36)

The philosophy that inspires me to keep going with an open heart and mind is this: *All is evolving toward some greater good.* I am being led toward self-mastery and enlightenment. I know my turn will come again to deal with a crisis involving a loved one or myself, and I will deal with that when it happens. For my health and well-being, I make it a habit to look at the world through "rose-colored glasses." It works for me! Honoring how people get through their struggles, I do not suggest that others do it my way. However, hoping for the best or seeing the pearl of wisdom in any situation is one possibility for coping with life's disappointments and tragedies. From my limited perspective, I cannot see the bigger picture, and I certainly cannot judge what I do not understand. By bringing acceptance to every situation and having gratitude every day, I keep grace close by my side. I have faith it will lift me in my time of need, even though I cannot predict when or how it will intervene.

If we want to experience a more complete and lasting healing, we must take a step beyond what we can merely see or touch and listen to the inner wisdom of our hearts and souls as well. This inner wisdom, expressing itself through gratitude and unconditional love, is the most powerful healing force there is. No condition, illness, or disease exists that cannot be helped by its pure energy.

— Dr. John F. Demartini, *The Healing Power of Gratitude and Love* (2003, p. 1)

Healing involves mind, body, spirit and lifestyle.

I know that emotions, thoughts, diet, exercise, relationships, lifestyle, environment, worldview and history played a part in my getting cancer and my personal healing. To heal the body without addressing negative emotions, thoughts and lifestyle seems alien to me. Using any one of these approaches alone is not enough if I want to achieve optimal health and wellbeing. Taking a pill or supplement does not eliminate the stressful situations in my life that may be contributing to an illness. Unresolved negative emotions and trauma from the past cannot be eliminated with a healthy diet. A pessimistic view of the world will not be eliminated with exercise.

Healing and wholeness happened for me because I threw every healing method I could understand and afford at it. I used the cancer to heal myself and my life, not just cure my body. Healing connects me to others, life, a Creator and myself in positive uplifting ways. I feel at peace and connected to all parts of me, including the not so beautiful parts. My personality and multifaceted approach to healing serve me well. Life is good! Perfect, no! But I will take good enough and run with it.

Truth is liberating.

As each limiting pattern from childhood came up for review during my period of self-examination, I worked on it until I felt free of the constriction it had placed in my body and soul. I shattered beliefs that constricted my connection to an abundant universal flow and replaced them with higher truths that took me to my authentic self. Giving and receiving took on a new meaning after cancer. I now accept that receiving is an important part of life. Therefore, I can more easily attract and receive the special people, things and outcomes that reflect abundance. Receiving new clients who find me on the Internet feels really good! I think I have made some progress on living this truth.

Personal truth is a priceless treasure. When an epiphany lights up the mind and brings with it a new awareness, old limiting beliefs get shattered. Most important, the shift happens at the cellular and energy levels of the body. What a great barometer the body is for testing truth! When truth lands within me, or my clients, it brings with it a deep stillness that touches the body, mind and soul. It says, *"You are home. All is well."*

The present moment works.

At times on my healing journey, I felt lost and anxious about my ability to find the right treatments, stay healthy and create a viable income. I resisted the unknown instead of trusting the process. Striving to see a future outcome just raised my level of stress and kept me feeling frustrated. I found a way to hold the space of uncertainty by having gratitude every day and allowing the next step of the journey to reveal itself.

During that first year after diagnosis, I learned to deal with one phase of the healing journey at a time. If I tried to jump too far ahead of myself, I got out of the ease and flow of the present moment. Taking the necessary actions to accomplish short-term goals kept me feeling in charge. By staying positive and empowered, my body produced the internal chemicals that it needed to get healthy, and I was able to stay connected to a semblance of serenity in spite of the stress. I allowed the journey to unfold one moment at a time. Everything and everyone I needed came to me. Out of the rubble and uncertainty, my new life emerged.

When you become comfortable with uncertainty, infinite possibilities open up in your life. It means fear is no longer a dominant factor in what you do and no longer prevents you from taking action to initiate change.

— Eckhart Tolle, *A New Earth: Awakening to Your Life's Purpose* (2006, p. 274)

Anything is possible.

Necessity often brings out unexplored parts of a person. The healing journey forced me to go deeper and claim the parts of myself that enabled me to become a more complex person. In the process I touched my inner gold, that pure potential from which I was created. I do not know what part of me showed up for the Hawaiian cleanse, but somehow I did what needed to be done and even experienced moments of enjoyment. For a person who hates having needles put into her body, I survived two weeks of intravenous drips. For someone who likes financial stability, I started a new career during a time of financial hardship.

I have learned that I can take risks and survive, and right now it feels like I am thriving. The adventurer within me leads the way more and more. Certainly, I would prefer to jump off a four-foot ledge rather than a thousand-foot cliff. But like the Fool in the deck of Tarot Cards, I step into the open space of possibility and trust I can do whatever is being asked of me. I am willing to flow with life, prepare myself for the next adventure and hope for the best. I am learning that I can do things I have not yet imagined. Biting off more than I can chew may just be a part of my life's journey. It makes life exciting and meaningful. Onward and upward!

Don't sweat the small stuff.

I have been through enough of life's ups and downs to realize that everything besides facing serious disease and death is the small stuff. Perhaps I have turned my big stuff into small stuff (those rose-colored glasses again), or unimaginable bigger stuff awaits me. I can only talk about my experience, which taught me to take charge of my health and well-being. Forced to face a life-threatening illness, my eyes focused on the love and support all around me, as well as the abundance of possibilities for healing.

The following golden insight has taken root in me: *As the inner stillness gets louder, the small stuff gets smaller.* When I remain connected to my spiritual core in the face of a life crisis or challenge, I am more able to cope with the unexpected and unknown. Observing any situation from a higher perspective, I can make choices that serve me instead of create more challenges. I can even approach death with a sense of peace and wonder. I have a new relationship with life, death, and myself after taking on cancer.

Grow, Grow, Grow

Breast cancer became another wake-up call in my life. It placed me on a quest for healing and wholeness and catapulted me into new levels of awareness and truth. I recognize that I am on a continual journey of learning, loving and personal transformation. I am not who I was eleven years ago, and ten years from now I will be very different as well. Life is constantly growing me. I wish I could move forward without the tears, but they are a natural part of my future. One thing I know is that I will have wonderful people standing by me as I stumble and fall, and they will be there to cheer me on when it is time to "go for the gold."

As a result of my many life experiences, I am prepared to show up and do my best in any life challenge. The adventurer within me is alive and well. As a kid, I lived on the streets with a gang of cousins. Every day held new prospects for learning and fun. Looking out of the window on a rainy day, I felt imprisoned. Forced to stay inside, I was cut off from the excitement of the day. Though not a camping or outdoors type of person, I do need to feel the expansion and freedom of the adventure.

I never had any inclination to climb Mt. Everest. However, breast cancer placed me on an inner quest of life and death. The climb to the peak of my inner Everest showed me how healing works and allowed me to discover more of who I am. But, there are more heights to scale. While my body is basically healthy, there is still work to do. I want to increase my physical energy, strengthen my lungs, improve my digestion and fortify my immune system, as well as live with passion and purpose. I have another 20 to 30 years to live in this body and participate in life.

I am curious to see what can be done to cheat the physical decline of old age. The mind is the builder of my internal chemistry and the spirit is ageless. The more I apply both to my physical body, who knows what is possible?! My body tells me a lot more can be accomplished to achieve optimal health, and I am listening. Why stop ascending just because the cancer is behind me? Reaching for higher levels of great health, personal fulfillment and inner peace just feels right. I am on another quest with a joyful heart.

Afterward
A Wisp of Wisdom

The journey toward healing and wholeness is unique for each person. When life brings anyone a serious illness, she or he needs to find the healing path that feels right and gets results. The first step is to be curious and gather relevant data. The second is to make informed choices about treatment options, and the third is to take action based on knowledge and inner knowing. Once an individual commits to the healing journey with an open mind and heart, an unseen process guides that person to the next steps. The right doctors, health care providers, products and protocols will show up for the seeker who is focused, positive and passionate about getting well. Through awareness and trust, the way is made clear.

People can boost their immune systems, find inner peace or detoxify their bodies in so many different ways. It may take some effort to find the right option that does the job. But, by asking questions and advocating for what they want from the experts, people can take charge of their health and lives. When they are willing to listen to their bodies, they will receive feedback about what is working and what is not. They soon become the experts of their own bodies. Armed with their unique personal truth, they can make the healing choices that lead to successful results.

The chances for healing are greater when people approach the process from a holistic perspective. To heal the body, mind and soul takes a team of health care providers and other helpers who will accurately identify and treat the symptoms. Some experts may even be able to identify root causes. Such an integrative approach requires that an individual participate and become an important part of the treatment equation.

There are so many exciting methods and gifted healers in the marketplace today. If an individual is not making progress with one method or provider, she or he needs to try another. This is a journey that requires awareness, persistence and patience. The best of the conventional and alternative medical communities has much to offer when an individual is willing to take charge and explore. The number of treatment options is increasing rapidly. It does take attention, time, energy and money, as well as discernment, to find the ones that make a difference, but the rewards are invaluable.

When a person does the right things for her or his healing and wholeness (not just cure the disease), she or he begins to feel hopeful and empowered. Ease and flow replace physical tension, increased energy replaces fatigue, and serenity replaces inner turmoil. Optimal health and wellbeing are possible once a person takes the necessary actions to participate in her or his own healing. The adventure begins with self-acceptance and self-love. For anyone embarking on this journey, may grace carry you!

****

To help you on your journey toward healing and wholeness, this book includes reference sections:

Appendix A (pp. 183-185) provides basic instructions for performing EFT tapping, the Emotional Freedom Technique.

Appendix B (pp. 187-189) provides a list of alkaline and acid forming foods and beverages.

Appendix C (pp. 191-194) provides some recipes from Dr. LindaJoy Rose. All recipes shared by Dr. Rose are from her book *Raw Fusing Living*, copyright© 2010, Quantum Mind Press, LLC.

Appendix D (pp. 195-214) includes statements by twelve cancer patients who chose to take charge of their healing rather than be treated by their doctors alone. They stepped outside conventional "standard of care" treatments, explored options that felt right for them and accomplished amazing results.

Following these appendices, you will find information about the **Experts** whose excerpts and contributions have been included this book (pp. 215-223) and helpful information about the published and online **Resources** referenced in this book (pp. 225-233).

Appendix A
Basic Instructions on How to Do EFT

by Ruth Stern MA, AAMET EFT Certified Trainer and
Practitioner, and Certified EMDR Clinician
(www.taptotransform.com)

Step 1: **Choose a problem to work on and try to be as specific as you can be.**

Example: I have stress (general problem).

Specific: I am stressed. I can't do what I need to do.

Step 2: **Rate your stress or discomfort on a scale of 0-10.**

This is called the SUDS scale (0 = no disturbance and 10 = highest disturbance). When you think about it right now, how disturbing or upsetting is your stress? Write down your number.

Step 3: **Perform the Set-Up phrase.**

(See the tapping points below.) While tapping on the Karate point, say the following phrase three times:

"Even though I feel _____, I deeply and completely accept myself."

Example: Even though I'm stressed and I can't get things done, I deeply and completely accept myself.

Now, use a short reminder phrase that represents the problem, such as "this anxiety" or "this stress of chores" when you tap on the stress points.

Step 4: **Tap on the stress points (see picture).**

As you tap on each point, say your reminder phrase (for example, "this anxiety"). You will be tapping with your fingertips (using 2 or 3 fingers) and tapping at least 7 times on each stress point. (I tap pretty quickly.)

EB	this anxiety (tap)
SE	this anxiety (tap)
EU	this anxiety (tap)
UN	this anxiety (tap)
CH	this anxiety (tap)
CB	this anxiety (tap)
UA	this anxiety (tap)
Head	this anxiety (tap)

Take a deep breath!

Step 5: **Now rate your anxiety or stress.**

Ask yourself how stressful or disturbing this is to you now on the 0-10 scale. If the SUDS number is going down, perform another round of tapping, starting with the Karate chop and say, "Even though, I still have some of this stress, I deeply and completely accept myself." Then, tap on all the rest of the stress points, using a short reminder phrase such as "this remaining anxiety" on each point.

Step 6: **If the number is not going down or going down very little, ask yourself:**

"What else am I feeling about this?" Or, if you are not sure, ask yourself, "What could I be feeling about this?"

Take a guess and go with that guess. Often your guess is very accurate. This is important because you want to tap on all the feelings that are feeding into the problem.

Example: I am also feeling angry that I have no time for me.

Step 7: **Start with the Set-Up again with your new phrase:**

Example: "Even though I'm angry that I have no time for me, I deeply and completely accept myself."

Tap on all the stress points with your new reminder phrase "this anger." Measure your upset feeling again on the SUDS scale. Do another round until you feel little or no upset.

Karate Chop Point (KC)

With the fingertips of the index and middle finger, you tap the other hand vigorously. You are tapping on the fleshy part of the outside of the hand—the part of your hand you do a karate chop. You can tap on either hand and switch hands if you like.

Eyebrow (EB)

Tap at the beginning of the eyebrow, just above and to one side of the nose.

Side of the Eye (SE)

Tap on the bone bordering the outside corner of the eye.

Under the Eye (UE)

Tap on the bone under the eye about 1 inch below the pupil.

Under the Nose (UN)

Tap between the bottom of your nose and the top of your upper lip.

Chin (CH)

Tap in the crease of your chin.

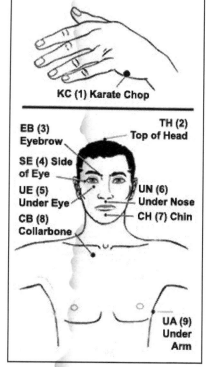

KC (1) Karate Chop

EB (3) Eyebrow
TH (2) Top of Head
SE (4) Side of Eye
UE (5) Under Eye
UN (6) Under Nose
CB (8) Collarbone
CH (7) Chin
UA (9) Under Arm

Collarbone (CB)

Tap where your breastbone and collarbone and first rib meet. To locate it, put your finger in the U-shaped notch at the top of the breastbone (above where a man would knot his tie). From the bottom of the U. move your finger down toward your navel and then go 1 inch to the left or the right. You are tapping an indent under the collarbone.

Under the Arm (UA)

Tap about 4 inches down from your armpit on the side of your body. For men, it is even with the nipple and for women it is where your bra strap would hit.

Top of the Head (H)

Tap on the top of head in a circle towards the front.

Appendix B
Alkalizing and Acidifying Foods

Below is a list of alkaline and acid forming foods and beverages. Many versions of acidifying and alkalizing food charts are available in books and on the Internet. Discrepancies exist within the various charts and lists. However, for optimal health, eat lots of fresh vegetables and fruits. (A **bold** word below means a specific food is a high alkaline or high acid forming food.)

ALKALIZING FOODS		ACIDIFYING FOODS	
Alkalizing Vegetables		***Acidifying Vegetables***	
Alfalfa grass	Peppers	Corn (a grain)	
Asparagus	Pumpkin	Olives	
Beets	Sea Veggies	Winter Squash	
Broccoli	Spinach		
Brussel sprouts	Sprouts	***Acidifying Beans & Legumes***	
Cabbage	Squashes		
Carrot	Sweet potatoes	Black Beans	Pinto Beans
Cauliflower	Wheat Grass	Chick Peas	Red Beans
Celery		**Cocoa beans**	Soy Beans
Chard		Green Peas	White Beans
Collard Greens		Kidney Beans	
Cucumber		Lentils	
Dandelions		Lima beans	
Eggplant		Navy beans	
Garlic			
Green beans		***Acidifying Grains***	
Kale			
Kohlrabi		Amaranth	Rye
Lettuce		Barley	Spelt
Mushrooms		Bran, wheat	**Wheat**
Okra		Bran, oat	Wheat Germ
Onions		Corn	
Parsley		Kamut	
Parsnips		Oats	
Peas		Quinoa	
		Rice	

ALKALIZING FOODS

Alkalizing Fruits

Apple	Raisins
Apricot	Raspberries
Avocado	Rhubarb
Banana	Strawberries
Berries	Tangerine
Blueberries	Tomato
Cherries, sour	Tropical Fruits
Coconut, fresh	**Watermelon**
Currants	
Dates	
Figs	
Grapes	
Grapefruit	
Kiwi	
Lemon	
Lime	
Mangos	
Melons	
Nectarine	
Orange	
Papayas	
Peach	
Pear	
Pineapple	

Alkalizing Dairy

Acidophilus
Buttermilk
Milk, raw
Whey
Yoghurt

Alkalizing Oils

Olive Oil
Flax Seed Oil
Canola Oil

ACIDIFYING FOODS

Acidifying Fruits

Cranberries
Prunes

Acidifying Nuts, Seeds & Butters

Brazil
Cashews
Peanut Butter
Peanuts
Pecans
Pumkin seeds
Sunflower seeds
Tahini
Walnuts

Acidifying Animal Protein

Beef	**Oyster**
Chicken	**Pork**
Clams	Rabbit
Fish	Sardines
Lamb	**Shellfish**
Lobster	Turkey
Mussels	Veal

Acidifying Dairy

Butter
Cheese (all)
Homogenized Milk
Ice Cream

Acidifying Oils

Avocado Oil	Sesame Oil
Corn Oil	Sunflower Oi
Hemp Seed Oil	
Lard	
Safflower Oil	

ALKALIZING FOODS	ACIDIFYING FOODS
Alkalizing Sweeteners	*Acidifying Sweeteners*
Maple Syrup Raw Honey Raw Sugar Rice Syrup **Stevia**	**Artificial Sweeteners** Carob Corn Syrup Molasses Processed Honey Processed Sugar
Alkalizing Beverages	*Acidifying Beverages*
Herbal Teas **Ionized Water** **Lemon Water** Green Tea Mineral Water Fresh Veggie and Fruit Juices Kombucha	Alcoholic beverages Distilled Water Tea Coffee Cocoa **Beer** **Soft Drinks**

Appendix C
Raw Fusion Recipes

Green Smoothie: Raspberry Razzle Dazzle
© *Raw Fusion Living*

Ingredients: 1/2 bunch of Swiss chard or baby spinach
1 apple
¾ cup fresh or frozen raspberries
1 banana
1/2 cup fresh or frozen strawberries
filtered water
ice (optional)

Directions: Place washed greens first in blender or Vitamix, cut apple, discarding the seeds, add the rest of the ingredients and add about 2 inches of water. If you like it cold, add some ice. Blend until smooth and add sweetener, if needed.

Soup: Cream of Mushroom Soup
© *Raw Fusion Living*

Serves 2-4.

Ingredients: ¼ cup tahini or raw almond butter
1 cup white or bella mushrooms, quartered
1 cup shitake or forest mushrooms
½ cup soaking water from mushrooms
2 TB. Vidalia onion, chopped
1 TB. Bragg's liquid aminos
½ tsp. Celtic sea salt
2-3 large mushrooms, minced
1 scallion, minced

(Continued on the next page...)

Prep: Cover 1 cup of shitake or forest mushrooms with warm (not hot) water and soak for at least 1 hour. Remove mushrooms but retain liquid.

Directions: In a blender, combine the nut butter, quartered mushrooms, rehydrated mushrooms, onions, Bragg's, salt and water. Blend until smooth. Mix in minced mushrooms and top with minced scallions.

Note: Can be used as soup or gravy for veggies, nut burgers or seed loafs. Reheat in dehydrator or in glass container on cooktop, but do not exceed 115 F degrees.

Salad: Raw-Some Caesar Salad
© *Raw Fusion Living*

Ingredients:
2 oz raw pumpkin seeds*
1 tsp. Celtic sea salt
½ lemon, juiced

1/4 cup olive oil
1 garlic clove
black pepper (optional)

*Use darker Austrian (Styrian) variety if available

Options: Replace lemon with apple cider vinegar. Use tamari or nama shoyu to replace salt.

Directions: Grind pumpkin seeds in coffee/spice grinder. Place in bowl and stir in olive oil and lemon juice. Press garlic clove and whisk into seed mixture, adding salt to taste. This salad dressing should keep for at least 5 days, tightly covered and refrigerated. Serve over romaine lettuce with your favorite chopped veggies.

Main Course: Raw Fusion Asian Stir Fry
© *Raw Fusion Living*

Serves 1-2. (Vegan optional – you can add sliced chicken or shrimp. If you are eating this vegan and need it to be more filling add some boiled rice vermicelli noodles.)

Ingredients:
1 cup baby spinach
½ cup arugula or dandelion leaves

(Continued on the next page...)

2 baby bok choy (or 2 cups regular bok choy)
1 large Portobello mushroom cap
½ cup mung bean sprouts
2 TB. coconut oil
1-2 tsp. toasted sesame oil
1 clove garlic sliced or chopped
1 tsp. fresh ginger, sliced thinly
1 TB. tamari or nama shoyu
½ cup nuts or seeds (cashew, pine nuts, walnuts,
     sunflower seeds – whichever you prefer!)
2/3 cup snow peas (can substitute with fresh or frozen
     English peas)
2 green onions
1-2 TB. sesame seeds

Prep: Slice Portobello thinly and marinate in tamari/nama shoyu for 2-3 hours.

Optional: ½ cup sliced water chestnuts, 2 TB. coconut aminos (These are sweeter — if you use Bragg's, which are salty, use only a small amount!)

Directions: Put the spinach and arugula/dandelion leaves at bottom of deep salad or soup bowl. Chop bok choy and green onion and set aside. Wash and de-string snow peas and cut in half and put in separate bowl. Boil 1 cup of water and pour over snow peas and temper for 1-2 minutes until bright green. Drain, rinsing with cool water. In a glass or non-teflon frying pan heat coconut and sesame oils on moderate heat. (Do not allow to smoke.) Stir in garlic and ginger. Stir fry bok choy, bean sprouts, green onions and nuts until thoroughly heated but not too hot. Pour over greens in bowl and toss well, allowing the stir fried veggies to wilt the leaves. Top with marinated Portobello slices, coconut aminos and sesame seeds. Serve immediately.

Dessert: Apple Betty with Cashew Cream Sauce
© *Raw Fusion Living*

Ingredients: *Filling*
             8 apples
             2 cups raisins
             1 1/2 TB. orange zest
             1 TB. cinnamon
             3 TB. raw honey   *(Continued on the next page...)*

Crust
3 cups raw pecans
1 cup dates
1 TB. olive or coconut oil

Sauce
1 tsp. nutmeg
¾ cup raw cashews
1 cup water
3 TB. honey
½ tsp. cinnamon
1 tsp. vanilla extract (or ½ tsp. butterscotch flavoring)

Prep: Soak raisins for 1-2 hours. Soak cashews (separately) for 2 hours.

Directions: In food processor, pulse 3 apples with 1 cup raisins, cinnamon, nutmeg and honey. Dice remaining apples into small pieces and put in bowl with remaining raisins. Pour the processed mixture over and ideally marinate several hours. Process pecans, dates and oil until fine. Press 2/3 of the mixture into baking pan. Pour apple mixture over. You can warm this in oven at lowest temperature with door ajar for 3 hrs. Put cashews, water, honey, extract and cinnamon in blender and blend until smooth. Remove pan from oven and drizzle cream sauce over top.

Snack: Chocolate Mousse
© *Raw Fusion Living*

Ingredients: 1 cup dates soaked until very soft with pits removed
3 medium avocados
3/4 to 1 cup almond milk (or 1 C coconut water)
1/2 cup almond butter (or 1/2 C coconut meat)
3/4 cup Organic Fair Trade cacao powder
      (can substitute carob powder)
2 TB. coconut oil, melted

Directions: Process avocados in food processor until smooth. Blend avocados with remaining ingredients in blender. (Blend immediately after adding coconut oil to keep it from hardening). Add almond or coconut milk 1/4 cup at a time to keep from over-thinning.

Appendix D
Twelve Cancer Patients Who Participated in Their Own Healing
(In Their Own Words)

In this appendix, you will read the stories of twelve courageous cancer patients who made alternative and integrative treatment choices. May each personal story be a source of inspiration and hope about what is possible when you participate in your own treatment and healing. They remind you to:

* Gather information.
* Explore possibilities and take risks.
* Listen to your body.
* Take responsibility for your healing.
* Improve the health of your body, mind and spirit.
* Reduce and manage the stress in your life.
* Trust that you know what is right for you.
* Understand you have many options for integrating conventional medical therapies with alternative medical practices.
* Intentionally laugh, love, appreciate today and enjoy life.

PATIENT 1

"I am a 64-year-old woman. It has been 19 years since I was first diagnosed with cancer."

Diagnosis: Stage I invasive lobular breast carcinoma, 1993; and stage IV, 1997. (I had several recurrences from initial diagnosis to stage IV.)

Conventional Treatment: I had a lumpectomy in 1993 and a second lumpectomy in 1995. I had multi-focal disease, but the first surgeon failed to do a biopsy so misjudged the situation. More tumors appeared throughout the breast, ending with a mastectomy after the third lumpectomy. I had chest wall recurrences for several years and was finally given a stage IV diagnosis in 1997.

Treatment Options Refused: I refused chemo due to Multiple Chemical Sensitivity (including systemic candida). The oncologist I consulted treated me like the cancer in room 7 paying no attention to my comments about MCS. I walked out feeling I could NOT have a therapy that was not about me. I refused radiation because I had large breasts, the chest wall area was HUGE and included my heart and left lung. I also did not use hormonal therapy.

Integrative Choices: I chose to explore integrative medicine.

* Used Arnica before most of the many surgeries.
* Tried metabolic enzyme therapy.
* Did coffee enemas (started in 1995 and still use them).
* Ate much more fruits and veggies — organic whenever I could.
* Did Gerson therapy in Mexico — It improved my candida, but did not "cure" the cancer.
* Used many supplements, including high dose vitamin A and Maitake mushroom extract, both of which stopped the growth of some tiny chest wall tumors.
* Used Chinese herbs from a true Chinese herbalist. They stopped the growth of tumors, and I have been free of cancer since I STARTED them in 1999.

Successful Outcomes: First MRI indicated a proven chest wall "involvement" (3.5 cm tumor). I took Chinese herbs for months. The next MRI in September 2001, proved that I was free of cancer and was given a diagnosis of "No Discernible Disease." And there has been no evidence of disease since then. I had two bone scans, both of which were clear.

Conventional Doctor's Responses: I really did not have any mainstream docs except for a breast cancer surgeon. Many times over the years as she and I spoke, I brought journal articles to support the things I planned to do or take. She placed them in my files; I thought the information was for sharing.

Lifestyle Changes: Still maintain a mostly organic and mostly raw vegan diet, take lots of supplements, use coffee enemas, juicing, and other detox protocols, exercise, practice happiness, and run a national nonprofit that provides information to people with cancer:

www.annieappleseedproject.org

Words of Wisdom: There are many paths to wellness so choose what you feel comfortable with. It is possible to combine conventional treatments with natural approaches; that's called *Integrative Oncology*. If your doctor doesn't know about it, talk to her/him or find one who does. If, for example, you are allergic to or uncomfortable with any specific protocol, happily there are others. Combining eating fruits and vegetables with some exercise, a way to relax and enjoy life, a simple detox plan, and some supplements is a really good background for better health. And finally, I am not special so if I was able to find natural substances and therapies that worked for me, I am sure others can too.

PATIENT 2

"I am a 48-year-old woman. It has been almost 3 years since I was first diagnosed with cancer."

Diagnosis: Left breast cancer, DCIS (ductal carcinoma in situ).

Conventional Treatment: My surgical oncologist recommended a mastectomy, due to family history and my relatively young age. Fortunately, the surgery was all that was required, as the cancer was non-invasive and all the pathology margins and lymph nodes were clear!

Treatment Options Refused: None

Integrative Choices:

* Signed up for membership at Inspire Health, Canada's world-famous integrated cancer care centre. I signed up for a "Life Course," which taught many facets to integrative cancer care including diet, exercise, stress management, etc.

* I went for relaxation and meditation classes at various facilities as well.

* Began a regimen of vitamin supplements specially formulated for cancer patients.

* Had EFT sessions after treatment was finished to get at core issues causing me stress.

* I also went for lymphedema massage and learned how to administer it on myself.

Successful Outcomes: My overall stress levels have been reduced in general, and I feel more able to let certain things slide that might normally have gotten me frazzled. Lymphedema is not a problem, and if I feel a bit swelled at times, I can do some self-massage to help it out. My mammograms have been normal, and my blood work looks really good.

Conventional Doctor Responses: In general doctors were very supportive of my integrative cancer care. However, I did get the impression from one health care provider that all I was doing to change my lifestyle in order to live cancer-free might be overwhelming for most patients.

Lifestyle Changes: I am trying very hard to improve my eating habits and my responses to stress, with varying degrees of success.

Words of Wisdom: Be positive and release the stress. Laugh. Look for the funny in everything. But also allow yourself to feel what you feel. Don't hold anything back.

PATIENT 3

"I am a 75-year-old man. It has been six years since first diagnosis in February 2006."

Diagnosis: Prostate cancer (aggressive but no stage specified).

Conventional Treatment:

* Watchful waiting for 18 months while the PSA continued to rise.
* Dec-07: Cryoablation surgical procedure of the whole prostate gland. I was told that this may not stop the cancer, but several doctors thought it was a good choice.
* May-09: PSA 35, 2-3 cm lymph nodes. Given approximately 18 months to live and placed on Antiandrogen therapy.
* Several ups and downs of the PSA over next 18 months.
* Nov-10: PSA began to rise; over next eight months had a series of scans: MRI, CT, Bone, PET Cystoscopy. Nothing abnormal.

* Aug-11: PSA 325. Saw a medical oncologist at a cancer center. Stopped one of the antiandrogens, continued Luprin, and a vaccine was suggested.

Treatment Options Refused: I refused other surgery options for prostate removal. Cryoablation seemed likely to provide the best result. Radiation of various forms were suggested, but I refused them. Recently, a vaccine was suggested, but I refused it because the benefits were too small to be useful.

Integrative Choices:

* During the watchful waiting period, I consulted a biochemist who had a set of chemical remedies which he believed would help and I used them for many months. Apparently did not work.
* I went to an MD who did alternative treatments and took IV vitamin C — up to 75gm in a session. I did this weekly for several years. Her office identified the doctor who did the cryoablation.
* Modified my diet by reducing the amount of red meat to about once a week and greatly reduced my sugar consumption. I eat organic chicken and fish several times, grass-fed beef and other anti-inflammatory foods.
* Began vegetable juicing daily.
* In early 2011, began the Budwig protocol, which uses a combination of flaxseed oil, flaxseeds and cottage cheese.
* Practiced meditation to work the mind-body connection for healing.
* Did rebounding to stimulate internal organs and cleanse the lymph nodes.
* Used a variety of supplements to stimulate my immune system and detoxify my body.
* Used EFT to clear core issues causing me stress.
* Began using several homeopathy remedies prescribed by Beth Poindexter in April 2011.

Successful Outcomes: Today my PSA is holding at below 0.1, down from 325 in five months. The alternative therapies have been instrumental in my current health status.

Conventional Doctor Responses: The MDs have been extraordinarily surprised by my test results. Most of my doctors have been open to my additional choices although they did not expect much from them. One MD was particularly negative. On the other hand, two MDs asked me to write up my other choices. They thought the information might be valuable.

Lifestyle Changes: I have been eating in a much more "aware" manner. I have reduced red meat, sugars, and gluten products. I intend to meditate and exercise more than in the past; I have not achieved the level I want.

Words of Wisdom: Listen to your doctors, ask many questions, and research their answers. Be aware that although the MDs claim to value only "evidence-based" treatments, in fact, only about 20% of current medical treatments are actually evidence-based! That is not much different from many of the alternatives that are available.

PATIENT 4

"I am a 54-year-old woman. It has been ten months since diagnosis."

Diagnosis: Stage IV breast cancer (a very fast growing cancer)

Conventional Treatment: Biopsies (3), surgeries (4), chemo (8 rounds for a total of 6 months, and finally radiation (31 sessions—5 days a week for 6 weeks).

Treatment Options Refused: I did everything they told me to do. Half way through the chemo, I started taking my juice plus again even though the doctor had told me not to take it.

Integrative Choices:

* I did have a couple of sessions of Reiki and a couple of sessions of Healing Touch (provided free to cancer patients via the doctor's office).

* Now that I'm at the tail end of my treatment, I am exercising (walking for now).

* I am eating a better diet (no white or brown sugar, no white flour, only organic meats, vegetables and fruits, and cutting meat out of my diet as much as possible).
* I am doing meditation to work on my type A personality and the stress at work.
* I took the Juice Plus, but did not tell the doctors.

Successful Outcomes: After chemo was finished, we did a second PET scan that showed no signs of cancer; all my "hot" spots were gone. Also, my tumor marker blood test was in the normal range. I am getting stronger every day. I feel invincible again, and I haven't felt this good for years. In fact, I am not even getting the colds and flu that are going around at my office. It's like my immune system is working again.

Conventional Doctor Responses: I tried talking to both my oncologists about diet... How can I help my body with food/nutrition? The only advice I got was to eat no soy because it mimics estrogen. Controlling my cancer and my immune system are really not topics that my doctors want to discuss, but they did offer consultations with nutritionists and other integrative healing professionals.

Lifestyle Changes: Now that I'm feeling better I have been able to read books and articles about surviving cancer. I am now much more educated about controlling cancer and helping my immune system fight it. I don't feel like this is a death sentence any more. I know that many people survive a "long" time with stage IV cancer through improved diet, stress control and exercise. Now that I'm done with chemo (I'll be 3 months out of chemo on March 9, 2012), and I'm getting stronger every day, I feel like there is much I can do, and I'm excited about living. I am cutting way back on meat (no more than 20% of my diet), eating only organic foods, and focusing on foods that fight breast cancer specifically (i.e., cauliflower and blueberries). I am open to possibilities now that before I might have thought were silly (like Healing Touch). I am working on stress reduction and plan to change jobs within a year or two after I get my medical bills under control. I'd like a less stressful job, something that is less consuming so I have time after work to exercise. (I am a chief financial officer.)

Words of Wisdom: Believe in yourself. Believe that you know what's best for you because you do. Listen to your mind and your body. Embrace hope.

PATIENT 5

"I am a 65-year-old woman. It has been three years since diagnosis."

Diagnosis: Breast Cancer — Stage I tubular carcinoma

Conventional Treatment: I had a lumpectomy. I also stopped natural hormone replacement therapy.

Treatment Options Refused: I did not have radiation. There was no trace of cancer cells in the breast tissue pathology report; however, they still wanted to radiate my entire breast.

Integrative Choices: The main focus of my treatment included:
* Heavy metal detoxification under the care of Beth Poindexter, naturopath and homeopath health care provider
* Immune building – vitamin C, better diet, more water, less stress, more relaxed life style, and improved breathing
* Continued brisk walking and Pilates

Successful Outcomes:
* Follow-up mammograms have been normal.
* Mercury has been reduced from significantly high to a negligible amount.
* I no longer have candida or tooth plaque.
* I have improved energy.

Conventional Doctor Responses: The doctors did not respond well to my decision. They tried to pressure me to have the radiation because it is considered the standard of care.

Lifestyle Changes: I have reduced the stress in my life, have a better diet, and exercise regularly. I began reading *A Course in Miracles* and have been attending local groups since I found out about the cancer.

Words of Wisdom: Fear not; cancer is a teacher to become the new you.

PATIENT 6

"My mother was 75 years old at the time of her lung cancer diagnosis. She died 18 years after this diagnosis. She was also diagnosed with uterine cancer at age 65."

Submitted by Dr. Mary Ann Block, author of *Today I Will Not Die*, www.blockcenter.com

Diagnosis: Metastatic, terminal lung cancer, stage IV. She was given two months to live by a prominent cancer treatment center.

Conventional Treatment: She received palliative radiation and chemotherapy.

Treatment Options Refused: None

Integrative Choices: As a physician in my first year of practice, I researched and tried natural treatments while my mother received radiation and chemotherapy. Her significant treatments included:

* Hypnosis and visualization
* Nutrition IV drips with high doses of vitamin C
* Elimination of sugar
* Magnesium injections
* Oral supplements—vitamins and minerals
* Staphage lysate immune enhancer injected under the skin to increase the immune response. (Only veterinarians can use it today.)
* Pau d'arco tea to boost her immune system

Successful Outcomes: She was cured in four months and remained cancer free for the rest of her life, dying at the age of 92 after breaking her hip. We never dreamed it was possible, but a very large tumor in the middle of her chest, which spread outside of the lungs, disappeared after four months of treatment. The chemo and radiation treatments were stopped once the tumor disappeared. My mother was a positive thinker. She said that she did not have a role model for dying, so she was not going to do it.

Conventional Doctor Responses: The doctors were thrilled by the results; however, they never referred any of their patients to me.

Lifestyle Changes: My mother took supplements and magnesium injections for the rest of her life and reduced her sugar intake. She continued to be a positive thinker and did not let things get her down.

Words of Wisdom: Cancer patients need to do their research thoroughly and not just go to one doctor. They need to locate the doctor who has the best success with their particular cancer and is willing to look at combining conventional and alternative treatment approaches. People with a positive outlook, who take control of their treatment, have better outcomes. Too often doctors tell their patients not to take supplements or do anything alternative. Patients must educate themselves and then choose the route that is best for them.

PATIENT 7

"I am a 49-year-old man. It has been 20 months since first diagnosis in July 2010."

Submitted by Evan Katz

Diagnosis: Stage III melanoma cancer (lymph node involvement, not metastasized)

Conventional Treatment: Within weeks after the diagnosis, an oncology surgeon removed the tumor on my right upper back and took a sentinel lymph node. The node contained cancer. Six weeks later, the surgeon removed 32 lymph nodes under my right arm to prevent the cancer from spreading. The statistics for stage III Melanoma suggest that less than 17% of patients survive more than five years.

Six weeks after the second surgery, I began chemotherapy with a drug called Interferon. Interferon gave me very negative side effects, including high fevers, night terrors, shakes that felt like seizures, and a suicidal depression.

Approximately two weeks after I started the Interferon, I began having severe pain under my right arm. Three weeks into chemo I was hospitalized for an infection. I was in massive pain for five days, waiting for the lab results. After learning that it wasn't a staph infection, I checked myself out of the hospital and discontinued chemotherapy.

Treatment Options Refused: I did what the doctors recommended before discontinuing chemo.

Integrative Choices: During the six weeks between the second surgery and the chemotherapy, my brother, who healed his colitis through nutrition and Chinese herbs, took me to see Dr. Susan Russell, an acupuncturist and healer in Marietta, Georgia. After one acupuncture treatment, my body felt different. I had no pain. However, I was still committed to treating my cancer with chemotherapy.

Between the second surgery and starting chemo, my brother also took me to New York City to see Dr. George Wong, MD, a fourth generation Chinese Herbalist. Dr. Wong prescribed herbs to protect my body during the interferon treatments. He and my oncologist consulted throughout the chemo treatment. After Western medicine became ineffective, my oncologist (originally from South Africa) recommended that I work with Dr. Wong full force.

After the infection crisis, I began working with Dr. Russell again—first to get the toxins out of my body and then, in conjunction with Dr. Wong, to treat my cancer. I went to her three days a week. After five weeks of acupuncture and Dr. Wong's herbs, the infection was gone. I continue to see her once a week and take Dr. Wong's herbs every day.

Dr. Wong's herbs focus both on eliminating my cancer and softening my "type A" personality. Both he and Dr. Russell suggest specific foods and meditation techniques. My entire person feels different on these herbs. When I run out, I start to get depressed. My body gets tired and I do not do the right things to stay healthy. Dr. Wong had me taking a Reishi mushroom extract to boost my immune system. Then in November 2011, there were problems, resulting in six excisions, four of them in one month. Dr. Wong discontinued the capsules and now has me taking Reishi spores, which are a thousand times more powerful.

The Chinese believe my cancer is curable, and now I do, too.

Successful Outcomes:

* My scans continue to show no cancer, and the inflammation continues to lessen.
* I feel healthy and am less intense (less fire).
* I'm a different person today. I am a happier and better person than before I was diagnosed with cancer.

Conventional Doctor Responses: I only go to seasoned doctors who agree with what I am doing.

Lifestyle Changes:

* I follow Dr. Wong's recommendations and take the herbs he prescribes.
* I see Dr. Russell for acupuncture, Reiki and whatever she feels is necessary.
* I've changed at a very deep level of my being—now believing there is a connection between cellular functions and pure energy. Without these changes, I don't believe I would have survived.
* I eat better, meditate and view life holistically.
* I have a new understanding of energy and how it can improve my life.
* I no longer subscribe to western medicine. I see everything as alive and having medicinal qualities.

Words of Wisdom: Be open-minded. Do not let fear close your mind. Chinese medicine has been around for 5,000 years. Western medicine has only been around for 200 years.

PATIENT 8

"I am 30+ years old. It has been eight years since initial diagnosis in July 2004."

Submitted by Maria Valdivia

Diagnosis: Multifocal infiltrating lobular carcinoma intraepithelial neoplasia, stage IV breast cancer (lymph tumors in the side of my neck)

Conventional Treatment: Recommendations by two hospitals:

1) Double radical mastectomy (amputation of both breasts)
2) Radiation therapy to reduce the size of tumors first, and
3) Chemotherapy after the mastectomy. The scan before radiation therapy, detected that the cancer was already in the lymph nodes on the side of my neck.

Treatment Options Refused: I refused all of the recommendations.

Integrative Choices: I learned about a doctor in Mexico who was having much success with cancer through a science created by Isaac Goiz Duran, MD, called "BIOMAGNETISM." He has discovered that microorganisms (bacteria, viruses, parasites, etc.) are the cause of cancer, and they can be destroyed without affecting human tissues by using regular low intensity magnets (a few dollars each). The magnets placed in certain ways change the pH (acid/alkaline ratio) of the organs and rapidly destroy these microorganisms. The tumors lose force and begin to reduce, until they disappear. (These magnets have been used in the USA for more than 40 years.)

Successful Outcomes: Twenty days after returning from Mexico, a scan showed that the tumors on the side of my neck had disappeared. At that point I decided to do nothing more conventionally than have evaluations and examinations from time to time. Each time I was feeling much better and healthier.

Currently, I live with an extraordinary quality of health. My cholesterol, sugar level, blood pressure, and corporal weight (that is to say all parameters that I have now) correspond to a 23-year-old person, and many of the small conditions that I had before cancer have disappeared.

Conventional Doctor Responses: My breast cancer was rare (10% of women) and invasive. The group of physicians who attended me in 2004 warned me that in just a few months they would not be able to treat my cancer and death was imminent. They made me sign a document stating that I voluntarily rejected any treatment, taking full responsibility for the consequences of my decision. I had no objections to signing it.

Today doctors still don't understand how it is possible that I'm alive and well, since my cancer had metastasized and the central tumor was three centimeters in diameter.

Lifestyle Changes: I continue to use Biomagnetism for myself and others. Two years after being cured, I was invited to study with Dr. Issac Goiz Duran in Mexico City. In 2007, I opened the first clinic of Biomagnetism in the USA. To learn more, visit my website:

www.biomagnetismushealth.com

Words of Wisdom: If someone has recently been diagnosed with cancer, I suggest investigating Biomagnetism. This system is one hundred percent safe. If it is done professionally, the improvements are going to be reflected in the laboratory tests.

PATIENT 9

"I am a 44-year-old woman. It has been five years and five months since diagnosis."

Diagnosis: Breast cancer — stage IIa — invasive ductal carcinoma (2.9 cm lump with no lymph node involvement). Eight months later, I found a second tumor (1.5 cm).

Conventional Treatment: I had two lumpectomies. Doctors recommended a double mastectomy, 20 cycles of chemotherapy, four rounds of Herceptin, twelve weeks of radiation treatments, and tamoxifen hormone therapy for five years.

Treatment Options Refused: I refused all of their treatment recommendations.

Integrative Choices:

* CUT out ALL SUGAR/processed foods from diet!
* Changed to a vegetarian raw diet for six months to restart my immune system. I began to drink vegetable juice and green smoothies every day; I have not missed a day since I started! Currently, I eat 70% healthy cooked foods and 30% raw foods. Sometimes all raw, depending on what my body asks for each day.
* Received Christian Science Treatment with a practitioner for six months.

* Did White/Red ozone treatments and Alkaline/MSM/Thymus/Vitamin C/Amigdalin/Laetrile/Alpha Lipoic Acid drips twice a week for one year.
* Received acupuncture treatments.
* Increased vitamin D—tanning naked outside for 15 minutes on each side.
* Began giving myself nutrition before and after running; regularly run marathons/blindfold marathons.
* Observed my thoughts constantly, making "I AM healthy and perfect" a predominant thought.
* Began nurturing myself emotionally and spiritually. I prayed and knew that "ALL IS WELL."

Successful Outcomes: I was bulimic/anorexic for 20 years, so when I began to give myself nutrition, I had energy, was clear minded, and had a great sense of wellbeing for the first time in my life. Today I am cancer free. All PET scans, breast MRI's and check ups were clear after the second lump, but I knew that! I was done with the cancer.

Conventional Doctor Responses: My oncologist told me that if I did not do the chemo/radiation/tamoxifen, I would be dead in five years. At every three-month follow-up visit, he offered chemo. Now I have yearly visits. I saw 20 oncologists and none supported my choice to strengthen my immune system.

Lifestyle Changes: I did not go back to a high pressure ABC News job. I got rid of the negative people/situations in my life, which is an ongoing process. I started to grow my own food/garden. Instead of abusing myself with food, I nurture myself with food. I practice GRATITUDE, GRATITUDE, GRATITUDE! I have started to take steps toward my lifelong dream:

The Couch Show: www.facebook.com/CouchShow

which was and is a big part of my healing process. By sharing it with the world, I hope to heal others as well.

Words of Wisdom: Take 100% responsibility for your healing — mind, body and soul. Don't be a victim of circumstances; create your own circumstances. Ask yourself why cancer showed up in your life, and then listen. You might be surprised by what you hear.

PATIENT 10

"I am a 67-year-old man. It has been almost two years since diagnosis."

Diagnosis: Prostate Cancer (metastasized to bones and lymph nodes). PSA 254, Gleeson Score 4+4 some 4+5. CT and bone scans showed skeletal metastases in the thoracic and lumber spine, multiple ribs, throughout the pelvis and elbow joint.

Conventional Treatment: I began hormone treatment (Zoladex) 24 months ago and continue with it in spite of the horrible side effects: short term memory loss, lack of motivation, penile shrinkage, weight gain, very emotional, short tempered, loss of strength, headaches, fatigue, broken sleep, easily upset, and increase in blood pressure. The total inability to obtain an erection affected my mind. I was given antidepressants and referred to a counselor. Twelve months later, I have a different outlook on life. I have also been attending a monthly support group meeting since August 2011; this has also been very helpful.

I have been on a clinical trial of mdv3100 for six months. Some of the new treatment options that are in the final stages of testing or have just been approved look very exciting. They are giving a better prognosis to men who have metastasized prostate cancer.

Treatment Options Refused: I did what was recommended. However, the doctors gave me little information about the treatment and side effects. I believe it is really important for the doctors to give you the full information, not leave you to find out along the journey. While I wouldn't or couldn't change my treatment option, I would have preferred to have been informed.

Integrative Choices: I try to eat a really healthy diet: lots of fresh fruit and vegetables, more grilled fish and chicken, red meat only once a week, reduced salt, and no sugar. I exercise and have always been active, but I do need to get motivated and do more regular exercise.

Successful Outcomes: My PSA showed a dramatic drop over the first ten months and has been going up and down steadily since April,

2011. The CT and bone scans showed some reductions in bone cancers, but by December, 2011 they showed some new bone cancers. Had bone and Ct scans in June, 2012. The CT scan report reads "metastasis, measurable nil, but there is non-measurable metastatic disease present," the bone scan done at the same time says "stable skeletal metastatic disease." This is almost a miracle! While it is early, the initial trial is very encouraging.

Lifestyle Changes: I made changes to my diet and continue to exercise. I continue to do a lot of research using the Internet and reading books in order to understand prostate cancer, including treatment options and side effects.

Words of Wisdom: If you want to survive, don't give up. You need to read and educate yourself about prostate cancer, join a support group, talk to others and encourage men to get screened. Every patient and their partner should be referred to a counselor to help them through the maze and shock associated with prostate cancer. I believe that diet and exercise are very important factors in helping you along the way. Live a healthy lifestyle, give up smoking, restrict your alcohol intake. Talk to your male friends, encourage them to seek medical advice on PC early. If you are in a club, organize a PC speaker to give a talk at your next meeting. We males need to be better educated about our health.

PATIENT 11

"I am a 57-year-old woman. It has been three years since diagnosis."

Diagnosis: Aggressive Breast Cancer

Conventional Treatment:

1. My oncologist prescribed eight chemotherapy treatments before surgery: one every 21 days, providing my T-cells were high enough. One week after the fifth chemo treatment, my T-cell count was 0.04.

2. After 14 days, I increased the Hyperimmune Egg supplement, also called i26, which brought my T-Cell count up to 10.37. My oncologist was amazed, but was not aware of my using the Hyperimmune egg. During the chemo and Hyperimmune Egg treatments, I was able to walk downtown. I was always in the presence of many people, prepared my own meals, did my household chores and traveled by bus and subway to get to Mass each day. On the evening of my last chemo treatment, I went directly to the airport and flew to Florida, a 1300-mile trip, with no side effects.

3. Thirty days after chemotherapy, I had a mastectomy.

4. Thirty days after surgery, I started 25 consecutive radiation treatments.

Treatment Options Refused: I did everything my oncologist recommended.

Integrative Choices:

* I took the Hyperimmune Egg, a dietary supplement, with over 100 global patents, designed to help the immune system function properly. This all natural, protein supplement contains concentrated amounts of immune cofactors (bioactive molecules) and IgY antibodies delivered through 100% all natural egg protein. I was very grateful that Dr. Hellen Greenblatt worked very closely with me and appreciated her expertise on being the foremost authority on Hyperimmune Egg, and it's impact on the immune system. (See www.i26forhealth.com/geetaferris for more information.)

* I juiced vegetables three times per week.

* I stayed away from acidic foods and meats.

Successful Outcomes:

* My tumor disappeared after my fifth chemotherapy treatment.

* I had energy during treatment, especially compared to my colleagues at the clinic.

* My blood count remained satisfactory.

* I experienced no lymphadema, which was another plus.

* Blood work and other tests were good at the time of my annual oncologist visit in April, 2012.

Conventional Doctor Responses: When it was all over, I told my oncologist that I had taken the Hyperimmune Egg throughout the entire treatment. She asked questions about the Hyperimmune Egg and was considering trying it in her clinic, but that has not happened so far.

Lifestyle Changes:

* I continue to exercise daily and do Zumba 2-3 times a week.
* I juice and eat healthy foods.

Words of Wisdom: Be strong and positive, and take the Hyperimmune Egg.

PATIENT 12

"I am a 56-year-old woman. It has been ten years since diagnosis."

Diagnosis: Stage II breast cancer

Conventional Treatment: I had a lumpectomy with only three sentinel lymph nodes removed, not the majority of lymph nodes they wanted to remove from my left arm. Doctors also recommended radiation and chemotherapy.

Treatment Options Refused: I chose to keep more lymph nodes, and I did not have radiation or chemo.

Integrative Choices: I did the Gerson Therapy treatment. We had a Gerson specialist come into our home for a week to help us set up the required equipment, supplies and then "coach" me in the first few days of adapting to the therapy. The treatment required a very strict vegan diet for about a year.

Successful Outcomes: My system was purged of all toxins to an extreme. I don't remember at any point in my life feeling that "clean." I don't think even in my childhood I had that kind of well-balanced feeling in my body. I was only getting tested for signs of cancer, not other health markers. The cancer tests have been clear for ten years.

Conventional Doctor Responses: Other than the lumpectomy, their official acknowledgement of what I chose to do is on record as being "cancer untreated."

Lifestyle Changes: Although I decided not to continue with a vegan diet once I was cleared, I have maintained healthy eating habits.

I made a very conscious decision to stay alive. I had the horrendous experience of losing both of my children in an accident with their father when I was in my thirties. I had carried on with my life but always believed that whatever finally came to claim my life I would go willingly and secretly gratefully. Once I was diagnosed, I surprised myself by realizing I truly wanted to live. That realization opened my eyes to a gratitude for the life I had after the death of my children. I never would have allowed that realization previously.

Words of Wisdom: Do not let anyone dictate to you. Listen to what people say, ask questions, but the most important thing about whatever course you decide to take with your treatment, conventional or otherwise, is that you should have confidence in that treatment.

The Experts Who Shared Their Wisdom in This Book

Judith Ansara, MSW
www.sacredunion.com
Radiation Prayer

Judith Ansara has served as a psychotherapist, coach, and spiritual guide for over 35 years teaching at universities and growth centers such as Omega and Esalen Institutes. She co-founded the Peacemaker Institute training students in the inner and outer arts of peacemaking and social action. Judith offers training in Transformational Coaching and with her husband of 40 years, Robert Gass, leads retreats for couples on the arts and skills of intimate relationship. As a writer, artist and dancer, mother and grandmother, Judith is committed to helping create a just and sustainable world.

Russell L. Blaylock, MD
www.russellblaylockmd.com
Understand Good Fats and Bad Fats

Dr. Blaylock is a board certified neurosurgeon, author and lecturer. He is the author of *Natural Strategies for Cancer Patients, Health and Nutrition Secrets That Can Save Your Life, Excitotoxins: The Taste That Kills*, and *Bioterrorism: How You Can Survive*. He offers a newsletter: *The Blaylock Wellness Report*. (Thanks go to Kensington Publishing Corporation for permitting the publication of Dr. Blaylock's excerpts.)

Maria E. Belluccio, DOM, AP, RN, CCT
www.lotuspathwellness.com
Thermography: Another Breast Screening Option

Dr. Belluccio is a Doctor of Oriental Medicine and Certified Clinical Thermographer. She is the owner of Lotus Path Wellness Center. Her center offers Chinese medicine and acupuncture, thermography, NAET (Allergy Elimination), diet and nutritional counseling, Functional Medicine, bio identical hormone therapy, weight management and smoking cessation.

Jack Challem
www.jackchallem.com
The Role of Inflammation in Disease

Jack Challem is known as The Nutrition Reporter™. He is the author of *No More Fatigue, Stop Prediabetes Now, The Inflammation Syndrome, The Food-Mood Solution, Feed Your Genes Right* and *Syndrome X*. He writes a newsletter and blog, offers nutrition coaching and gives presentations and speeches. (Thanks go to John Wiley & Sons, Inc. for permitting the publication of Mr. Challem's excerpts.)

Dr. Nalini Chilkov, LAc, OMD
www.doctornalini.com
The Benefits of Acupuncture in Cancer Care

Dr. Chilkov has combined her diverse training in Traditional Oriental Medicine, Modern Biomedicine and Cell Biology in her private practice for the past 30 years. Dr. Nalini primarily serves patients with cancer and complex, chronic illnesses alongside her Optimal Health and Wellness practice. She is a respected expert in Collaborative Integrative Cancer Care. She integrates modern and traditional healing paradigms and partners with physicians to provide best outcomes for patients. She has been a lecturer at the School of Medicine at UCLA and UC Irvine in California as well as many schools of Traditional Oriental and Naturopathic Medicine over her long career. Dr. Nalini is a regular contributor to the Healthy Living Section of the *Huffington Post* (www.huffingtonpost.com/nalini-chilkov).

Robert A. Eslinger, DO, HMD
www.renointegrativemedicalcenter.com
Darkfield Live Blood Analysis and The Body's Immune System and "Terrain" Promote Wellness

Dr. Eslinger is the director of the Reno Integrative Medical Center and is one of 15 doctors worldwide, who are featured in the book *Defeat Cancer* by Connie Strasheim. The Center specializes in cancer treatment and offers diagnostics tests, osteopathic medicine and many treatment options: vitamin-mineral infusions, mega dose ascorbate infusions, homeopathic remedies, herbs and nutrients, chelation therapy, oxidative therapies, laetrile, insulin potentiated therapy, Revici remedies, German Biological Medicine, pre and post operation immune boosting, ultraviolet blood irradiation, hyperthermia, Poly-MVA nutritional supplement, and the RIMC HCG diet.

Raymond Fracis, MSc
www.beyondhealth.com
The Problem with Most Cancer Treatments

One of the few scientists to achieve a breakthrough understanding of health and disease, Raymond Francis has created an entirely new concept of health along with a simple program for achieving it called the *Beyond Health Model*. He is chairman of Beyond Health International, which supplies highly advanced health education and world-class health-supporting products to the public, and the author of *Never Fear Cancer Again, Never Be Sick Again,* and *Never Be Fat Again.*

Mimi George, PhD
www.hawaiiancleanseprogram.com
Colon and Detoxification Cleanse the Hawaiian Way

Dr. George has led these cleanses for the last ten years at the request of Auntie Margaret Machado. The cleanse foods and formulas are 100% organic, highest quality, non-inflammatory, and provide the cleansers with the opportunity to follow up their ten days at the cleanse with self-testing for food sensitivities that they may not be aware of. The food preparations are done in a completely open way so that cleansers can access and participate in all techniques and recipes. Experts in ho'oponopono, nutrition, naturopathic medicine and Iyengar yoga work with cleansers daily. Dr. George may be emailed at george.mimi@gmail.com.

Ann Louise Gittleman, PhD, CNS
www.annlouise.com
Parasites—The Silent Epidemic

Dr. Ann Louise™ First Lady of Nutrition is the creator of Fat Flush, the detox/diet connection to weight loss, and author of over 30 books on health and wellness: *Guess What Came to Dinner?, Fast Track Detox Diet, Why Am I Always So Tired?, Super Nutrition for Women, Beyond Pritikin, Fat Flush for Life, Lose Weight Cookbook, Before the Change, Super Nutrition for Men,* and *How to Stay Young and Healthy in a Toxic World.* (Thanks go to Penguin Group (USA) Inc. for permitting the publication of Dr. Gittleman's excerpts.)

Christine Horner, MD
www.drchristinehorner.com
10 Tips to Lower Your Risk of Breast Cancer

Dr. Horner is a board certified and nationally recognized surgeon, author, professional speaker and relentless champion for women's health. She spearheaded legislation in the 1990s that made it mandatory that insurance companies pay for breast reconstruction following mastectomy. She is the author of *Waking the Warrior Goddess: Dr. Christine Horner's Program to Protect Against and Fight Breast Cancer*—winner of the 2006 IPPY award for "Best book in health, medicine and nutrition." Dr. Horner worked in collaboration with Enzymatic Therapy to create Protective Breast Formula, a combination of seven different supplements that powerfully promote breast health. She offers telephone consultations, an online newsletter, and is available as a keynote speaker on various topics on natural health.

Joan Kasich, CNHP
www.herbspecialist.com
www.bemeramerica.com/joankasich
Balance Your pH; Balance Your Life

Joan is a Certified Natural Health Professional and Herb Specialist. Since 1999 she has helped over 2,000 clients get healthier. Joan is currently promoting a bioenergetic device called the BEMER. The BEMER emits a signal that increases vasomotion in the vessels thus improving microcirculation (capillary activity) by 30%. Because your capillaries take up 74% of your circulation, you produce more energy, feel less discomfort, get a more restful sleep, and achieve an overall sense of wellbeing.

Michael Lam, MD, MPH, ABAAM
www.drlam.com
The Basics of Estrogen Dominance

Dr. Lam is Board Certified by the American Board of Anti-aging Medicine. His clinical focus is on adrenal fatigue and natural hormonal balancing. His organization offers nutritional coaching services worldwide. DrLam.com is a free educational website that focuses on holistic nutrition. His mission is to empower people to take control of their health. He is the author of *Beating Cancer with Natural Medicine, How to Stay Young & Live Longer, Adrenal Fatigue Syndrome, Five Proven Secrets to Longevity*, and *Estrogen Dominance*.

Gail S. Lebovic, MA, MD, FACS
www.asbd.org
Oncoplastic Surgery: A Creative Surgical Approach for Breast Cancer Patients

---

Dr. Lebovic is credited as one of the few pioneers in the field of Oncoplastic Surgery. She has developed new techniques in the diagnosis, treatment and post-operative care of patients. In addition to her clinical work as an Oncoplastic Surgeon, she is well known around the world as the inventor of the MammoPad™ and other innovative devices in women's healthcare. She has served as Associate Director of the Lee Breast Center at USC and developed and led the program for Preventive Services as Director of Women's Healthcare at the Cooper Clinic. Currently she serves as a healthcare educator and physician/patient advocate throughout the world. For additional information about oncoplastic breast surgery, visit the website of the American Society of Breast Disease, a medical society advancing a multidisciplinary approach to breast care.

Carol Look, LCSW, DCH, EFT Master
www.attractingabundance.com
Tapping into Abundance

Carol Look is an EFT Founding Master, the leading success and abundance coach in the energy psychology field, and an international workshop presenter. She is the author of *Attracting Abundance with EFT* and *Improve Your Eyesight with EFT.* She is a highly sought after advanced trainer for practitioners and offers additional audio and video training products on a variety of topics including: *Abundance, Public Speaking, Clearing Clutter, Law of Attraction, Healing Pain and Illness,* and *Weight Loss.*

Dustin Maher
www.dustinmaherfitness.com
Physical Fitness and Optimal Health Go Hand in Hand

Dustin Maher is a fitness professional with a degree in Kinesiology Exercise Science. He is the creator of Fit Fun Bootcamps and author of *Fit Moms for Life.* He has created home workout DVDs that get results: *FMFL: Buns Guns Back and Shoulders, Babytone, FMFL Got Core,* and *FMFL Ultimate Buddy Bootcamp.* He also offers a *Fit Moms for Life* monthly DVD program.

Barb M. Mahlmeister, RD, LD/N
www.naturalchoicenutrition.com
Your Gut Is Your Lifeline to Happiness!

Barb Mahlmeister is a Registered Dietitian and Nutritionist and graduate of the Institute of Functional Medicine. In her approach to healing, she addresses primary prevention and underlying causes instead of symptoms for serious chronic diseases. She specializes in treating digestive disorders, food allergies and sensitivities, cardiovascular disease, diabetes, gastric bypass, sports nutrition, and weight loss.

Christiane Northrup, MD
www.drnorthrup.com
Inner Wisdom Contributes to Health

Dr. Northrup is a *New York Times* best-selling author and the world's leading authority in the field of women's health and wellness. Her visionary approach acknowledges the integration of mind, body, emotions and spirit. She has authored many bestselling books: *Women's Bodies, Women's Wisdom; The Wisdom of Menopause; The Secret Pleasures of Menopause; The Wisdom of Menopause Journal;* and *Mother-Daughter Wisdom*. She writes a blog and e-newsletter, and shares her wisdom in a weekly radio show on www.HayHouseRadio.com. (Thanks go to Bantam Books, a division of Random House, Inc., for permitting publication of Dr. Northrup's excerpts.)

Beth Poindexter, ND, MPH
www.naturalmedicinetucson.com
Detoxification: Pathway to a Healthy Body

Dr. Poindexter is a licensed naturopathic doctor and classically trained homeopath. She also holds a Masters Degree in Public Health. At Creative Health Professionals, a disease-state is considered to be a complex relationship comprised of the environment, lifestyle, thoughts and genetics. Dr. Poindexter works with her clients to address specific health challenges, remove obstacles to recovery and create a research-based multifaceted treatment approach. The areas of expertise include fatigue/thyroid conditions, naturopathic/homeopathic cancer treatments, customized weight loss and low cost laboratory testing.

Dorothy Ratusny, PhD
www.dorothyratusny.com
Living a Purposeful Life

Dr. Ratusny is a certified psychotherapist in Toronto, Canada, who specializes in Cognitive Therapy. She counsels individuals and couples, consults in the corporate workplace, and offers workshops and retreats. She is a leader in the area of self-actualization and personal growth. She speaks on a variety of topics offering strategies for living consciously and making empowering choices by living your truth. She is the author of *Live Your Life's Purpose: A Guidebook for Creating* and *Living a Purposeful Life and The Purpose of Love: A Guidebook for Defining and Cultivating Your Most Significant Relationship.* (Thanks go to Insomniac Press for permitting publication of Dr. Ratusny's excerpts.)

Wayne C. Rebarber, DC
www.rebarberchiro.com
Spinal Alignment Results in Optimal Health

Dr. Rebarber offers holistic health care for the entire family in central New Jersey. His centers offer chiropractic adjustments, functional diagnostic testing, nutritional diagnostic testing and education, health coaching, Isagenix Cleansing System, acupuncture, and massage therapy. The centers also sell nutritional supplements and many items for healthy living. The Rebarber Family Chiropractic centers focus on creating health and affirming wellness.

Rev. Maria Antonieta Riveros-Revello
www.reikishrine.org
Reiki: Radiant Energy

Reverend Riveros-Revello offers training and treatments in several energy modalities. She is a PhD Candidate at the University of South Florida and has studied many forms of bioenergetics in her search to find natural ways of healing. She travels internationally teaching and learning. She is also a member of the International Center for Reiki Training (ICRT). The Reiki Shrine is a non-profit organization that offers classes for healthy living.

LindaJoy Rose, PhD
www.rawfusionliving.com
www.drljrose.com
Optimal Health Benefits from a Raw Food Diet

Dr. Rose is a Life Makeover Therapist, Wellness Chef, and pioneer of the Raw Fusion movement. As a counselor and coach, she uses a multi-disciplinary approach to facilitate a client's "life makeover" on many levels. She has over 25 years of international experience helping people get to the root cause of behavioral patterns. Through *Raw Fusion Living* she offers lifestyle and nutritional guidance to enhance vitality for the entire family. She is the author of *Your Mind: The Owner's Manual, Raw Fusion Living, Raw Fusion Recipes, A Year of Positive Habits: The 21-Day Secret to Changing Your Life*, and *Parallel Lives*. (Thanks go to Quantum Mind Press, LLC for permitting publication of Dr. Rose's excerpts.)

Brian Luke Seaward, PhD
www.brianlukeseaward.net
A Mind-Body-Spirit Approach to Managing Stress

Dr. Seaward is a renowned international expert in stress management and mind-body-spirit healing. Through Inspiration Unlimited & The Paramount Wellness Institute, a health and wellness consulting company, he speaks on topics that inspire others to make lifestyle changes and achieve their human potential. Topics for his workshops are: *Stand Like Mountain, Flow Like Water; Letting Go of Stress; Spirits on a Human Path; Mind-Body-Spirit Healing;* and *Care for the Care Giver*. He is the author of *Stand Like Mountain, Flow Like Water; Stressed Is Desserts Spelled Backward; The Art of Calm; Achieving The Mind-Body-Spirit Connection: A Stress Management Workbook; Hot Stones & Funny Bones;* and *Quiet Mind, Fearless Heart*. He has created an *Earth Songs* DVD and journal. (Thanks go to Jones & Bartlett Learning for permitting publication of Dr. Seaward's excerpts.)

Deb Shapiro
www.edanddebshapiro.com
Repressed, Denied and Ignored

Deb Shapiro is the author of *Your Body Speaks Your Mind: Decoding the Emotional, Psychological and Spiritual Messages that Underlie Health* and co-author with Ed Shapiro of *Be the Change: How Meditation Can*

Transform You and The World, Voices from the Heart, and Meditation. Deb and Ed are available for corporate consulting and coaching, private sessions on personal development, and spiritual counseling. They are featured bloggers on www.Oprah.com, www.HuffingtonPost.com, www.Care2.com, www.Lohas.com and www.VividLife.me. They have a monthly radio show on www.VividLife.me radio and write monthly articles for *Change Your Attitude Change Your Life 24/seven* magazine. (Thanks go to Sounds True Publishing for permitting publication of Ms. Shapiro's excerpts.)

Molly Snow, LMT
www.neosmassage.com
CranioSacral Therapy and Epigenetic Programming

Molly Snow is a licensed massage therapist and the owner of Neos Massage. She offers energetic healing through three primary modalities. She offers CranioSacral Therapy and Unwinding Meridians therapy, both eliminate restrictions and emotional patterns locked in the body and organs. She received her CranioSacral Therapy training from the Upledger Institute in Palm Beach, FL. She also offers Epigenetic Programming which allows her to influence a client's healing at the cellular level by changing the energy surrounding each cell. She offers sessions in person and over the telephone and is getting great results with her clients through her integrative approach to energy bodywork.

Ruth Stern, MA
www.taptotransform.com
What Is EFT?

Ruth Stern is a licensed Mental Health therapist, AAMET EFT Certified Trainer and Practitioner, and Certified EMDR Clinician. She provides individual EFT sessions both in person and on the phone. She has been a health care professional for over 29 years and has led various workshops on stress and anxiety, chronic pain and weight loss with EFT. She offers Levels 1, 2, and 3 EFT training for mental health therapists. She created a DVD program, *Four Steps to Blissful Sleep,* and a CD program, *Tap Into Happiness!*

Book Resources
for Self, Health & Wealth

Self

A Book of Miracles: *Inspiring True Stories of Healing, Gratitude, and Love* by Dr. Bernie S. Siegel—Through personal stories, quotes, suggestions and reflections, the book guides us into a deeper understanding of the perceptions and attitudes we must cultivate to attract miracles. This book is a must read for anyone who is going through a difficult life situation and feels alone and powerless. It uplifts our souls, gives us hope and empowers us to keep going. It provides the guidance we need to live with more love, peace and gratitude. (2011, New World Library)

A New Earth: *Awaking Your Life's Purpose* by Eckhart Tolle—Tolle offers significant guidance to free ourselves from the distorted, limiting perceptions created by the dictates of the individual and collective ego. He offers a prescription that promotes authenticity, passion, inner peace, harmonious relationships and a purposeful life. His new way of being offers hope toward achieving a world free of destructive strife and struggle. (2006, Plume published by Penguin Group)

A Search for God Book I by Edgar Cayce—The channeled lessons in this book cover how to meditate and the wisdom that enables us to develop a closer relationship and attunement to God. (1982, Association for Research and Enlightenment Press)

Achieving The Mind-Body-Spirit Connection: *A Stress Management Workbook* by Brian Luke Seaward, PhD — Dr. Seaward offers a self-help workbook that describes the emotional, mental, physical and spiritual aspects of promoting wellness and eliminating stress. He provides self-assessment exercises and the strategies necessary to design a personal relaxation program from a holistic perspective. (2005, Jones and Bartlett Publishers, Inc.)

Cancer as a Turning Point: *A Handbook for People with Cancer, Their Families and Health Professionals* by Lawrence LeShan, PhD—Dr. LeShan encourages cancer patients to cope with the losses and disappointments of their past and do what makes them feel more alive. He describes how people can make psychological shifts and create lives with personal meaning and passion. This mind-body approach influences the body's ability to heal itself. (1994, Plume published by Penguin Group (US))

Chicken Soup for the Surviving Soul: *101 Healing Stories About Those Who Have Survived Cancer* by Jack Canfield, Mark Victor Hansen, Patty Aubrey, Beverly Katherine Kirkhart, and Nancy Mitchell-Outio—Cancer survivors share their personal cancer stories. With courage, hope and determination, they tackled cancer, integrating body, mind and soul in the healing process. (1996, Health Communications, Inc.)

Count your Blessings: *The Healing power of Gratitude and Love* by Dr. John F. Demartini—This book describes 25 principles that will enable us to live a healthy and fulfilling life. As we change our thinking, turn adversity into opportunity for growth and live his uplifting principles, we create the future we want. He offers affirmations, examples, exercises and meditations to help us master the art of living fully. (2003, Element Books, HarperCollins Publishers, Ltd.)

Getting Our Bodies Back: *Recovery, Healing, and Transformation through Body-Centered Psychotherapy* by Christine Caldwell, PhD—Dr. Caldwell shares a process for transforming unconscious addictive behaviors into conscious awareness and action. The Moving Cycle includes awareness, owning, acceptance and action. She highlights the power of direct experience in the body-mind healing process. (1996, Shambhala Publications, Inc.)

Getting Well Again: *The Bestselling Classic about the Simontons' Revolutionary Lifesaving Self-Awareness Techniques* by O. Carl Simonton, MD, James Creighton, PhD, and Stephanie Simonton—This book offers self-help techniques for learning positive attitudes, relaxation, visualization, and more to help cancer patients heal. Positive expectations, self-awareness and self-care can contribute to survival and minimize the negative effects of stress and other emotional factors. (1992, Bantam Books, a division of Bantam Doubleday Dell Publishing Group. Inc.)

Heal Your Body: *The Mental Causes for Physical Illness and the Metaphysical Way to Overcome Them* by Louise Hay—This book lists hundreds of specific illnesses, their probable mental causes and the new mindset that will overcome them. It gives the reader a deeper perspective about the negative thought patterns that may be contributing to an illness and is filled with healing affirmations. (1982, Hay House, Inc.)

Love, Medicine and Miracles: *Lessons Learned about Self-Healing from a Surgeon's Experience with Exceptional Patients* by Bernie S. Siegel, MD—Dr. Siegel explains the importance of the mind-body connection in the process of healing. The book offers anecdotal stories of patients who survived the odds against cancer. Self-awareness, self-love and determination are important aspects for a patient's survival. (1986, HarperCollins Publishers, Inc.)

Live Your Life's Purpose: *A guidebook for Creating and Living a Purposeful Life* by Dorothy Ratusny, PhD—Dr. Ratusny takes us on a journey of inner healing. She shares specific strategies to help us connect with our authentic self—core truths and values. She facilitates our finding our life purpose and developing daily practices that enable us to live with purpose and passion. (2008, Insomniac Press)

Living Your Best Life: *Discover Your Life's Blueprint for Success* by Laura Berman Fortgang—This book provides strategies to help us connect with our inner wisdom and move forward with our true desires. When we discover what we really want and take purposeful actions to get it, we create a personally fulfilling life. By staying focused on our desires on many levels, we easily live our "lucrative purpose" and become a magnet for success. (2001, Penguin Putnam Inc.)

Quantum Healing: Exploring the Frontiers of Mind/Body Medicine by Deepak Chopra, MD—Dr. Chopra describes how awareness, attention and intention are an important part of the physical healing process. He describes the individual going to the deepest core of the mind-body system to the point where consciousness starts to affect healing. Bringing the body back into balance and harmony reawakens its own healing ability. (1990, Bantam Books, a division of Bantam Doubleday Dell Publishing Group, Inc.)

Prescriptions for Living: Inspirational Lessons for a Joyful, Loving Life by Bernie S. Siegel, MD—This book offers a collection of stories based on Dr. Siegel's life experiences that are meant to inspire lessons and guidance for a joyful, loving life. He offers wisdom that will help people get to the brighter, lighter side of life. (1998, HarperCollins Publishers, Inc.)

Remembering Wholeness: A Personal Handbook for Thriving in the 21st Century by Carole Tuttle—Carol Tuttle provides insights into the life principles that help each of us remember who we really are, spiritual beings having a human experience. She provides guidance in how to put into practice our innate creative powers to create the life we want. (2002, Elton-Wolf Publishing)

The Dynamic Laws of Healing by Catherine Ponder—Catherine Ponder describes the laws of healing that can change the negative thoughts and feelings causing our diseases. She describes how our mental, emotional and spiritual powers contribute to our health and healing, including our life situations. She reminds us that the power to heal comes from the divine source within us. (1966, DeVorss & Company)

The Healing Secret of the Ages by Catherine Ponder—This book describes, in detail, aspects of mental and spiritual healing. Catherine Ponder reports that the glands are centers of vital mind powers and are associated with the seven natural powers and twelve mind powers located within the vital nerve centers in the body. She discusses and gives examples of proven methods of healing and shares affirmations that lead to healing our lives. (2000, DeVorss & Company)

The Path of Transformation: How Healing Ourselves Can Change the World by Shakti Gawain (1993, 2000, New World Library)—This book provides a unique perspective on personal development and how it impacts constructive change in the world. Healing and integrating the spiritual, mental, emotional and physical levels of our existence contribute to healing our world. The book identifies seven action steps that lead to transformation. (Quote reprinted with permission of New World Library, Novato, CA, www.newworldlibrary.com)

Transforming Stress: The HeartMath ® Solution for Relieving Worry, Fatigue, and Tension by Doc Childre and Deborah Rozman, PhD—This book gives us strategies to gain control of the automatic stress responses in our bodies. It shares strategies that use our heart rhythms to counteract stressful feelings, change our perceptions, and increase our energy. In minutes we learn to go from an incoherent heart rhythm to a coherent rhythm that promotes health and wellbeing. (2005, New Harbinger Publications, Inc.)

The Healing Code: Six Minutes to Heal the Source of Your Health, Success, or Relationship Issues by Alexander Loyd, PhD, NK with Ben Johnson, MD, DO, NMD—This book describes the prominent role stress and insufficient energy at the cellular level play in the development of illness and other life issues. Traumatic memories stored in the cells of our bodies negatively affect our health and wellbeing. Dr. Loyd describes the Healing Code and explains how to apply this simple energy technique. (2010, Grand Central Life & Style, Hackette Book Group)

The Promise of Energy Psychology: Revolutionary Tools for Dramatic Personal Change by David Feinstein, PhD, Donna Eden and Gary Craig—This book offers an in depth understanding of the field of energy psychology. It offers a detailed description of how to use meridian tapping and other ways to move energy through our bodies in order to overcome negative emotions and thoughts, change unwanted behaviors and increase our ability to have more of want we want in our lives. (2005, Penguin Group (USA))

The Writings of Florence Scovel Shinn: The Game of Life & How to Play It, Your Word Is Your Wand, The Power of the Spoken Word and The Secret Door to Success by Florence Scovel Shinn—Florence Scovel Shinn shares real-life stories to demonstrate the power of having a positive attitude and using affirmations to bring about positive change. The book is filled with timeless wisdom that places our feet on the path to enlightenment. (1988, DeVorss & Company)

You Can Heal Your Life by Louise Hay—Louise Hay offers practical steps in using our own creative powers to eliminate the emotional and mental blocks to healing. The book describes the emotional/mental causes of many ailments and provides healing affirmations to overcome them. Louise Hay healed herself of cancer using mind-body techniques. (1984, Hay House, Inc.)

Your Body Speaks Your Mind: Decoding the Emotional, Psychological, and Spiritual Messages That Underlie Illness by Deb Shapiro—Deb Shapiro explains how emotions and thoughts contribute to illness. She offers techniques to ask, listen and decode what our bodies are trying to express through illness. The book lists a variety of diseases and the right questions to ask so the body is able to communicate the truths that promote healing. (2006, Sounds True, Inc.)

Health

AntiCancer: *A New Way of Life* by David Servan-Schreiber, MD, PhD—Dr. Servan-Schreiber addresses the current developments in cancer research and offers tips on how people living with cancer can fight it by making lifestyle changes, including anti-inflammatory factors. He also addresses mind-body approaches to reduce stress. Reading this book is a must for anyone who wants to stay healthy and prevent cancer. (2009, Viking Penguin, a member of Penguin Group (USA))

Beating Cancer with Natural Medicine (My Doctor Says Series) by Michael Lam, MD—Dr. Lam discusses the difference between traditional and natural approaches to healing cancer. He gives us a framework from which to understand and assess the value of many alternative treatment options. His treatment approach focuses on the use of antioxidants and other supplements to boost the immune system. He also covers the benefits of detoxification, the importance of a balanced internal terrain, and the fundamentals of an anti-cancer diet. (2003, Dr. Michael Lam)

Beating Cancer with Nutrition by Patrick Quillin, PhD, RD, CNS—Dr. Quillin is a leading expert in nutrition and cancer. In this book, he describes how nutrition increases the effects of chemotherapy and radiation and treats the underlying causes of cancer. Nutrition improves a cancer patient's outcome, longevity and quality of life. The information in this book is evidenced based. (2001, Nutrition Times Press, Inc.)

Cancer: 50 Essential Things To Do by Greg Anderson—Based on interviews with thousands of cancer patients through the Cancer Recovery Foundation International, Greg Anderson found six basic strategies that cancer survivors have in common. The categories include medical, nutrition, exercise, attitude, support and spiritual. The book describes 50 things people can do as they design their integrated treatment program and beat the cancer odds. (1999, Plume published by Penguin Group (USA))

Fit Moms for Life: *How to Have Endless Energy to Outplay Your Kids* by Dustin Maher—This book reveals five strategies that will result in rapid fat loss that lasts. It provides a workout plan and roadmap to help moms make lifestyle changes that lead to trim, healthy bodies. Dustin emphasizes strength and burst training, proper nutrition and a positive mindset. In each chapter, moms share their success stories. (2011, Morgan James Publishing)

Guess What Came to Dinner? *Parasites and Your Health* by Ann Louise Gittleman, PhD, CNS—Dr. Ann Louise discusses the role of parasites in many ailments and the rise of parasitic infections in the United States. The book offers practical advice on protecting your food and water from parasites. Methods of detection, anti-parasitic treatments and herbal cures are included. (2001, Avery, a member of Penguin Putnam, Inc.)

KNOCKOUT: *Interviews with Doctors Who are Curing Cancer and How to Prevent Getting It in the First Place* by Suzanne Somers—Suzanne Somers speaks with doctors who treat cancer using integrative approaches that build up the body rather than tear it down. The book also includes interviews with experts on nutrition, lifestyle and dietary supplementation. Testimonials by people who are surviving cancer give a message of hope to others. (2009, Three Rivers Press)

Life Over Cancer: *The Block Center Program for Integrative Cancer Treatment* by Keith I. Block, MD—Based on his 30 years of experience, Dr. Block developed a researched-based model of integrative cancer treatments. He gives patients instructions on how to improve their quality of life while living with cancer and undergoing traditional treatments. He also emphasizes the body-mind connection to defeat disease. (2009, Bantam Dell, Division of Random House, Inc.)

More Health, Less Care: *How to Take Charge of Your Medical Care and Write Your Own Personal Prescription for Lifelong Health* by Peter J. Weiss, MD—Dr. Weiss creates a blueprint about how people can develop their own plan to achieve total health —body, mind and spirit. He advises the reader to play a role in treating his/her illness and preventing disease. (2010, LaChance Publishing LLC)

Natural Strategies for Cancer Patients by Russell L. Blaylock, MD—This books points out the power of good nutrition and supplements for those fighting cancer. It describes ways to minimize the side effects of chemotherapy and radiation while increasing their effectiveness. It also discusses ways to fortify your immune system and maintain physical strength and vitality. (2003, Twin Streams Books, Kensington Publishing Corp.)

Never Fear Cancer Again: *How to Prevent and Reverse Cancer* by Raymond Francis, MSc—In simple language, Raymond Francis describes the cancer process as malfunctioning cells and indicates what can be done to eliminate the toxicity and deficiency that promote cancer cells. The six pathways to health or disease highlight what the reader can do to turn the cancer process off. This is a must read for anyone who wants to take the mystery out of cancer and learn about natural, non-toxic ways to beat cancer. (2011, Health Communications, Inc.)

Options: The Alternative Cancer Therapy Book by Richard Walters—This book offers a comprehensive overview of the many types of alternative treatments available to the cancer patient. Through unbiased reporting and easy to understand language, Walters gives the reader the supporting research and underlying scientific rationale for each method. The book also provides important guidelines in helping the cancer patient make informed decisions about treatment as well as referral resources. (1993, Avery Publishing Group, Inc.)

Outsmart Your Cancer: *Alternative Non-Toxic Treatments that Work* by Tanya Harter Pierce, MA, MFCC—The book explains why non-toxic cancer treatment methods can be more effective than conventional ones based on research findings. Tanya Harter Pierce discusses the underlying causes of cancer and describes leading alternative treatment approaches in easy to understand language, including Protocel. The book also includes stories of people who recovered from late stage cancer using alternative approaches. (2009, Thoughtworks Publishing)

Raw Fusion Living by LindaJoy Rose, PhD—This book guides us toward introducing more raw foods into our diets on a daily basis. It explains how living foods will improve our quality of health and life. Dr. LindaJoy inspires us to make informed choices about the best foods to give us more energy and get into a Raw Fusion lifestyle. The book includes testimonials from others who embrace a raw foods or raw fusion way of life. (2010, Quantum Mind Press, LLC)

The Biology of Belief: *Unleashing the Power of Consciousness, Matter & Miracles* by Bruce H. Lipton, PhD—Dr. Lipton discusses the new science of Epigenetics and how it is changing our understanding of the link between mind and matter. He describes the process by which cells receive information: The DNA of the cell is controlled by signals from outside the cell, including energetic messages emanating from our thoughts. (2008, Hay House, Inc.)

The Genie in Your Genes: *Epigenetic Medicine and the New Biology of Intention* by Dawson Church, PhD—Dr. Church cites hundreds of studies that show how thoughts and emotions can trigger the expression of genes. He applies the insights from the emerging field of Epigenetics (control above the level of the gene) to healing. He focuses on a class of genes called "Immediate Early Genes" and shows how the expression of these genes influences our health every day. (2007, Elite Books)

The Inflammation Syndrome: *Your Nutrition Plan for Great Health, Weight Loss, and Pain-Free Living* by Jack Challem—This book provides a powerful nutrition and supplement program that safely prevents and overcomes inflammatory disorders within the body. Chronic inflammation is a growing health problem and is one of the major causes of many illnesses. Jack Challem's approach to healing inflammation is based on the latest research from all over the world. (2010, John Wiley & Sons, Inc.)

Third Opinion (Third Edition): *An International Directory to Alternative Therapy Centers for the Treatment and Prevention of Cancer & Other Degenerative Diseases* by John M. Fink—This comprehensive listing of doctors, centers and treatment approaches serves as a guide for anyone who wants to make informed choices about treatment options for cancer and other chronic health issues. Contact information and approximate costs of treatment are included. (1997, Avery Publishing Group)

Ultraprevention: *The 6-week Plan That Will Make You Healthy for Life* by Mark Hyman, MD and Mark Liponis, MD—Drs. Hyman and Liponis break free of the quick-fix prescription cycle and have designed a program that identifies and eliminates the cause of disease instead of masking symptoms. The book lists the Five Forces of Illness and describes three simple steps to stop these forces so people can maintain good health throughout life, getting older without aging. (2005, Simon & Schuster)

Waking the Warrior Goddess: *Dr Christine Horner's Program to Protect Against and Fight Breast Cancer* by Christine Horner, MD—Dr. Horner explains the various foods, supplements, and health-promoting strategies that enable women to fight breast cancer and achieve optimal health. She shares what the warrior goddess should avoid and what she should embrace in order to heal and become a breast cancer thriver. The resources section lists contacts to purchase various nutrients and toxin-free products. (2007, Basic Health Publications, Inc.)

Women's Bodies, Women's Wisdom: *Creating Physical and Emotional Health and Healing* by Christiane Northrup, MD—Dr. Northrup gives a multi-dimensional understanding of a woman's body and its processes and offers strategies for any woman to participate in achieving optimal health and wellbeing. Dr. Northrup integrates a body-mind-spirit approach to healing. She offers strategies which allow a woman to decode the language of the body in order to promote healing on many levels. (1994, 1998, 2006, 2010; Bantam Books, a division of Random House, Inc.)

Wealth

Attracting Abundance with EFT: *Emotional Freedom Techniques* by Carol Look—Carol Look combines EFT, abundance games and principles of the Law of Attraction to help readers increase their financial abundance and magnetize the success they want in their lives. It contains 45 different EFT exercises and scripts to release any blocks or limiting beliefs to receiving abundance in all aspects of your life, including wealth and happiness. The book teaches fun, simple ways to focus and harness the power of the Law of Attraction in order to boost your magnetizing power and attract the success you want. (2005, Authorhouse)

Excuse Me Your Life Is Waiting: *The Astonishing Power of Feelings* by Lynn Grabhorn—Lynn Grabhorn reveals how the power of feelings unconsciously shapes and molds our reality. Being aware of our feelings and keeping them positive is the driving force to change our lives and make what we want become a reality. The book is filled with logical explanations, simple steps and true-life examples that empower readers to access feelings and change their lives. (2000, Hampton Roads Publishing Company, Inc).

Jack Canfield's Key to Living the Law of Attraction: *A Simple Guide to Creating the Life of Your Dreams* by Jack Canfield and D. D. Watkins—Jack Canfield shares his knowledge and experience working with the Law of Attraction. His proven tools and techniques for applying the principles associated with the Law of Attraction are listed in this book. He also includes helpful exercises. He addresses the issues of clarity, purpose and action. (2007, Health Communications, Inc.)

Leveraging the Universe: *7 Steps to Engaging Life's Magic* by Mike Dooley—This book emphasizes the value of mastering our own thoughts and beliefs and taking purposeful action to accomplish what we want. Mike Dooley reminds us to do our part by harnessing the powerful metaphysical principles within the creative process. He describes seven steps to harness life's magic. (2011, Atria Books, a Division of Simon & Schuster, Inc.)

The Success Principles: *How to Get from Where You Are to Where You Want to Be* by Jack Canfield with Janet Switzer—Jack Canfield shares the strategies he has studied, taught and lived which have led to great success for him and many others. He teaches us how to increase our confidence, tackle daily challenges, live with passion and purpose, and realize our potential. If we apply the 64 time-tested principles covered in the book, we will take the right actions that lead to extraordinary outcomes. (2005 HarperCollins Publishers)

Other Resources

www.naturalstandard.com

Natural Standard is an Internet resource for those seeking high-quality, evidence-based and peer-reviewed information about complementary and alternative therapies. It was created by healthcare providers and researchers who do not support any interest group, professional organization or product manufacturer.

www.ahha.org

American Holistic Health Association serves as a neutral clearinghouse to assist those who want to enhance their health and wellbeing. They offer free and impartial information through videos, articles, and other resources.

www.annieappleseedproject.org

The Annie Appleseed Project is a volunteer, non-profit organization that provides information, education, advocacy, and awareness for people with cancer and their loved ones who are interested in natural therapies from a patient's perspective. The website includes valuable information about complementary therapies (use of natural therapies with conventional medicine) and alternative therapies (used instead of or after conventional therapy).

www.cancerrecovery.org

The Cancer Recovery Foundation International is a group of charities and national organizations whose mission is to help people prevent and survive cancer. It provides integrative prevention and survival strategies for people with cancer. The founder, Greg Anderson, is a leading wellness authority and author of many books on integrative approaches to healing.

www.soulfulliving.com

Soulfulliving.com is an online resource for personal and spiritual growth. It covers topics related to spiritual growth, organic living and self-improvement. The website includes an online magazine, feature articles, bookstore and Internet links that guide your actions to live a fuller life with joy, inner peace and love.

www.aviewbeyond.com

Diane Sherman-Levine is a healer, a psychic medium, and a teacher. Her work is described in a book titled *Healing Tales*, edited by Stanley Krippner. She works under spiritual guidance, using energy and sound healing, and channels information regarding spiritual, psychological and emotional growth, as well as more mundane matters.

www.acourseinmiracles.com

A Course in Miracles (ACIM) is a self-study curriculum that aims to assist its readers in achieving spiritual transformation.

About the Author

Sandra has known life challenges from a very young age. She turned a traumatic childhood into fertilizer for her personal growth and emerged with a desire and tenacity to be and do more.

She decided to leave full-time mothering and start college at the age of 30. Her volunteer experiences helping inmates learn decision making skills in a county jail program inspired her to become a professional helper. The women's consciousness movement opened a door that had been closed to her. After six years, she left college with a Masters of Education Degree in counseling.

Learning never stopped for her. Sandra became a Licensed Professional Counselor, an energy worker, hypnotherapist, Emotional Freedom Techniques (EFT) practitioner, personal life coach, and executive leadership coach. She immersed herself in the human potential and personal transformation movement. As a result of her journey of self-discovery, she developed her intuitive skills. Listening to others from the deepest level of her being, she guides her clients to truth and enables them to discover and eliminate the core issues sabotaging their success. In her golden years, she is on her way to adding *author* and *speaker* to her list of accomplishments.

The Tampa Bay area of Florida has become Sandra's home, and she loves living there with her husband. She enjoys traveling to see her family, especially the grandchildren, and enjoys visiting special places and cultures throughout the world.

Sandra treated her stage I breast cancer as though it were stage IV. She used a systems approach to destroy cancer cells within her body and correct the deficiencies that created them in the first place. She continues to live a lifestyle that prevents a cancer recurrence and improves her health and wellbeing.

Sandra Miniere Offers...

Sandra feels fulfilled and energized when she is inspiring others to become their best and accomplish the extraordinary. Please feel free to contact Sandra for services provided in person, over the telephone and/or over the Internet.

You may e-mail Sandra via her websites:

◆ www.IntegrativeWellnessExpert.com

◆ www.ALighterSidetoCancer.com

Sandra's Services Include:

◆ Personal life and executive leadership coaching services

◆ EFT consultations

◆ Podium presentations, workshops, webinars, and teleseminars on a variety of motivational and integrative wellness topics

◆ Articles for newspapers, magazines and Internet websites

Sandra's Seminars Include:

◆ *Six Secrets to Living Well Longer!*

◆ *Turn Your Wake-up Call into a Call to Action!*

◆ *Five Tips to Become Your Own Truth Detective*

Free Download Bonus Gifts

Sign up at www.ALighterSidetoCancer.com/bonusgifts

Sandra's Supplement Program

You will receive a list of the supplements that I take to stay cancer free and improve my health. The list will include the name of the supplement, the brand, the dosage and the perceived benefit (the reason I take it).

The list offers suggestions and is not meant to be a recommendation. Dosages can be different for everyone and need to be given serious consideration in order to avoid negative side effects. Supplements should be taken with awareness, caution and professional guidance.

Four-Part e-Course: How to Turn Your Intuition into a Trusted Guide

Part 1 – Get centered! Discover mindfulness and breathing exercises to help you create a receptive presence. This inner stillness enables you to **hear clearly** and prepares your body to recognize truth.

Part 2 – Ask great questions! Discover tips on how to **develop appropriate questions** that will generate golden insights and accurate guidance. The questions you ask determine the answers you get.

Part 3 – Receive answers! Discover how to recognize truth through your body, mind, feelings, and energy. Learn to discriminate between ego-driven messages and intuitive messages. Discover tips on how to **interpret** an intuitive sign or insight accurately because the message you tell yourself influences your actions and the outcome.

Part 4 – Practice, Practice, Practice! Explore the do's and don'ts of acting on your intuition. Discover ways to **test** your guidance. Act with curiosity, caution and confidence.